CARRIAGE
AND
WAGON MAKERS'
MACHINERY AND TOOLS

Kenneth L. Cope

ASTRAGAL PRESS
Mendham, New Jersey

Library of Congress Control Number   2003117085
International Standard Book Number   1-931626-18-9

Cover design by Donald Kahn

Published by
THE ASTRAGAL PRESS
5 Cold Hill Road, Suite 12
P.O. Box 239
Mendham NJ 07945-0239

Manufactured in the United States of America

DEDICATION

Dedicated to the last remnants of the once great horse-drawn vehicle industry:
those who salvage, restore, collect and study the relatively few remaining vehicles.

ACKNOWLEDGMENTS

This work is based largely on information and illustrations gleaned from contemporary catalogs and periodicals. Special thanks for contributions of important catalog information is due to:

Kendall H. Bassett, Tacoma, WA, who furnished copies of several catalogs offering blacksmiths' and wheelwrights' tools of the 19th and 20th centuries.

Jack Devitt, Ottoville, OH, who loaned research material gathered for his book *Ohio Toolmakers and Their Tools*.

Robert Vogel, Washington, DC, who loaned his copy of the 1910 Defiance Machine Works catalog.

INTRODUCTION

The development of carriage and wagon makers' machinery, especially wheelwrights' machinery, began in the U.S. in the 1820s with the introduction of the Blanchard lathe. Thomas Blanchard's patent of September 6, 1819 (later changed by Congress to January 20, 1820), was for a machine which could automatically produce wooden parts of irregular shape by tracing a pattern piece mounted on the machine. First used to make gun stocks at the Springfield Arsenal, it was quickly applied to the manufacture of spokes, lasts, and other such products.

Other early developments appear to have centered around hub mortising and felloe making machines. The virtual automation of the three most important parts of the carriage and wagon wheel greatly simplified the most difficult and time consuming procedures done by the wheelwright. As a result productivity was greatly increased, with a corresponding decrease in the cost of the final product.

The degree to which woodworking machinery quite early supplanted hand work is clearly shown in the 1855 report of an English committee that visited a large number of American factories in 1854 to investigate the "American System of Manufactures." The portion of the report dealing with woodworking machinery stated:

> In those districts of the United States of America that the Committee have visited, the working of wood by machinery in almost every branch of industry is all but universal; and in large establishments the ordinary tools of the carpenter are seldom seen, except in finishing off, after the several parts of the article have been put together.
>
> The determination to use labor-saving machinery has divided the class of work usually carried on by carpenters and the other wood trades into special manufactures, where only one kind of article is produced, but in numbers or quantity almost in many cases incredible.
>
> The manufacture of carriage wheels frequently forms an important branch of the trade, and is carried on chiefly by the aid of machinery.

By 1866, wheel machinery was in almost universal use and, as shown in the ad below, available in great variety.

Production of carriage and wagon makers' machinery and tools, of course, declined as automobiles and trucks supplanted horse drawn vehicles. The extensive use of wooden spokes, body frames etc., in early automobiles kept the industry prosperous through World War I, but the decline became very rapid in the 1920s. The last significant listing of carriage and wagon makers' machinery noted is four machines offered in the 1929 Fay & Egan catalog.

It is noteworthy that carriage and wagon makers' machinery and tools were developed much earlier, and continued in production later, than most of us would have thought.

Continuing the pattern set by *AMERICAN LATHE BUILDERS, AMERICAN PLANER, SHAPER & SLOTTER BUILDERS, and COOPERAGE MACHINERY & TOOLS,* this book is meant to identify the inventors and builders of American carriage and wagon makers' machinery and tools; and to illustrate, as far as possible, their products. A few of the makers listed are well known, most are little known, and some are known only from a single advertisement or mention found in a contemporary magazine. None, as far as I know, remain in business.

GLOSSARY

AXLE—the transverse bar beneath a vehicle, on whose ends the wheels are placed. The wheels rotate on the AXLE SPINDLES, which are fastened to the AXLE TREE.

AXLE ARM—the spindle on the end of an axle, on which the box of the wheel fits.

AXLE BAR—an AXLE TREE with an arm at each end for a wheel.

AXLE BOX—a bushing inserted in the hub which acts as a bearing as it revolves on the spindle. The box is designed to take the wear incident to use and is replaceable when required.

AXLE-CLIP—a clevy or bow that unites another part of the vehicle with the axle.

AXLE NUT—a nut on the end of an axle spindle, to keep the wheel in place.

AXLE PIN—a linch pin; a small bar passing through a mortise near the end of the axle arm or spindle, to hold the wheel in place.

AXLE SETTING MACHINE—a machine for setting the spindles true on the ends of the axle-trees, giving them the required SET and GATHER.

AXLE-SKEIN—a band, strip or thimble of metal on the wooden arm or spindle of a carriage axle. Acts as a bearing and wear plate and prevents wood rubbing on wood.

AXLE-TREE—the axle, or transverse bar, on the ends of which the AXLE SPINDLES are fastened.

AXLE-TREE TURNING MACHINE—a machine for turning both ends of the axle-tree to the desired form and size.

BAND—see HUB BAND

BOX—the iron or other metal bushing of a NAVE or HUB. See AXLE BOX.

BOX SETTER—a device for setting AXLE BOXES in hubs so the wheel runs true.

CARRIAGE BODY KNIFE—see L. & I.J. WHITE entry for an illustration.

CARRIAGE MAKERS' DRAW KNIFE—see L. & I.L. WHITE entry for an illustration.

CARRIAGE ROUTER KNIFE—see L. & I.J. WHITE entry for an illustration.

COACH CURRIER—the maker of the leather parts of a carriage.

COACH FOUNDER—the maker of the framework or ironwork of carriages.

COACH MAKERS' DRAW KNIFE—see L. & I.J. WHITE entry for an illustration.

COACH MAKERS' VISE—a vise with smooth, larger than normal jaws to prevent marring the work. Also called a CARRIAGE MAKERS' VISE.

DISH—the projection outwardly of the tire beyond the plane of the insertion of the spokes in the hub. Not used when the spindle of the axle is cylindrical, but when the spindle is tapered it is necessary to give a GATHER and SWING to the spindle and a dish to the wheel.

FELLOE—the rim of a wheel or one of the annular segments thereof. Also seen as FELLY, and sometimes spelled FELLOW, in early writings.

FELLY—see FELLOE

FELLY AUGER—a pod auger for boring the holes in the felly to receive the spokes, or the dowel pin holes in the felly ends.

FELLY BENDER—a machine for bending straight pieces of heated and/or steamed wood into the proper shape for use as fellies.

FELLY BORING MACHINE—a machine for boring the spoke holes and dowel pin holes in a felly. It may be hand or power operated.

FELLY BORING AND COMPRESSING MACHINE—a form of felly boring machine that compressed the felly as the spoke tenon hole was bored. This resulted in an oblong hole that was believed to prevent splitting of the felly when the spoke was inserted.

FELLY COUPLING—a piece for enclosing the adjacent ends of fellies in the rim of a wheel. One type can be expanded by a taper screw to tighten the tire.

FELLY DRESSER—a machine for dressing the edges and periphery of fellies after the wheel was formed but before the tire was mounted.

FELLY ROUNDING MACHINE—a machine used to finish the inner curved surface of a felly.

FELLY SAWING MACHINE—a machine for sawing stock into fellies.

FOREAUGER—see SPOKE POINTER

GATHER—the forward inclination of the spindle relative to the line of direction of the axle-tree. This brought the forward edge of the taper spindle into a direction transversely across the vehicle, so as to prevent the riding out of the wheel against the hub.

HUB—the central portion of a wheel in which the spokes are fitted. Also called NAVE.

HUB AUGER—a special twist auger bit furnished in any diameter up to 2 1/2." It was used to bore a straight hole in the center of a hub block previous to being seasoned.

HUB BAND—a steel or iron band fitted around one or both ends of a hub to make it stronger and less likely to split. Some patent types covered almost the entire hub.

HUB BLOCK ROUGHING MACHINE—a machine used to rough size a hub block prior to mounting in a hub turning machine.

HUB BORER—a tool for boring hubs to accept the box, either straight or tapered. Both hand and power versions were made.

HUB BORING MACHINE—a machine for boring a center hole in the hub block.

HUB BOXING MACHINE—a machine for boring or reaming the hub to accept the box. See BOX.

HUB CENTERING MACHINE—a machine in which the hub is chucked while the hole for the axle-box is reamed out concentric with the outside diameter.

HUB LATHE—a special lathe for turning carriage and wagon hubs. Most use a form cutter, which is a single cutter in the shape and length of the hub to be turned.

HUB LATHE MANDREL—tapered mandrel designed for insertion in the tapered hole reamed in the hub block. The mandrels and hub blocks were then mounted in the Hub Lathe where the outside diameter was turned concentric to the tapered hole.

HUB MORTISING MACHINE—a machine in which a wheel hub was held on a mandrel so designed that a reciprocating chisel would cut the mortises for the spokes. The hub was rotated to an index for radial location of the mortise cuts.

HUB POLISHING MACHINE—a machine for sanding or polishing hubs prior to painting.

HUB REAMER—a special taper reamer mounted in a hub reaming machine used to bore and ream the center hole in a hub block. They were made in several sizes from 7/8" diameter at small end, 1 1/4" at the shank, and a length of 8"; to 2 1/2" at small end, 4" at the shank, and a length of 23".

HUB REAMING MACHINE—a machine that used a HUB REAMER to bore and ream the finished center hole in a hub block.

HUB TURNING MACHINE—a form of lathe used to turn hub blanks to final form.

NAVE—another term for HUB

POLE—see TONGUE

RIM PLANING MACHINE—a machine for planing simultaneously one curved and one flat surface of a wheel felly.

RIM WRENCH—see TIRE BOLT WRENCH

SHAFT AND POLE BENDING MACHINE—a machine for bending wagon and carriage shafts and poles to the desired shape.

SHELL—a formed sheet metal piece shaped to cover most or all of a carriage or wagon hub.

SPOKE—one of the radial arms that connect the hub with the rim of a wheel. The parts are; the foot, which is inserted into the hub; the shoulder of the foot; the tongue or tenon which is inserted into the felly; and the throat, a narrowed part of the body near the hub.

SPOKE AUGER—a hollow auger used to make round tenons on the outer end of spokes. It may be hand operated or part of a machine.

SPOKE DRIVING BENCH—a bench on which the hub is clamped and the spokes supported as they are driven into the hub.

SPOKE DRIVING MACHINE—a machine for driving spokes into their mortises in the hub. See J.A. FAY for an illustration.

SPOKE GAGE—an instrument for testing the set of spokes in the hub.

SPOKE LATHE—a lathe for turning irregular forms, usually to a pattern. Most are based on the Blanchard patent of 1828.

SPOKE POINTER—a cutting tool, usually mounted in a brace, for cutting a taper on the end of a spoke so it will fit into the hollow auger. Also called a SPOKE TRIMMER or a FOREAUGER. See CINCINNATI TOOL CO. for an illustration.

SPOKE POLISHING MACHINE—a machine for smoothing spokes after turning and before painting.

SPOKE SETTER—a machine for centering a hub, so that it may be bored accurately for the spoke mortises.

SPOKE SIZING MACHINE—a machine for planing the sides of spokes and bringing them to a uniform shape.

SPOKE TAPERING MACHINE—a machine for tapering the edge of the spoke tenon to fit the bevel heading of the mortise in the hub.

SPOKE TENON COMPRESS—a machine that compressed the spoke tenon to the size desired. It also usually left corrugations on the tenon surface that aided the gluing process.

SPOKE TENONING MACHINE—a machine for forming the tenons on the outer end of the spokes. This was usually done after the spokes were inserted in the hub so they could all be cut to identical length just before cutting the tenons.

SPOKE THROATING MACHINE—a machine to form the throat of a spoke. The throat is the portion of lesser thickness a short distance from the hub, to give some flexibility to the spoke.

SPOKE TRIMMER—see SPOKE POINTER

SPOKING MACHINE—a machine for setting spokes in a hub with a uniform dish.

STAGGER—to set the spokes in a hub so that they are alternately on each side of a median line, in order to give them a broader base, and therefore greater stiffness to the wheel against lateral strain.

STAGGERED WHEEL—one whose spokes are set in and out alternately where they enter the hub.

STRAP SKEIN—a flat iron strip let into the wood of an axle arm to act as a bearing. See AXLE SKEIN.

SWING—the outward inclination of the top of a wheel. Necessary with a conical axle so that the bottom edge of the spindle will be about horizontal.

TENON TRUING MACHINE—a machine for truing or sizing the tenons of spokes and cutting the tenons to the desired length at the same operation.

THIMBLE SKEIN—a sleeve over the arm of a carriage or wagon axle. See AXLE SKEIN

TIRE—an iron or steel band around the fellies of a wheel. The tire was usually expanded by heating, and then shrunk on so as to tightly compress the wheel, and bolted.

TIRE BENDER—a device for bending strips of iron or steel into a uniform circular shape for forming tires.

TIRE BOLT HOLDER—a tool for clamping tire bolts while the nut is being turned on or off. See WILEY & RUSSELL for an illustration.

TIRE BOLT WRENCH—a tool for installing and removing tire bolts. Also called a RIM WRENCH. See BYRNE & ZIEGAUS for an illustration.

TIRE COOLER—a tank of water, with means to raise and lower a wheel on which a heated tire is to be shrunk. See H.D. BOKOP entry for an illustration.

TIRE DRILL—a machine, either hand or power operated, for drilling bolt holes in tires.

TIRE HEATER—a furnace is which a tire is expanded by heat before it is shrunk on to the wheel.

TIRE MEASURER—a rotary gauge used to measure the circumference of wheels to determine the length of an iron strip to be formed into a tire. See WILEY & RUSSELL for an illustration. Also called a TRAVELER.

TIRE PRESS—a machine for driving the iron or steel tire on the rim of the wheel. Some were designed to do this without heating the tire.

TIRE SHRINKER—a device for shortening tires when they have become loose due to the shrinkage of the wooden wheel. Also see TIRE UPSETTER.

TIRE UPSETTER—a machine for shrinking tires without cutting. The tire is heated and then forcibly compressed endwise to shorten it. Also see TIRE SHRINKER.

TIRESMITH—one who makes tires and other ironwork for vehicles.

TONGUE—the single shaft or pole which, in two-horse vehicles, is attached to the fore-carriage, and is the means of guiding and drawing.

TRAVELER—see TIRE MEASURER

WAGON BOW—an arched shaped slat with it ends planted in staples in the wagon bed sides. Used to elevate the cover.

WAGON BOX BORING MACHINE—a multiple spindle drilling machine used to simultaneously bore all holes in wagon box sides.

WAGON MAKERS' KNIFE—see L. & I.J. WHITE for an illustration.

WAIN—a wagon

WAINWRIGHT—a maker of wagons.

WHEEL—a circular frame turning on an axle.

WHEEL BAND—another name for a tire.

WHEEL FACING MACHINE—a machine for facing the sides of wheels, reducing the fellies to a uniform thickness, and beveling them if desired.

WHEEL RIMMING MACHINE— a machine for installing the rim of felloe on the wheel.

WHEEL SCREWING MACHINE—a machine for boring the holes and fixing the screws in the rims or fellies of wheels.

WHEEL SPOKING MACHINE—see SPOKE DRIVING MACHINE

WHEELWRIGHT—a maker of wheels.

ABBOTT. &. CO., Hudson, MI

Operated by Adrian O.Abbot. Maker, beginning in 1875, of the LITTLE GIANT hub borer (Figs.1 & 2), patented January 13, 1874. Weighing 50 pounds, it was designed for bench mounting. Abbot's box puller (Fig.3), priced at $6.00, was offered in 1882. By 1891, Abbott introduced an improved version of the hub borer (Fig.4), patented May 5, 1891, and offered his box puller in two sizes. Both tools were offered well into the 20th century.

ABBOTT'S LITTLE GIANT HUB BORER.

ADAMS CO., Dubuque, IA

Formed in 1892 when Eugene Adams (1860-1952) and his brother Herbert Adams (1863-1945) bought and reorganized the Roberts & Langworth Iron Works. Eugene served as president; Herbert as secretary and treasurer.

One of its first products was the DIAMOND vise made from 1892 to well into the 20th century. As shown in the ad at right, the vise was furnished with an optional felloe boring attachment for wagon makers and blacksmiths.

ADAMS' DIAMOND VISES.

Net price each.

Complete, with Fellow Boring Attachment $4.00
Complete, without Fellow Boring Attachment 2.75

This is a fine little Vise for the money, and is giving good satisfaction wherever used.

ADAMS & SONS, JOSEPH, Amherst, MA

Maker, beginning in 1849, of a machine for cutting felloes of wheels out of planks (Figs.1&2). Patented June 12, 1849, and July 9, 1850, by Joshua and Levi Adams, the machine was claimed to "cut 60 good felloes in one hour" and was advertised as late as 1851 (Fig.3).

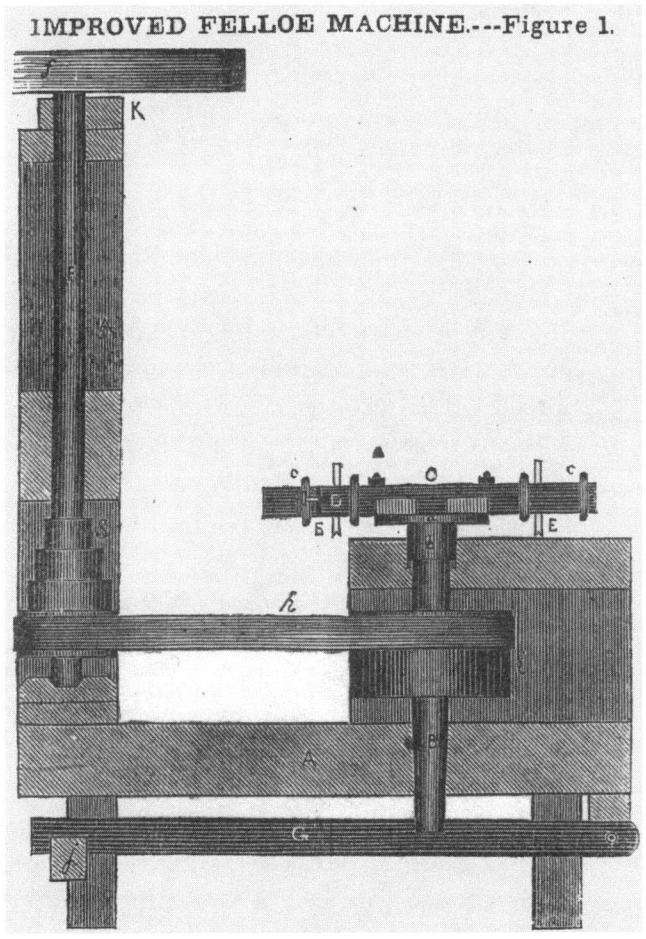

IMPROVED FELLOE MACHINE.---Figure 1.

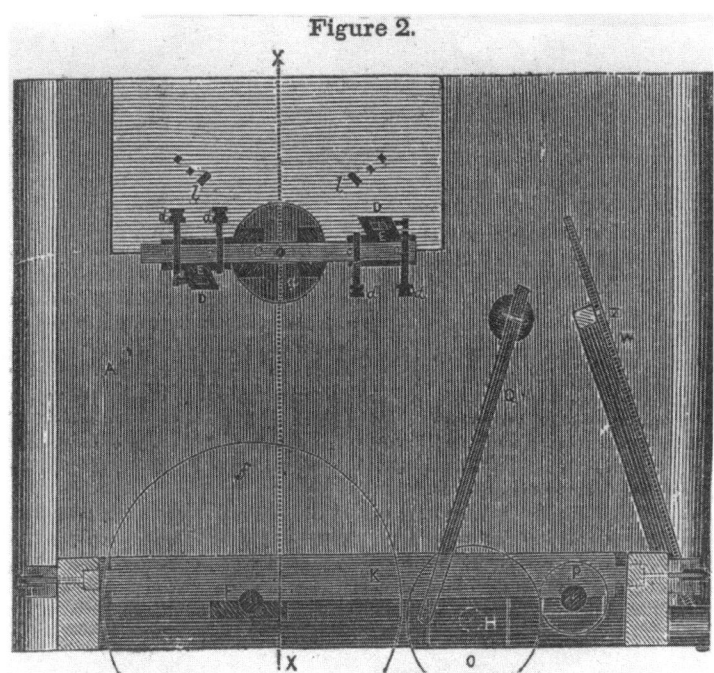

Figure 2.

Fig.3

FELLY CUTTING MACHINE.—MESSRS. JOSEPH ADAMS & SONS, Amherst, Mass., offer for sale town, county and State rights, or single machines, with the right to use, of this unrivalled Felly Cutting Machine, illustrated in No. 5, Vol. 6, Scientific American. It is portable, easily kept in order, requires but little power to drive it, and will execute in the most rapid and perfect manner, cutting 60 good felloes in one hour. 6tf

ALLEN BROTHERS, Homer, MI

Wagon makers and blacksmiths, the firm also made a Hub Centering Machine and Spoke Guide, patented July 11, 1871, by King P. Allen. In operation, the hub was mounted on two uprights and clamped in place. An expanding mandrel was placed in the bore of the hub and the spokes driven into the mortises. A rod, extending at right angles to the mandrel, carried a guide and scribe; the guide to set all spokes to the same dish and the scribe to mark each spoke so it could be cut to the same length.

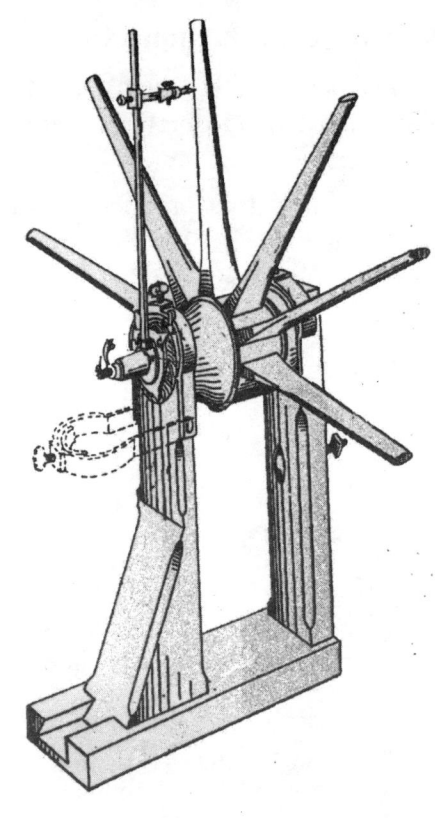

AMES & SON, OLIVER, Seymour, CT

See DOUGLASS MFG. CO. and JAMES SWAN CO.

MACHINE FOR THE MANUFACTURE OF SPOKED WHEELS.

ARCHIBALD, E.A., Methuen, MA

Maker of a complex machine for the manufacture of spoked wheels, patented December 28, 1869. The machine required two floors, the upper holding a clamping mechanism that forced wheel sections, consisting of one felly and two spokes, into the iron flanges forming the hub; the lower containing the power gearing and the operating rods for the clamps on the upper floor.

Advantages for the type of wheel produced were claimed to be: "In the iron-hubbed wheel the spokes are more than twice as large as a wooden hub wheels of corresponding size and a wheel made on this plan will not shrink, and that as the bases of the spokes are as firmly compressed against each other as it is possible for wood to be, and held by metallic flanges firmly bolted together, it is the most perfect method of constructing wagon wheels for heavy work yet devised."

ATKINSON, GEORGE, San Francisco, CA

Inventor and maker of a carriage makers' knife, patented March 7, 1871. As shown below, the tool had two cutting blades, one wide and one narrow, which could be adjusted in two planes relative to the handles.

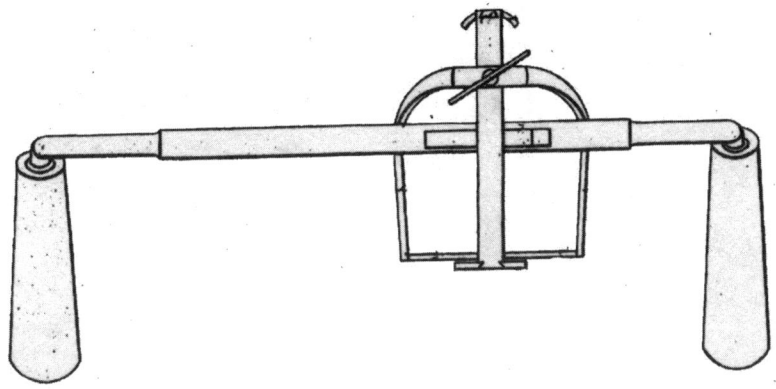

AVOCA WHEEL CO., Avoca, NY

Primarily a wheel maker, the firm also made spoke finishing machines, patented November 9, 1895, by C.D. Carroll. Note the foot pedal used to control the force with which the spoke was held against the sanding belt.

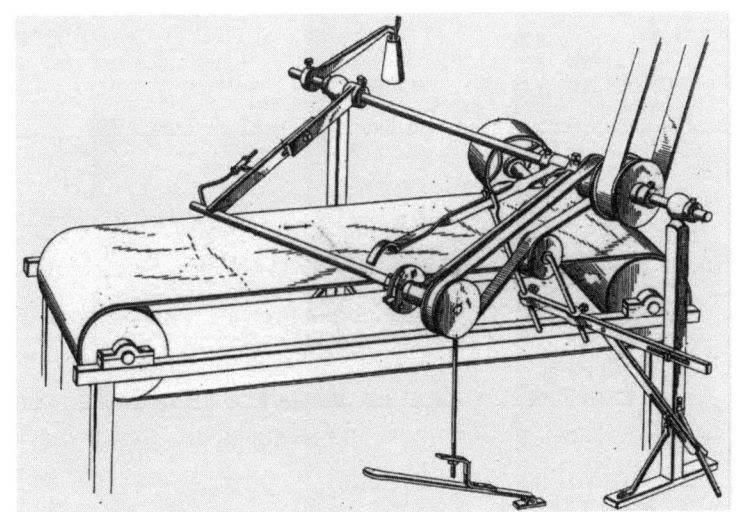

HUB MORTISING MACHINE.

BAILEY, T.R., Lockport, NY, later
BAILEY & VAIL, Lockport, NY

Bailey, beginning about 1851, was an inventor and maker of a variety of woodworking machinery such as lathes for turning broom handles and chair parts. In 1856, he introduced a hub mortising machine, patented August 5, 1856. The hub was held between centers, one of which was equipped with an index wheel to position the hub radially for slot location. A rotating mortising tool was then moved horizontally to cut the spoke slot.

By 1871, Bailey had formed a partnership with L.W. Vail to produce woodworking machinery and keyseating machines. The firm was reorganized as the MERRITT MFG. CO. in 1882.

BASHAW, JOHN N., Lake Geneva, WI

Inventor and maker of the Bashaw tire remover, patented October 11, 1898. As shown below, the tool was simple and probably quite effective.

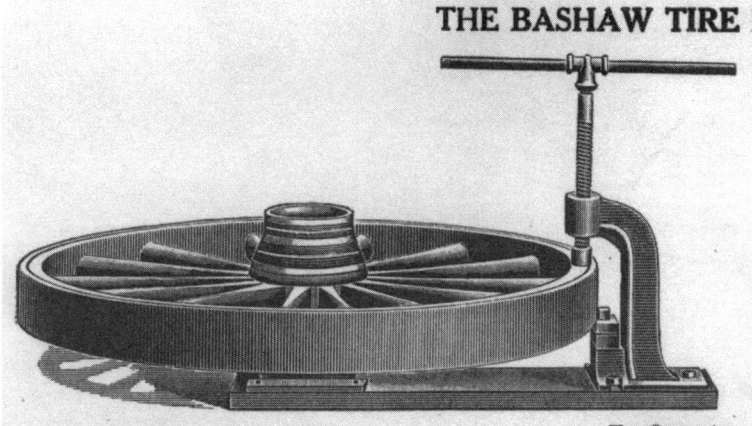

THE BASHAW TIRE REMOVER

A tool that no blacksmith can afford to be without who has tire setting to do. It saves time, patience, broken felloes and spokes. By using the Bashaw Tire Remover the wheel is not injured.

The tool is made of malleable iron with steel screw and bar, and no parts to wear out, is very simple and anybody can operate.

Directions.

This machine will remove any tire from ¼ to ¾ inches thick and 4 inches wide, no matter what the condition of the edges may be, by one man in a very few moments.

To Operate.

Screw the machine securely to the floor, place the tire on the block, corresponding to the thickness of the tire, turn the screw down against the felloe until the tire draws tight. Then turn the wheel directly over towards the machine, thereby bringing the opposite side of the felloe against the screw, which tighten down in the same manner as before and the tire will easily be removed and the wheel will be uninjured.
Price ....Each, $5.00

BASS FOUNDRY & MACHINE WORKS, Fort Wayne, IN

Established in 1853 as Cooper, Bass & Co. to operate a car wheel foundry. John H. Bass gained control in 1858 and, after several reorganizations, formed the Bass Foundry & Machine Works as a stock company in 1873.

The firm's most important product continued to be cast car wheels through the 19th century, but it also produced a variety of machinery including steam engines, grist mills, and saw mills.

In 1874, it advertised itself "Exclusive Manufacturers, under letters patent, in this state of Wisell's Spoke and Axe-Handle Lathe." The Wisell lathe, patented March 3, 1863, and also made by E.K. WISELL, was an improvement on the Blanchard design whereby a rotating pattern guided a set of rotating cutting wheels in machining a workpiece rotating in step with the pattern. The most obvious difference between the Blanchard and Wisell designs was the side-by-side mounting of the pattern and workpiece by Wisell vs. the upper-lower mounting found in most such machines based on the Blanchard design.

WISELL'S LATHE FOR IRREGULAR FORMS.

BATAVIA WHEEL CO., Batavia, NY

In common with many other wheel and axle manufacturers, Batavia designed and built many of the machines used to make its products. These machines included a wheel rim finishing machine (right), patented July 29, 1890, by J.M. Sweet. A complete wheel would be supported on a dovetail slide that had a roller arm to hold the wheel in the proper position as it was rotated against a sanding disc.

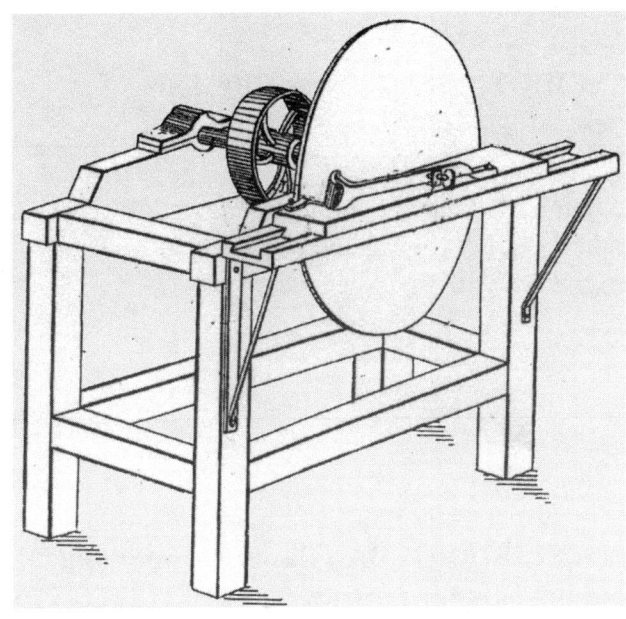

BEIDLER, PETER S., South Easton, PA

Maker, in 1868, of an automatic felly sawing machine (left). Two reciprocating saw blades A cut the felly to the desired width as it was rotated in an arc by a gear segment D of the proper radius. The segment could be changed when a different radius was required and the saw blades adjusted to change the width.

BEIDLER'S AUTOMATIC FELLY SAWING MACHINE.

BELDEN CO., R.A., Danbury, CT, later
BELDEN MACHINE CO., Danbury, CT

Formed by Russell A. Belden (1835-1899) ca.1882 as a reorganization of Hull & Belden, builders of machine tools. Belden incorporated in 1885 and by 1886 had added power hammers (Fig.1) to his product line.

In 1888 the firm became the Belden Machine Co., which continued to produce the same hammer (Fig.2). Production of the hammers continued when the line was taken over by SCRANTON & CO. in 1894.

Fig.1

UPRIGHT POWER HAMMER.

This Hammer possesses advantages superior to any other in the market. It has neither cylinders, valves or piston rods, consequently repairs are trifling. It takes up less space, less power to drive; strikes much harder and truer blows than hammers with double the weight of ram.

It can be worked to strike good alternate blows on a 3-inch and ¾-inch bar when a 100-pound hammer is used, and can be used on die work to a far greater advantage than any other hammer known. Manufactured by the

R. A. BELDEN CO., Danbury, Conn.

Fig.2

If You Use
Power Hammers

Write to us for Circulars.

BELDEN MACHINE CO.
NEW HAVEN, CONN.

BENEDICT, J.B., Michigan City, IN

Inventor and maker of a device for bending axle ends, patented September 13, 1881. It was used on newly made axles to set the "pitch" and "gather" of the wheels, and on damaged axles to straighten them.

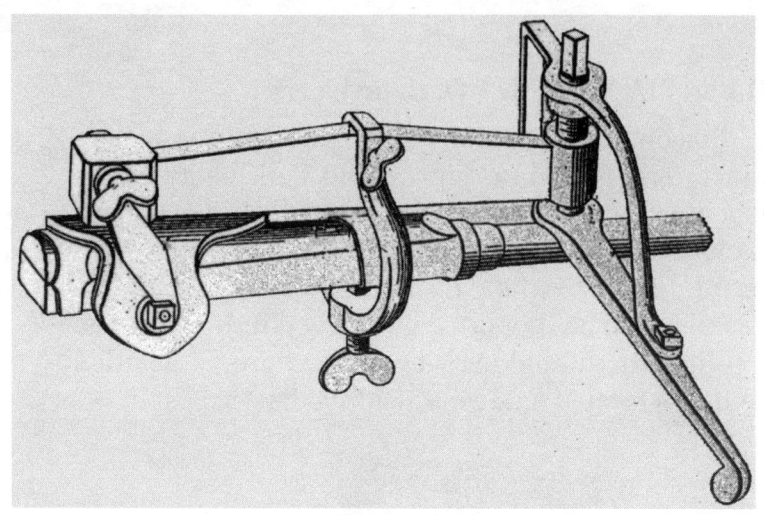

BENTEL, MARGEDANT & CO., Hamilton, OH, later
BENTEL & MARGEDANT CO., Hamilton, OH

A partnership of F. Bentel, W.C. Margedant and H. Climer formed in 1873 as a reorganization of McBETH, BENTEL & MARGEDANT. The firm continued production of a line of woodworking machinery including horizontal and upright boring machines, band and scroll saws, and planning and matching machines.

Production of carriage and wagon makers' machinery appears to have begun in 1874 with the introduction of Buffington & Forney's wheelwright machine (Fig.1), designed for planing the rims of wheels on three sides after the spokes were driven on. In 1887, a wheel-tread sanding and equalizing machine (Fig.2) was introduced.

The firm incorporated in 1886 as the Bentel & Margedant Co. and in 1891 advertised a variety of carriage and wagon makers' machinery in the *Carriage Monthly* magazine (Fig.3). Products included a felly rounding machine (Fig.4) for dressing the inside edges of the fellies and a wheel boxing machine (Fig.5) used to bore the hubs.

Fig.1

BUFFINGTON AND FORNEY'S WHEELWRIGHT'S MACHINE.

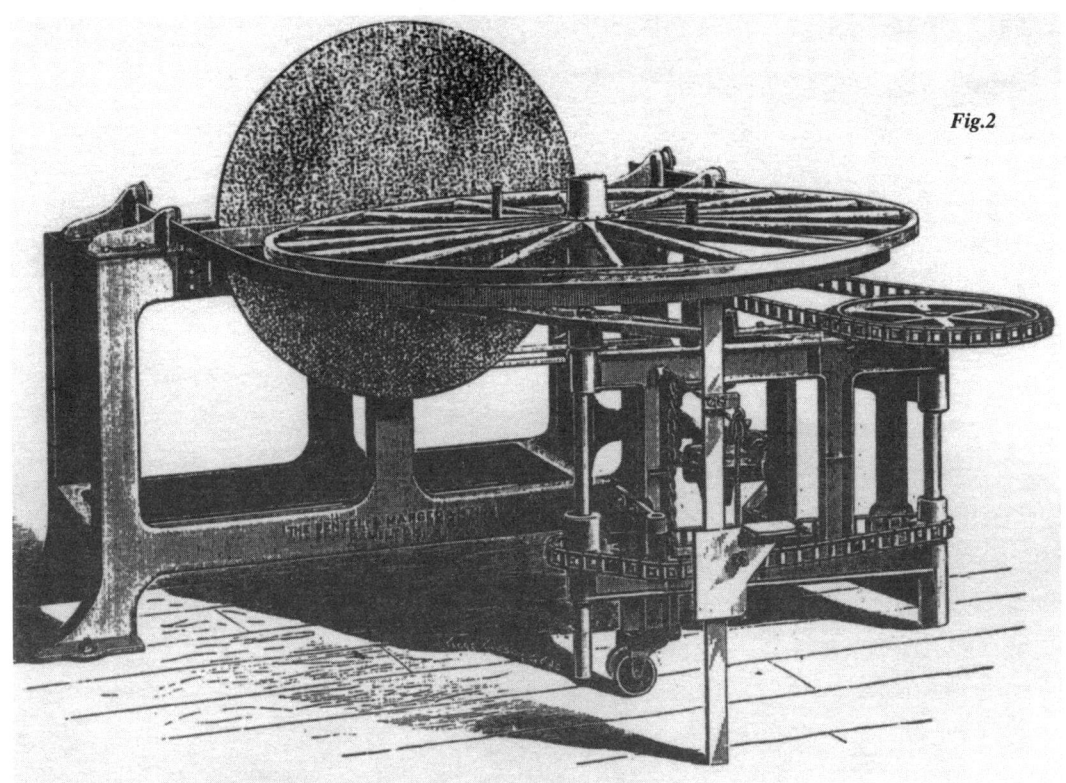

NEW WHEEL-TREAD SANDING AND EQUALIZING MACHINE.—(See description on this page.)

Fig.2

Wheel Polisher.

Felly Hand Planer.

Sand Belt Machine.

Automatic Railway Saw.

Spoke Tenoner.

9-Inch Moulder.

Wheel Boxing Machine.

THE BENTEL & MARGEDANT COMPANY. MANUFACTURERS OF WOOD WORKING MACHINERY. HAMILTON, O., U.S.A.

Felly Rounder.

Heavy Universal Saw.

Blanchard Spoke Lathe.

Heavy 2-Side Rim Planer.

Double Universal Wood Worker.

Hydrostatic Wheel Press.

Equalizing Cut-Off Saw.

Fig.3

IMPROVED FELLY ROUNDING MACHINE.

Fig.4

Fig.5

Fig. 6.—Wheel-boxing machine.

Fig.6

NO. 1 CUT-OFF BORING AND DOWELING MACHINE.

Fig.7

of assembled wheels for fitting of the wheel boxes. A felloe cut-off, boring and doweling machine (Fig.6) was introduced in 1892 and an improved spoke facing machine (Fig.7) in 1893.

1895 production included a power press "for starting and pressing on the various bands and shells on the hubs of vehicle wheels" (Fig.8), an improved rim planer (Fig.9) for planing two sides of a rim at one operation, and a new graduated stroke hub mortising and boring machine (Fig.10) for hubs up to 14" diameter and 18" in length. The mortising machine used hydraulic feed for the mortising operation rather than the commonly used direct mechanical feed powered by an operator's foot. "It will do away with the crippled and sore legs of operators."

The Bentel & Margedant Co. continued production of carriage and wagon makers' machinery into the 20th century. Catalog L, undated but issued ca.1905-1910, included 45 different machines as described in the 19 catalog pages reproduced on the following pages..

POWER CAM PRESS FOR WHEEL HUB BANDS, ETC.

GRADUATED STROKE HUB MORTISING AND BORING MACHINE.

IMPROVED RIM PLANER.

HAMILTON—OHIO—LINE

150

HAMILTON SPOKE TENON-ING OR MITERING MACHINE No. 222.

HAMILTON DIMENSION CUTOFF AND EQUALIZING SAW No. 221.

HAMILTON CENTER OR BOLT SAWING MACHINE No. 214.

HAMILTON SPOKE CUT-OFF RE-TENONING AND FACING MACHINE No. 257.

HAMILTON SPOKE TENON COMPRESSION MACHINE No. 380.

Larger Illustrations with full description on application.

HAMILTON—OHIO—LINE

148

HAMILTON AUTOMATIC BLANCHARD SPOKE LATHE No. 207.

HAMILTON—OHIO—LINE

154

HAMILTON AUTOMATIC SPOKE THROATER No. 299.

HAMILTON AUTOMATIC SPOKE TENONING AND MITERING MACHINES Nos. 298 and 199.

Larger Illustrations with full description on application.

HAMILTON—OHIO—LINE

152

HAMILTON DISK SPOKE FACER No. 179.

HAMILTON AUTOMATIC DOUBLE SPOKE FACER No. 258.

Larger Illustrations with full description on application.

HAMILTON—OHIO—LINE

HAMILTON AUTOMATIC HUB LATHE No. 297.

HAMILTON AUTOMATIC HUB LATHE No. 397.

Larger Illustrations with full description on application.

158

HAMILTON—OHIO—LINE

HAMILTON HUB BLOCK ROUGHING MACHINE No. 296.

HAMILTON HAND HUB-TURNING LATHE No. 245.

Larger Illustrations with full description on application.

156

HAMILTON—OHIO—LINE

HAMILTON HUB BLOCK REAMING MACHINE No. 197.

HAMILTON HUB BLOCK CUT-OFF SAW No. 328.

Larger Illustrations with full description on application.

162

HAMILTON—OHIO—LINE

HAMILTON HUB BLOCK BORING MACHINE No. 316.

HAMILTON HEAVY HUB BLOCK BORING OR REAMING MACHINE No. 317.

160

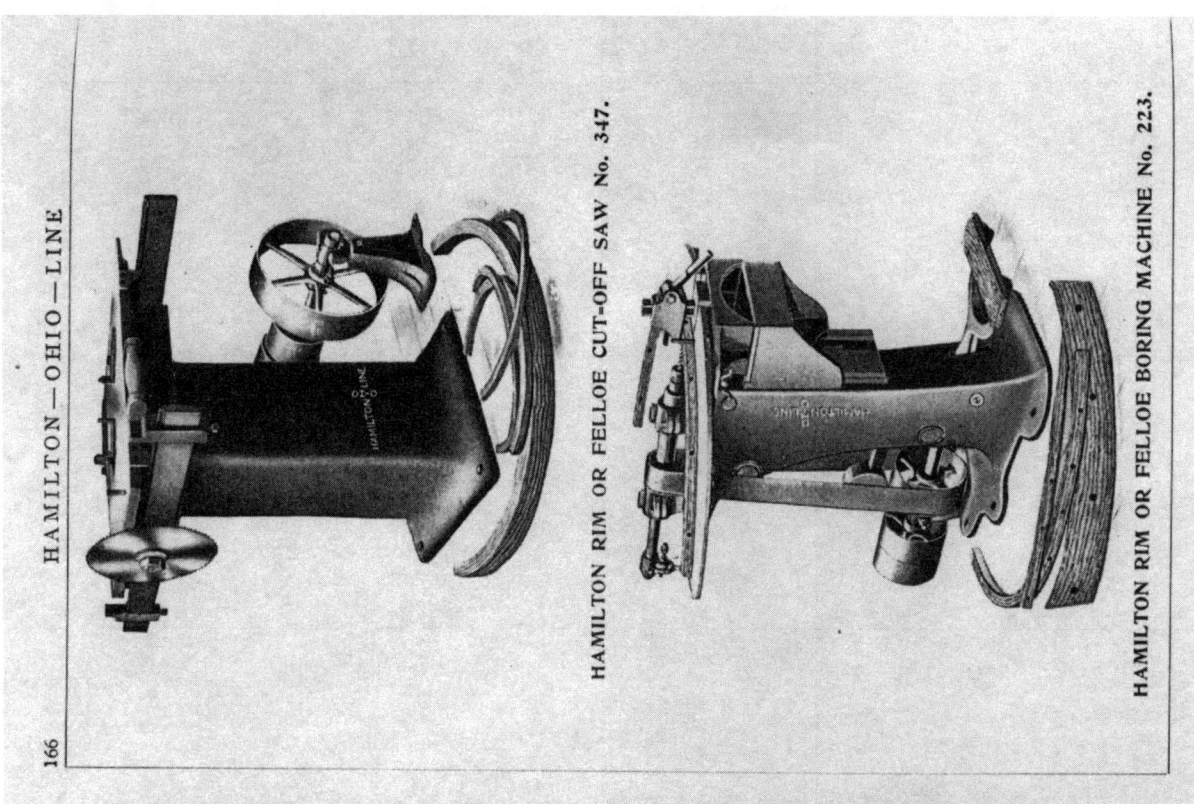

HAMILTON—OHIO—LINE

HAMILTON RIM OR FELLOE CUT-OFF SAW No. 347.

HAMILTON RIM OR FELLOE BORING MACHINE No. 223.

HAMILTON—OHIO—LINE

No. 157.

No. 164.

No. 264.

HAMILTON
HUB MORTISING
MACHINES.

Larger Illustrations with full description on application.

HAMILTON—OHIO—LINE

HAMILTON
TWO-SIDE RIM
OR FELLOE PLANER
No. 383.

HAMILTON
TWO-SIDE RIM
OR FELLOE PLANER
No. 384.

170

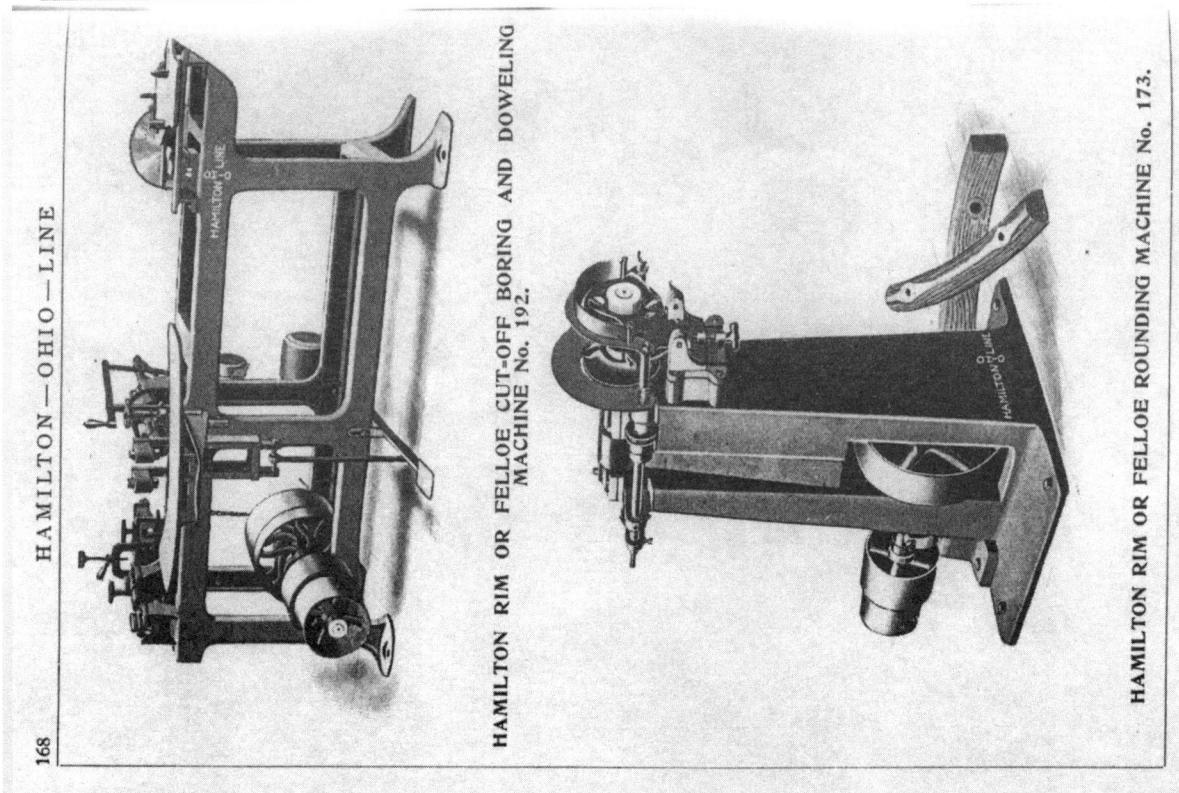

HAMILTON—OHIO—LINE

HAMILTON RIM OR FELLOE CUT-OFF BORING AND DOWELING
MACHINE No. 192.

HAMILTON RIM OR FELLOE ROUNDING MACHINE No. 173.

168

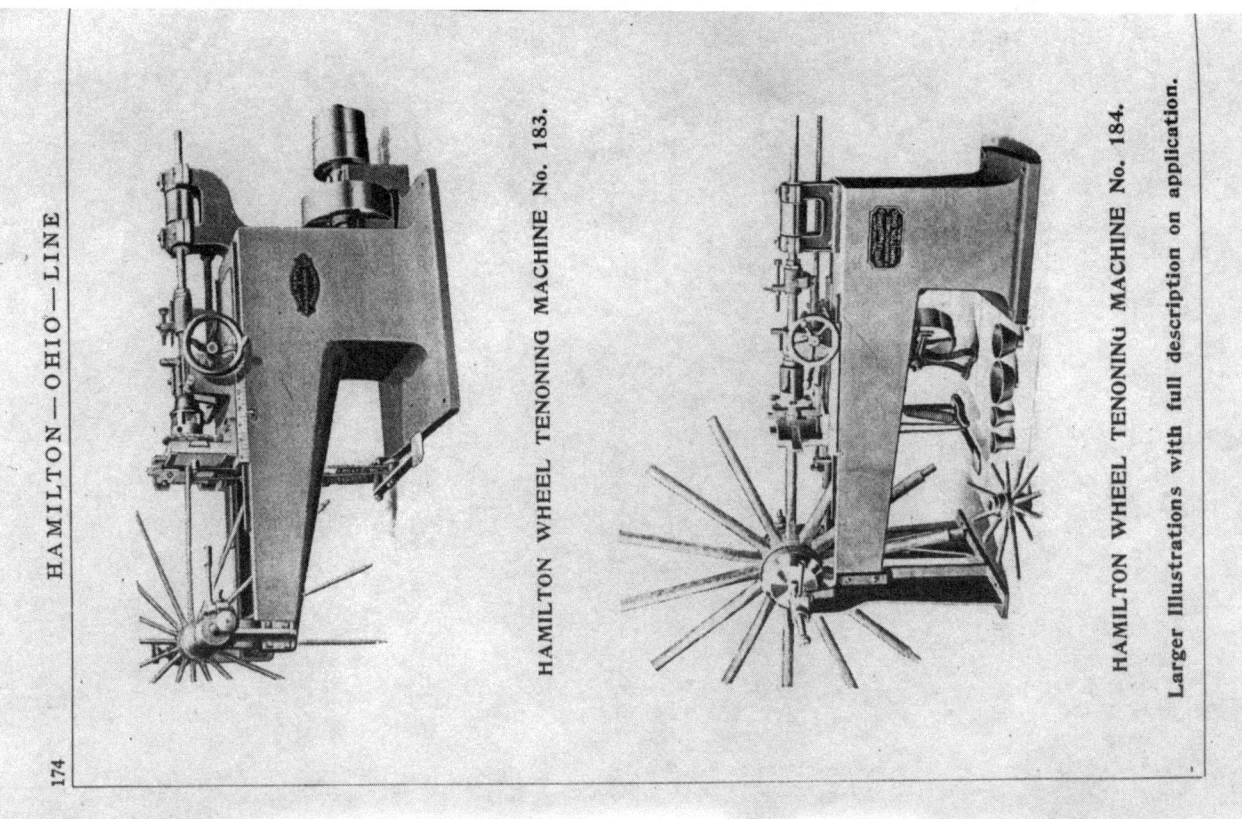

HAMILTON—OHIO—LINE

174

HAMILTON WHEEL TENONING MACHINE No. 183.

HAMILTON WHEEL TENONING MACHINE No. 184.

Larger Illustrations with full description on application.

HAMILTON—OHIO—LINE

172

HAMILTON TWO-SIDE RIM OR FELLOE PLANER No. 376.

HAMILTON FOUR-SIDE RIM OR FELLOE PLANER No. 188.

HAMILTON UNIVERSAL WHEEL MACHINE No. 186.

Larger Illustrations with full description on application.

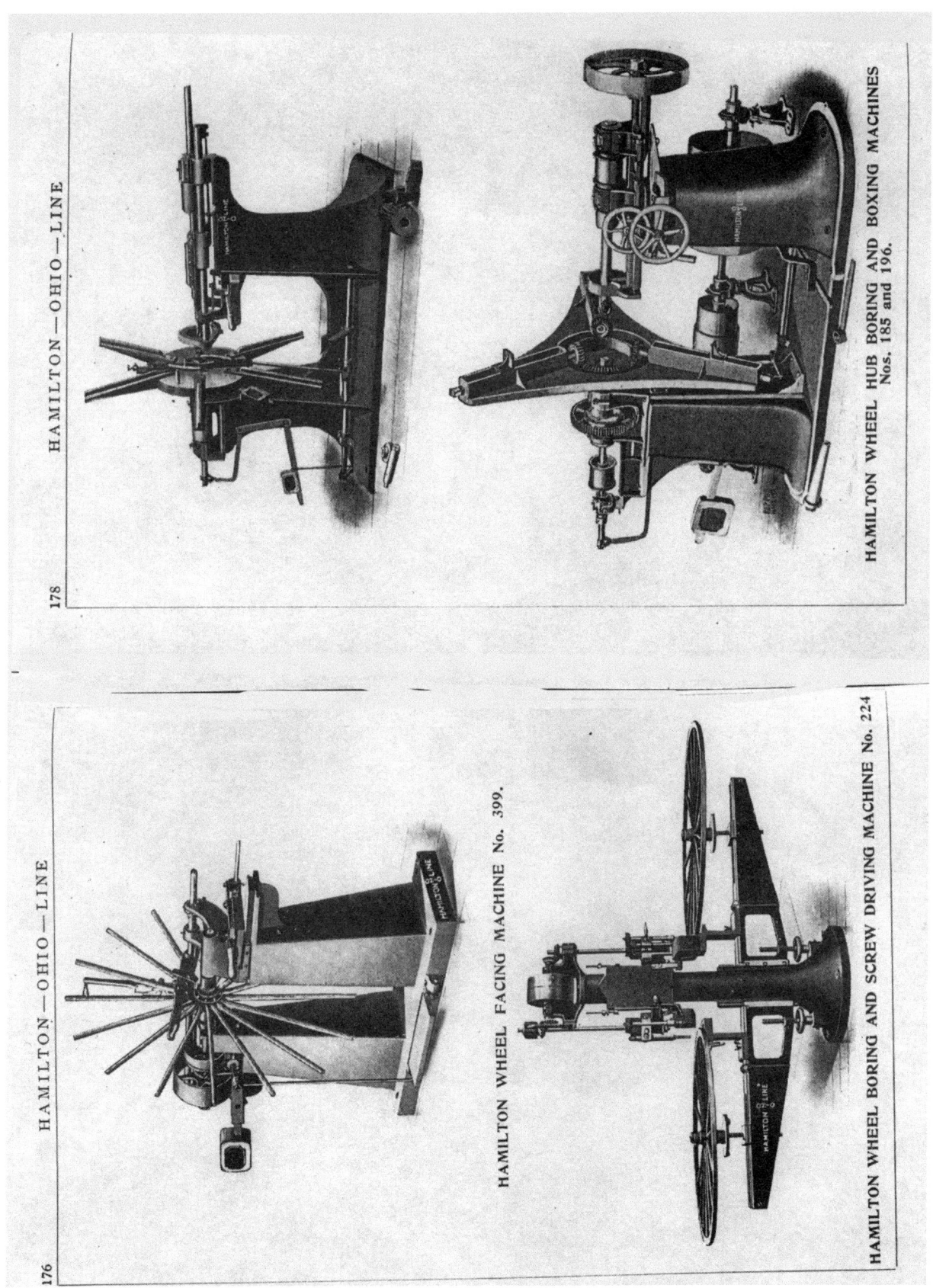

HAMILTON—OHIO—LINE

178

HAMILTON WHEEL HUB BORING AND BOXING MACHINES
Nos. 185 and 196.

HAMILTON—OHIO—LINE

176

HAMILTON WHEEL FACING MACHINE No. 399.

HAMILTON WHEEL BORING AND SCREW DRIVING MACHINE No. 224

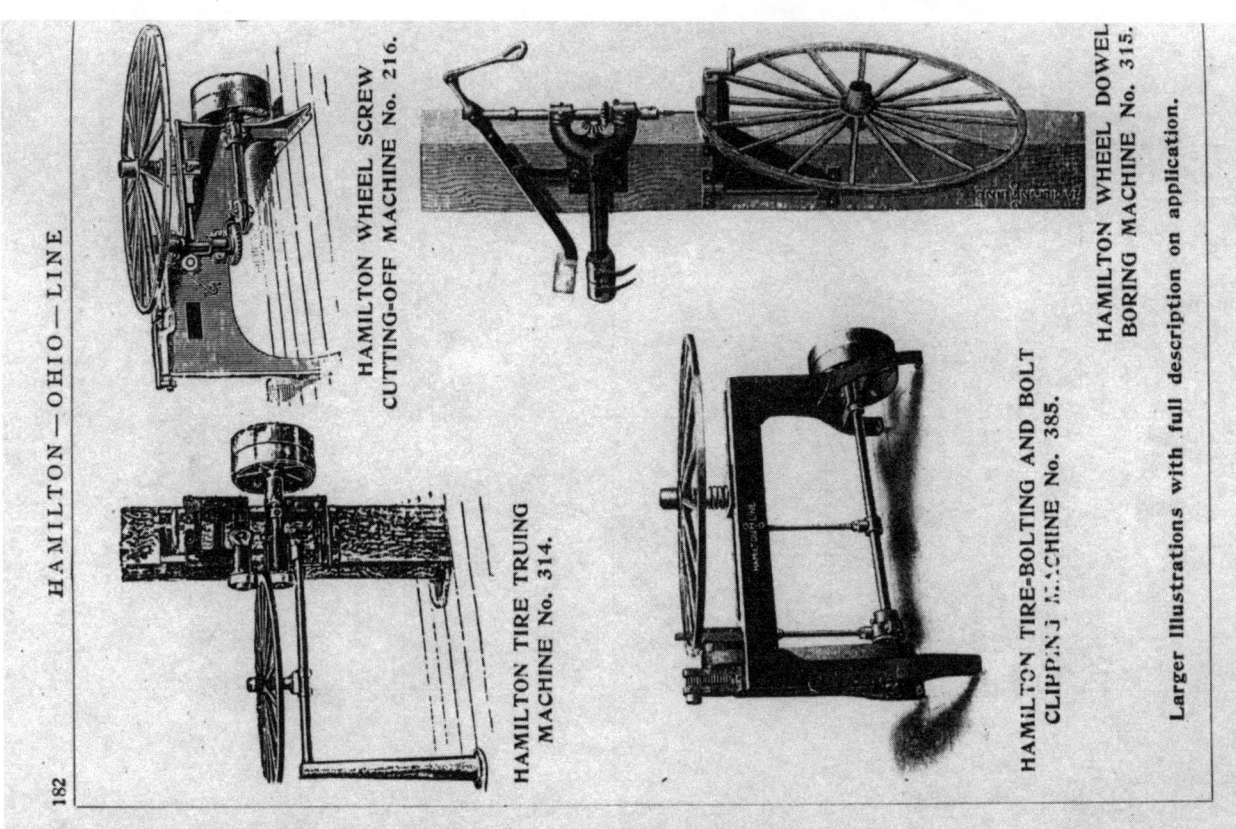

HAMILTON—OHIO—LINE

HAMILTON WHEEL SCREW CUTTING-OFF MACHINE No. 216.

HAMILTON WHEEL DOWEL BORING MACHINE No. 315.

HAMILTON TIRE TRUING MACHINE No. 314.

HAMILTON TIRE-BOLTING AND BOLT CLIPPING MACHINE No. 385.

Larger Illustrations with full description on application.

182

HAMILTON—OHIO—LINE

HAMILTON WHEEL POLISHING MACHINES No. 198 and No. 200.

HAMILTON SINGLE AND DOUBLE WHEEL TREAD SANDING AND EQUALIZING MACHINES No. 377.

Larger Illustrations with full description on application.

180

BOKOP, HENRY D., Defiance, OH

Maker, beginning about 1883, of a tire setter and cooler, patented March 20, 1883, (Fig.1). The machine consisted of a tub filled with water and a device for raising and lowering the heated tire and wheel into and out of the water. By 1894, Bokop also offered a companion tire heater (Fig.2) that could be placed over any appropriate fire.

(illustrations continued next page)

TIRE COOLER

THE BOKOP TIRE COOLER

No. 1—11 inch hole for tires up to 4 x ¾.
    Weight 450 lbs. Price complete...$60.00
    Price face plate only................ 20.00

No. 2—16 inch hole for heaviest tires.
    Weight 600 lbs. Price complete...$70.00
    Price face plate only................ 25.00

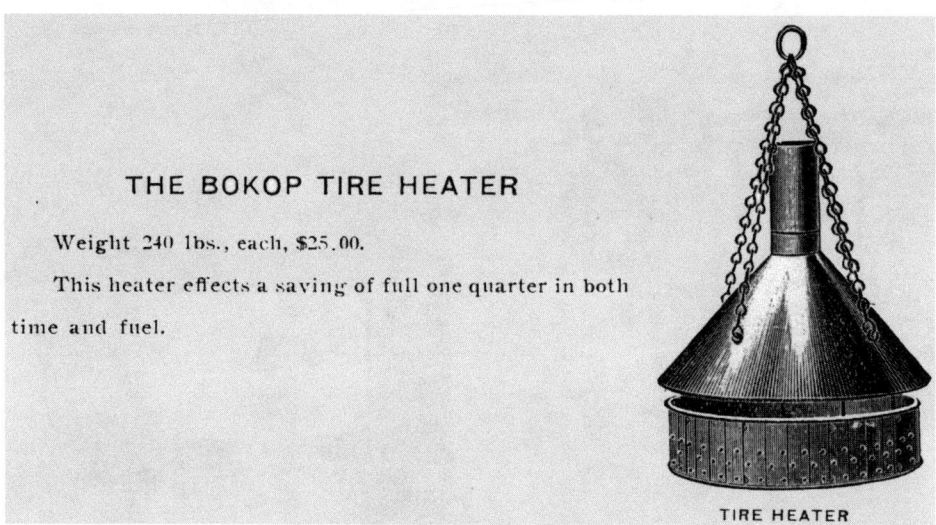

THE BOKOP TIRE HEATER

Weight 240 lbs., each, $25.00.

This heater effects a saving of full one quarter in both time and fuel.

TIRE HEATER

BOOTH, DULANEY & CO., Kuttawa, KY

Maker of spoke finishing machines (Fig.1), patented August 3, 1880, by F.A. Savage. The machine was designed to rotate three spokes past upper and lower sanding belts as each individual spoke also rotated. An improved version (Fig.2), was patented December 6, 1881.

Fig.1

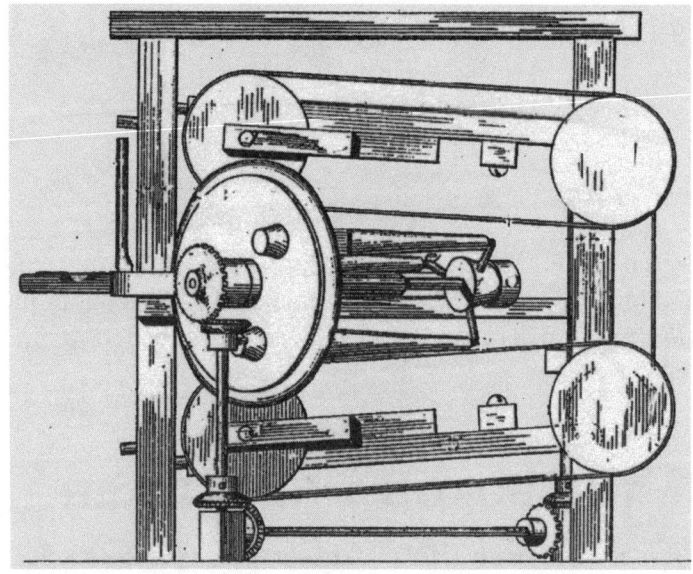

Fig.2

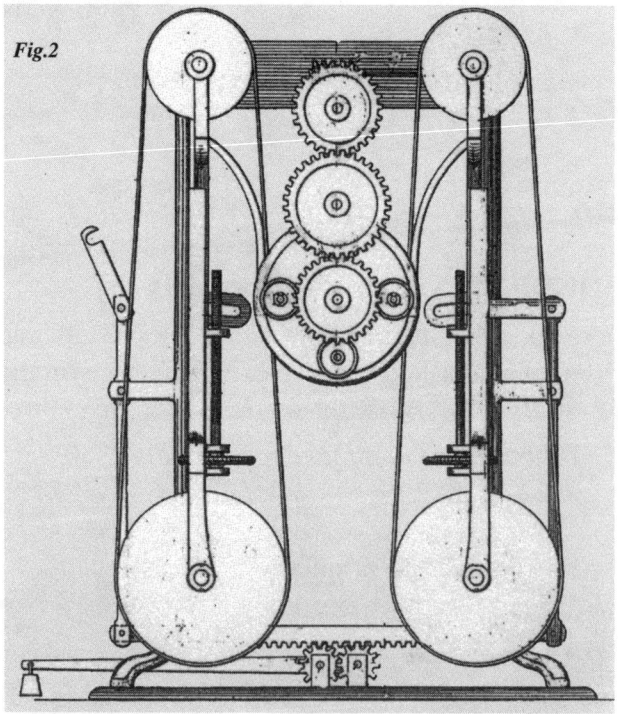

BOOTH, SON & CO.,A., Springfield, IL

Maker of a machine for turning the ends of axletrees to fit the thimble skeins, patented June 8, 1869. The workpiece was mounted on a rack driven slide which was adjustable in angle to secure the desired gather and pitch and then fed into a rotating cutter "made on the same principle as the tool ordinarily used by wagon makers for turning spokes." Unlike hand work, the machine cut all axles alike for a given setting, so that the gather and pitch was the same for all.

Made of iron, the machine weighed 1000 pounds and could turn out 200 axles in ten hours.

MACHINE FOR TURNING THE ENDS OF AXLETREES.

BOYNTON & PLUMMER,
Worcester, MA

Formed in 1880 by Edwin N. Boynton and Osgood Plummer (1835- 1916) to make small drilling machines and hand powered shapers. Boynton left the firm in 1888; Plummer continued to operate until selling out to his superintendent, Matthew G. Fitzpatrick, in 1915.

Products offered in 1883 included hand powered post drills, bench drills, and bolt cutters (Fig.1), tire shrinkers made in four sizes (Fig.2), and tire benders made in three sizes (Fig.3). In 1890, the firm introduced a power operated post drill (Fig.4) "adapted to blacksmiths' and carriage makers' use, being provided with a wheel-holding attachment, on which wheels are revolved when drilling holes in tires."

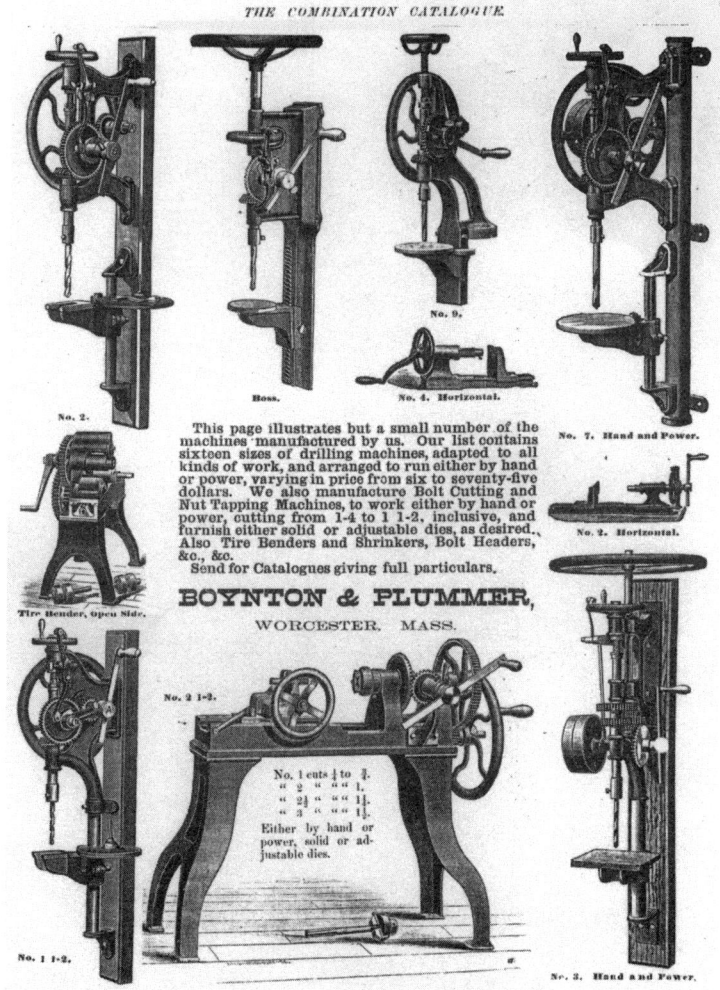

Fig. 1

Fig.2

Tire Shrinker.

No. 1 will upset tires ⅝″ thick by 4″ wide. Is furnished with clamp in centre, which is brought down on tire by means of wheel and screw, to prevent tire from kinking when being upset.
Weight, 150 pounds.   Price, $20.00.

NO. 2 TIRE SHRINKER.

Is the same as No. 1 without the clamp, wheel and screw, kinking of the tire being prevented by hammer in the hands of operator. Price, $15.00.

Fig. 1509.

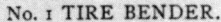

No. 3 TIRE SHRINKER.	No. 4 TIRE SHRINKER.
No. 3 is a large machine especially adapted for all sizes of tires, to 1¼″ thick, to 8″ wide. Weight, 400 pounds. Price, $60.00.	Same as No. 3, but smaller, taking tires to ⅞″ thick, to 5″ wide. Weight, 225 pounds. Price, $25.00.

Fig.3

Fig.4

Tire Benders.

No. 1 TIRE BENDER.

This is a strong and well-made machine, having open side, so that tires can be taken out without springing. The bearings or track of carriages on all our tire benders are planed perfectly parallel, which insures the tire going through the rolls and the ends coming together perfectly square. A pair of grooved rolls for bending iron edgewise is furnished when ordered. Also tight and loose pulleys can be fitted to the machine for power when desired. It will bend tires from the lightest to ¾″ thick by 5″ wide.
Weight, 500 pounds.
Geared 9 to 1.
Price, $45.00.   With grooved rolls, $60.00. With 16″x3½″ tight and loose pulleys, extra, $15.00.

No. 2 TIRE BENDER.

Same as No. 1 but smaller ; bending iron to ⅝″ thick by 3″ wide.
Weight, 250 pounds. Geared 9 to 1.
Price, $24.   With grooved rolls, $36. With 14″x3″ tight and loose pulleys, extra, $12.

No. 3 TIRE BENDER.

Weight, 1000 pounds. Geared 18 to 1.
Price, complete, for hand, $100.00. With 18x4 tight and loose pulleys, $120.00.

Fig. 1508.

22-INCH POST DRILL.

BOYNTON, RALPH H., Oshkosh, WI

Listed in the 1868 city directory as a spoke maker, Boynton was listed through most of the 1870's as a machinist. By the time he disappeared from the directory in 1884, he was listed as a lawyer.

Boynton was the inventor and maker of a machine for dressing spokes, patented January 23, 1866, (Fig.1). The machine dressed spokes as they were fed individually, by a conveyor, past a rotating cutting head. A much improved version, patented October 18, 1870, (Fig.2) used a continuous feed past upper and lower cutting heads via synchronized conveyers. A new design of spoke dressing machine, patented February 15, 1876, (Fig.3), was equipped with a reel that mounted three spokes, rotating them into position adjacent to an upper set of form cutters which formed the square part of the spoke and a lower set which formed the round, tapered section. The latter two machines would have been highly productive.

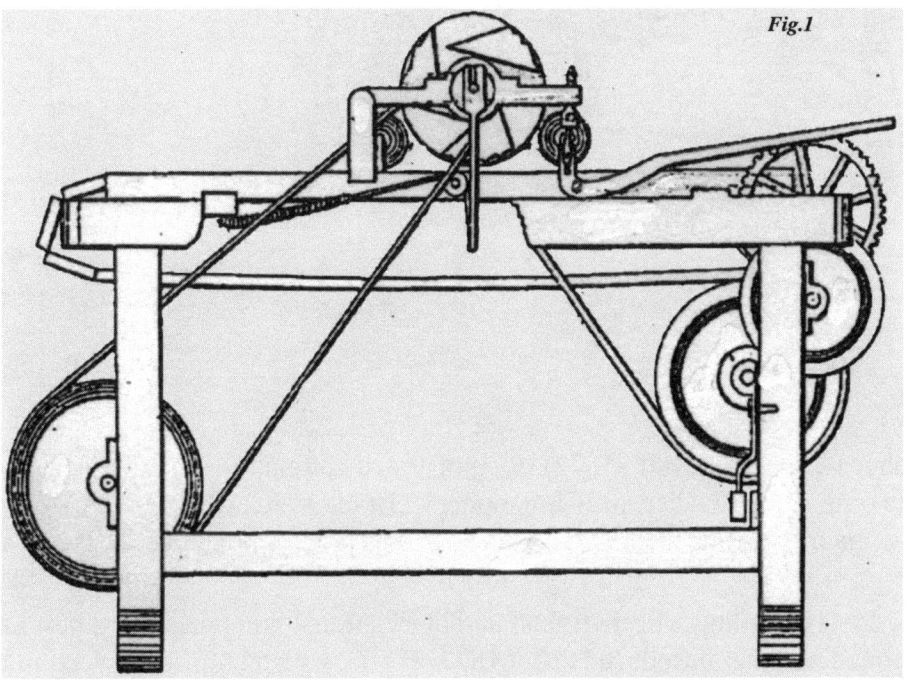

Fig.1

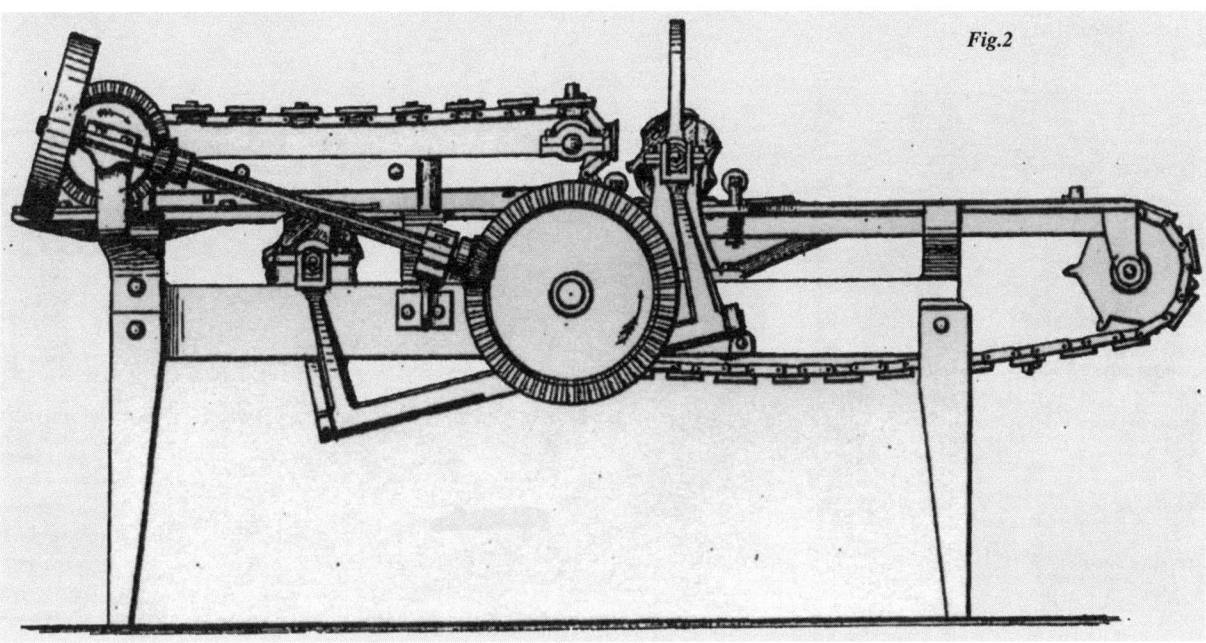

Fig.2

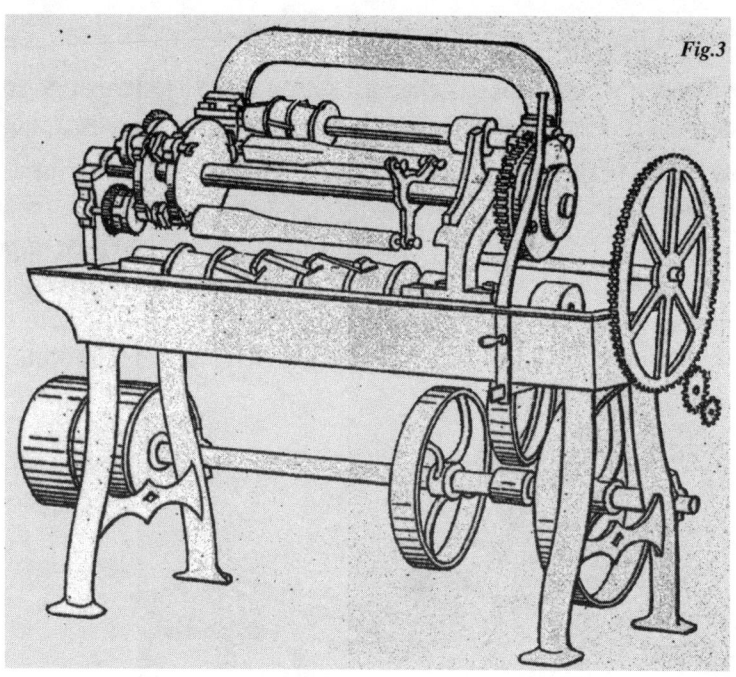

Fig.3

BRADLEY MFG. CO., Syracuse, NY, later
BRADLEY & CO., Syracuse, NY

Founded in 1832 by Christopher C. Bradley (1800-1872), who operated a foundry. The firm became the Bradley Mfg. Co. in 1872 when the senior Bradley died and Christopher C. Bradley, Jr. (1834-1916) took over. It became Bradley & Co. in 1878 and again reorganized, as C.C. Bradley & Son, when Christopher C. Bradley ILL (1874-1932) joined in 1894.

The firm made a variety of products including wheelwrights' and blacksmiths' equipment. The best known product was the BRADLEY cushioned hammer introduced about 1873 (Fig.1), with an improved version introduced by 1877 (Fig.2). A larger version, the BRADLEY upright cushioned strap hammer (Fig.3) was added by 1887. *(continued next page)*

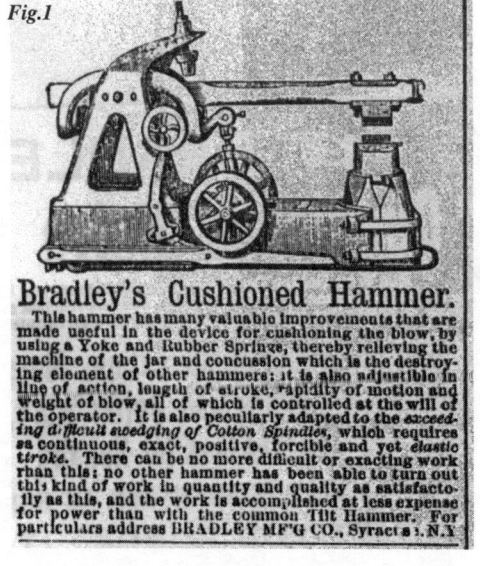

Fig.1

Bradley's Cushioned Hammer.

This hammer has many valuable improvements that are made useful in the device for cushioning the blow, by using a Yoke and Rubber Springs, thereby relieving the machine of the jar and concussion which is the destroying element of other hammers: it is also adjustible in line of action, length of stroke, rapidity of motion and weight of blow, all of which is controlled at the will of the operator. It is also peculiarly adapted to the *exceeding difficult swedging of Cotton Spindles*, which requires a continuous, exact, positive, forcible and yet *elastic stroke*. There can be no more difficult or exacting work rhan this: no other hammer has been able to turn out this kind of work in quantity and quality as satisfactoily as this, and the work is accomplished at less expense for power than with the common Tilt Hammer. For particulars address BRADLEY MF'G CO., Syracuse. N.Y.

Fig.2

BRADLEY'S
CUSHIONED HAMMER

BRADLEY'S CUSHIONED HAMMER

STANDS TO-DAY
WITHOUT
AN EQUAL.

It approaches nearer the action of the smith's arm than any hammer in the world.

Bradley & Company,
SYRACUSE, N. Y.
[Established 1832.]

Other products for wagon and carriage makers included the DUFFEY tire-heating furnace (Fig.4) offered in 1889. The furnace featured rollers that continuously rotated the tires through a fire. "As fast as one is removed nother is put in its place, the heating going on faster that the tires can be put on the wheels."

Fig.3

Bradley Hammers.

If you plate, draw, square, taper or weld iron and steel, you need a Bradley Hammer.
If you swage, collar, spindle, or do any manner of die work, a Bradley Hammer will soon pay for itself.
That the Bradley is the best Power Hammer in the market has never been questioned. Our circulars illustrate, describe, give sizes and prices.

BRANCHES: { 14 Warren St., New York.   BRADLEY & COMPANY,
{ 96-98 Sudbury St., Boston.   Syracuse, N. Y.

Fig.4

DUFFEY TIRE-HEATING FURNACE, BUILT BY BRADLEY & COMPANY, SYRACUSE, N. Y.

BRECHT BUTCHERS SUPPLY CO., GUS. V., St. Louis, MO

Primarily a maker of meat choppers and other meat processing devices, the firm also offered (right), beginning in 1868, a self-centering hub-boring machine, patented June 16, 1868, and widely sold. An improved version was introduced in 1891.

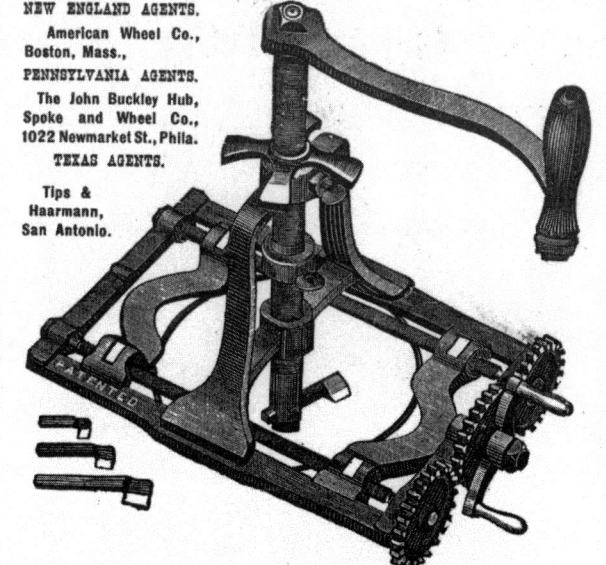

GUS. V. BRECHT'S
Patent Self-Centering Hub-Boring Machine
FOR WAGON AND CARRIAGE-MAKERS.

NEW ENGLAND AGENTS.
American Wheel Co., Boston, Mass.,
PENNSYLVANIA AGENTS.
The John Buckley Hub, Spoke and Wheel Co., 1022 Newmarket St., Phila.
TEXAS AGENTS.
Tips & Haarmann, San Antonio.

The most durable and practical machine in the market. Send for descriptive circular. Manufactured by the

PACIFIC COAST AGENTS,
TAYLOR & SNOOK,
710-712 FOLSOM ST.,
SAN FRANCISCO CAL.
Gus. V. Brecht Butchers Supply Co.
1201-1211 Cass Avenue, St. Louis, Mo.

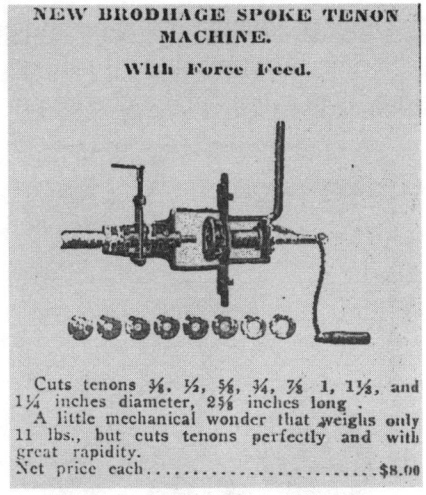

BRODHAGE, WILLIAM, Addieville, IL

Inventor and maker of the Brodhage spoke tenoning machine, patented April 11, 1899. Capable of cutting tenons from 3/8" to 1 1/4" in diameter and 2 5/8" long, it was offered as late as 1907.

BROOKS MACHINE CO., Wichita, KS

Maker of the Brooks cold tire setters, patented August 6, 1907, by Isaac M. Hackney. The machines were offered in hand power (Fig.1) and hydraulic (Fig.2) versions.

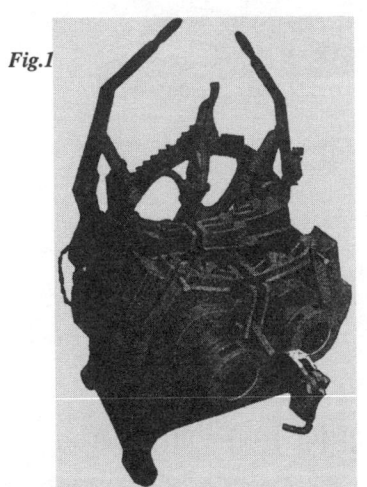

BROWN & VANARSDALE MFG. CO., Grand Crossing, IL

Maker, in 1886, of seamless thimble skeins, sad irons, tinsmiths' tools and hub reaming machines.

BRYAN, JAMES M., Penningtonville, PA

Inventor and maker of a combination tire bending and punching machine, patented June 2, 1868. The machine was a fairly simple lever punch with a set of rollers F on which a "fellow pattern" of the curvature of the tire to be bent, is placed and then forced against the tire material to form the desired radius.

BRYAN'S PATENT COMBINED TIRE BENDER AND PUNCH.

BUTTS & ORDWAY, Boston, MA

A partnership of Frederic H. Butts and Henry C. Ordway, formed in 1888 to make tools for carriage makers and blacksmiths. The firm incorporated in 1898 as a jobbing business; tool production appears to have ceased at that time.

Products included the SURE GRIP tire upsetter for tires up to 3" x 5/8" patented November 9, 1886, (Fig.1); the P&C hand operated hub-boring machine introduced in 1891 (Fig.2); a foot-operated vise weighing 150 pounds (Fig.3) offered in 1892; and the B & O tire bolt wrench (Fig.4) offered in 1896.

In 1893, the firm also offered the BOWE spoke extractor previously made by S.W. KENT and the BOSTON tire bender.

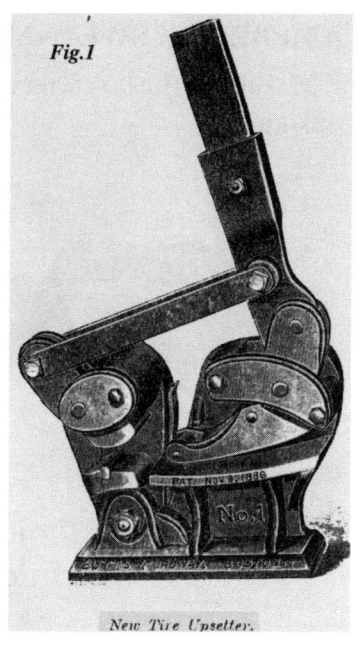

Fig.1

New Tire Upsetter.

Fig.2

P. & C. Hub Boring Machine.

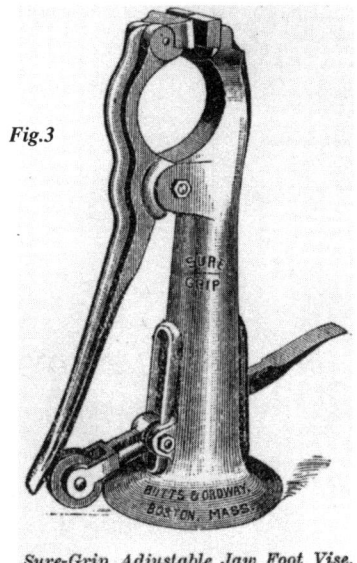

Fig.3

Sure-Grip Adjustable Jaw Foot Vise.

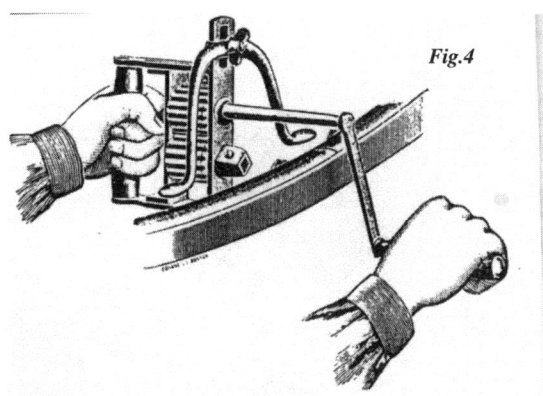

Fig.4

The B. & O. Tire Bolt Wrench.

BYRNE & ZIEGAUS, Sharon, WI

Maker, beginning in 1888, of a tire bolt clamp and wrench, patented March 13, 1888, by John Byrne.

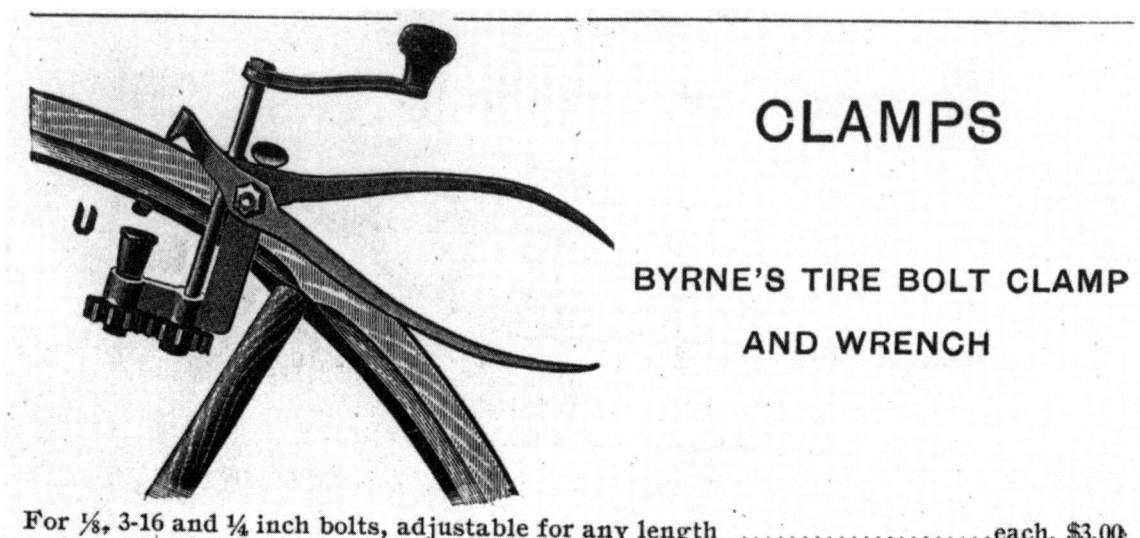

CLAMPS

BYRNE'S TIRE BOLT CLAMP

AND WRENCH

For ⅛, 3-16 and ¼ inch bolts, adjustable for any length ....each, $3.00

CAMPBELL & SWETNAM, Fairfax Station, VA

Maker of a tire bolt wrench, patented June 26, 1894, by Joseph E. Campbell. The design featured a removable crank handle.

Western Chief Tire and Axle Shrinker No. 1½

Use for Light and Rapid Work

This Shrinker is far superior to any other hot-metal shrinker on the market, and is guaranteed to operate with one-half the labor of any shrinker of equal capacity.

The Shrinking Lever pulls toward the machine, not away, as is the case with other makes, and with a powerfully arranged gearing a light man can operate this Shrinker to its full capacity.

The Bed has an open-and-shut movement of 1 5-6 inches.

The Jaws are machine-cut, tool steel, properly hardened.

Size of Jaws, 4½ inches wide, and will shrink from smallest to 4 x 1 inch round-edge tires, and 1¼ inch square axles.   Weight 400 pounds.

List Price $40.00

CANEDY-OTTO CO., Chicago Heights, IL

Formed in 1889 when William E. Canedy (1842-1914) moved his business, the Minnesota Anvil & Vise Co., to Downer's Grove, IL and took A.T. Otto as a partner. The firm moved to Chicago Heights, IL, in 1894.

Products included a wide variety of blacksmiths' tools and equipment such as forges, drills, etc. Carriage and wagon builders' equipment included the WESTERN CHIEF tire and axle shrinker offered in 1913 and shown at left.

CASSELMAN, W.J., Vernon, NY

Inventor and maker of a hub boring machine, patented May 9, 1854. Turning the hand crank rotated the wheel while also pulling the single point cutter through the hub by action of the threaded rod *c*. A tapered bore was formed by action of the lever *G* as it is moved by action of the cam *J* and follower *g*.

(see illustration next page)

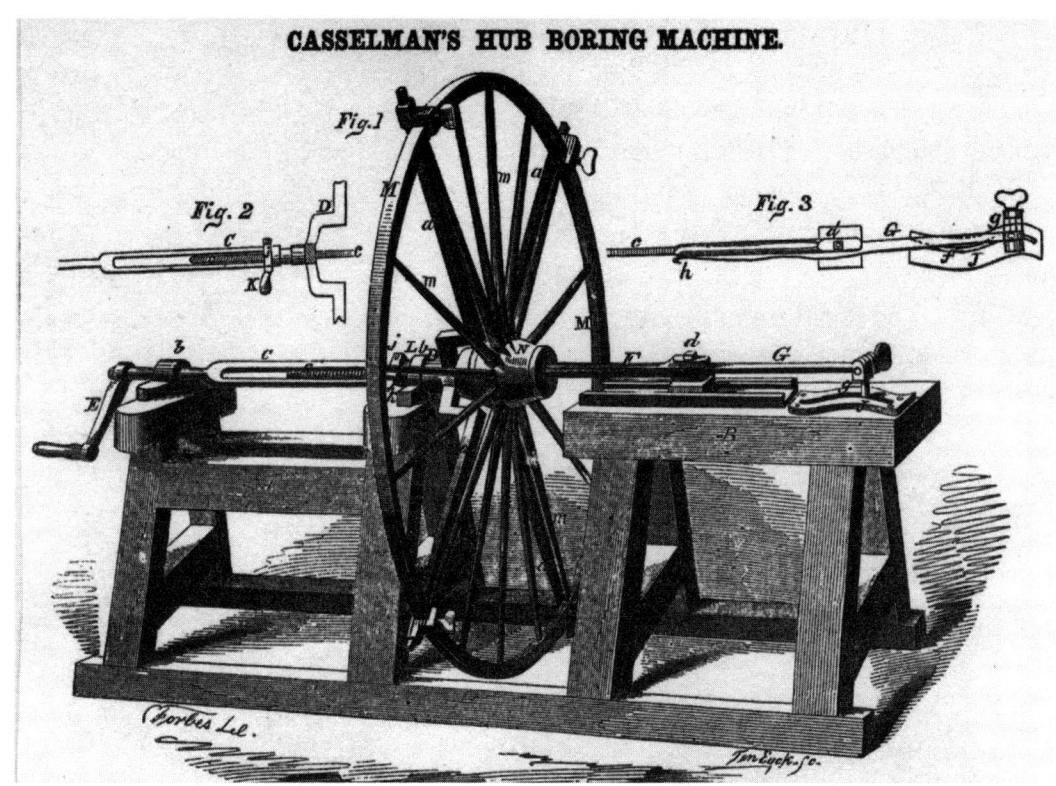

CASSELMAN'S HUB BORING MACHINE.

CHAMPION BLOWER & FORGE CO., Lancaster, PA

Founded in 1877 by Henry B. Keiper (1858-1920) to make blacksmiths' tools and equipment. Keiper served as president until his death in 1920.

Champion, beginning in 1887, offered a series of tire benders, patented March 15, 1887. These included the CHAMPION (Fig.1) for tires up to 3"x 3/4", the EUREKA (Fig.2) in two sizes, for tires up to 4"x 1"and 6"x 1", the GIANT (Fig.3) in four sizes for tires up to 6"x 1". Tire benders offered in 1906 included the COLUMBIAN (Fig.4), in three sizes, for tires up to 6"x 1", the NEW PATENT PEERLESS (Fig.5) in four sizes, for tires up to 6"x 1", the NEW PATENT GIANT (Fig.6) in four sizes, for tires up to 6"x 1", the NEW PATENT EUREKA (Fig.7) for 4"x 1" tires, and the CHAMPION NEW PATENT (Fig.8) for 3"x 3/4" tires. By 1918, Champion had added the large SAMSON (Fig.9) tire bender to the line. *(continued on next three pages)*

THE CHAMPION
OLD STYLE TIRE BENDER

Fig.1

Patented March 15, 1887.

THE CHAMPION
OLD STYLE EUREKA TIRE BENDER

Fig.2

Patented March 15, 1887.

Tire shrinkers offered in 1918 included the CHAMPION (Fig.10) for tires up to 4"x 1"and axles up to 1 1/4", the AMERICAN (Fig.11) for tires up to 4"x 1"and axles up to 1 1/4", the STAR (Fig.12), in two sizes for tires up to 7" x 1 1/2"and axles up to 3 1/2", the LANCASTER (Fig.13) for tires up to 4"x 1"and axles up to 1 1/2",and the STODDARD (Fig.14), made in five sizes for tires up to 6" and axles up to 2". Champion was one of a number of makers of the STODDARD tire shrinker, first marketed in 1875.

By 1916, the firm also offered the HERCULES power hammer (Fig.15).

Surprisingly, the firm continued to offer two models of tire benders, the NEW PATENT EUREKA and NEW PATENT CHAMPION, and one tire shrinker, the AMERICAN, as late as 1950.

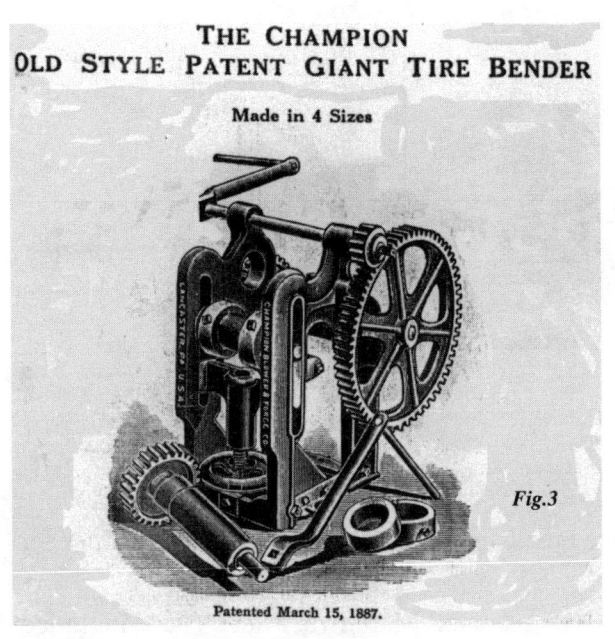

THE CHAMPION
OLD STYLE PATENT GIANT TIRE BENDER
Made in 4 Sizes

Fig.3

Patented March 15, 1887.

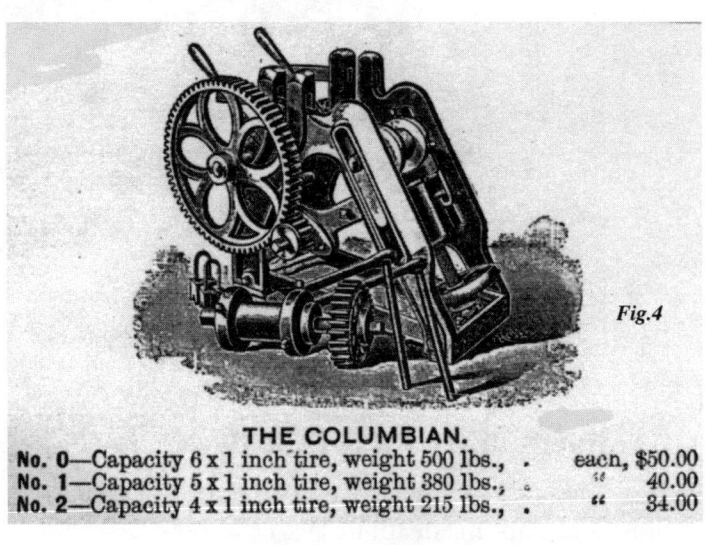

Fig.4

THE COLUMBIAN.

No. 0—Capacity 6 x 1 inch tire, weight 500 lbs., . . each, $50.00
No. 1—Capacity 5 x 1 inch tire, weight 380 lbs., . . " 40.00
No. 2—Capacity 4 x 1 inch tire, weight 215 lbs., . . " 34.00

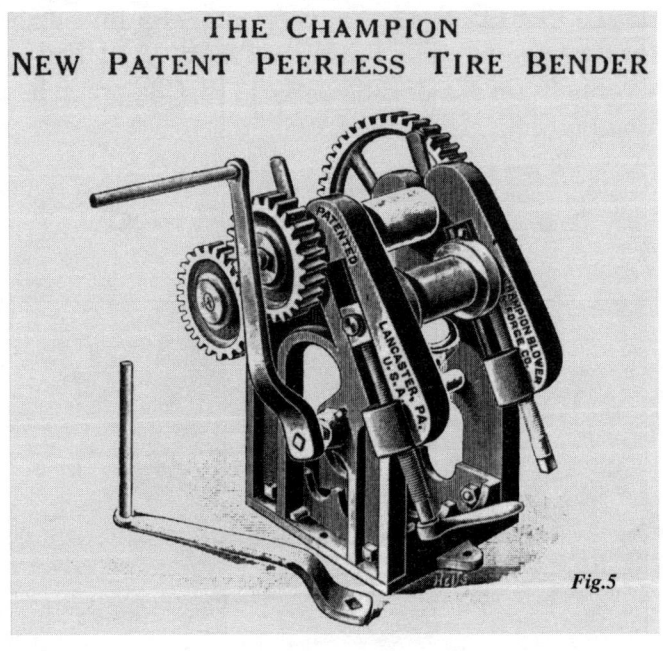

THE CHAMPION
NEW PATENT PEERLESS TIRE BENDER

Fig.5

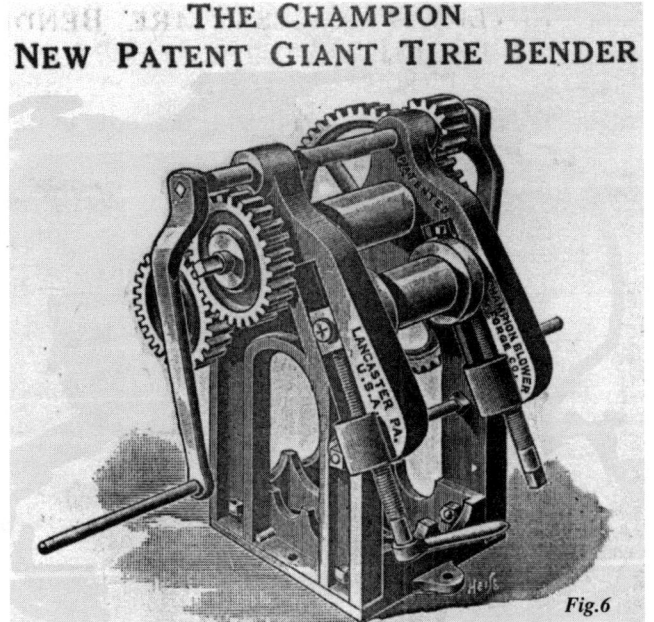

THE CHAMPION
NEW PATENT GIANT TIRE BENDER

Fig.6

Fig.7

Fig.8

CHAMPION "SAMSON" TIRE BENDER

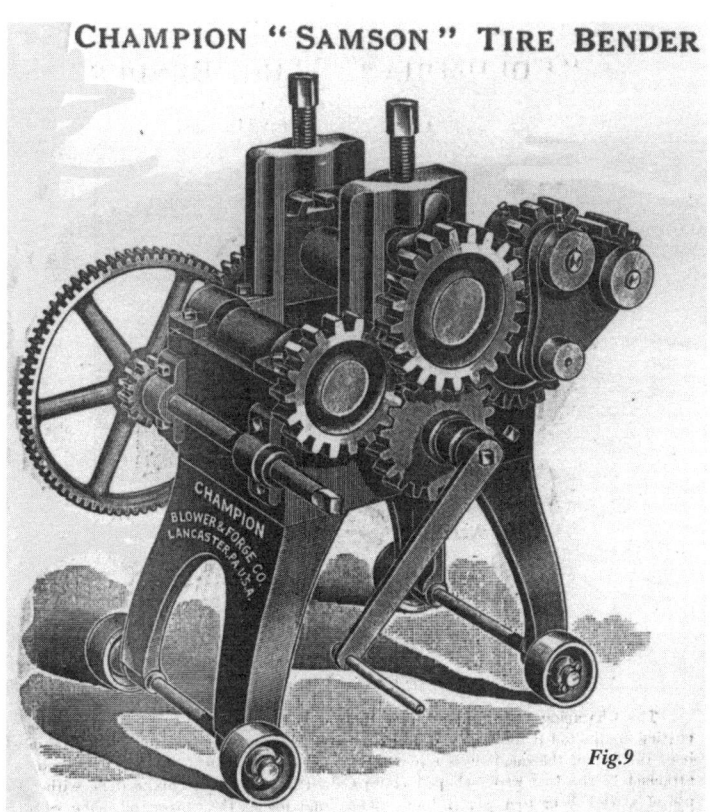

Fig.9

THE CHAMPION TIRE SHRINKER

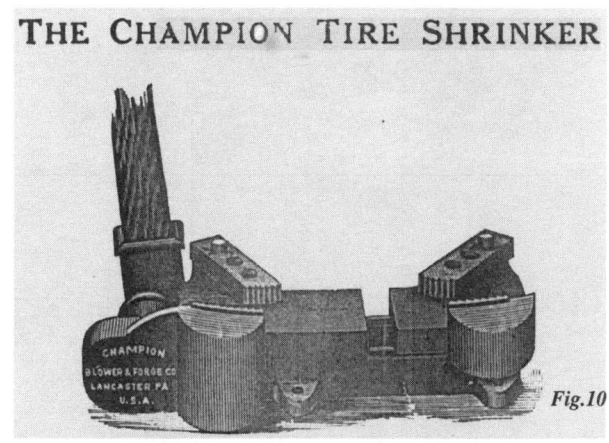

Fig.10

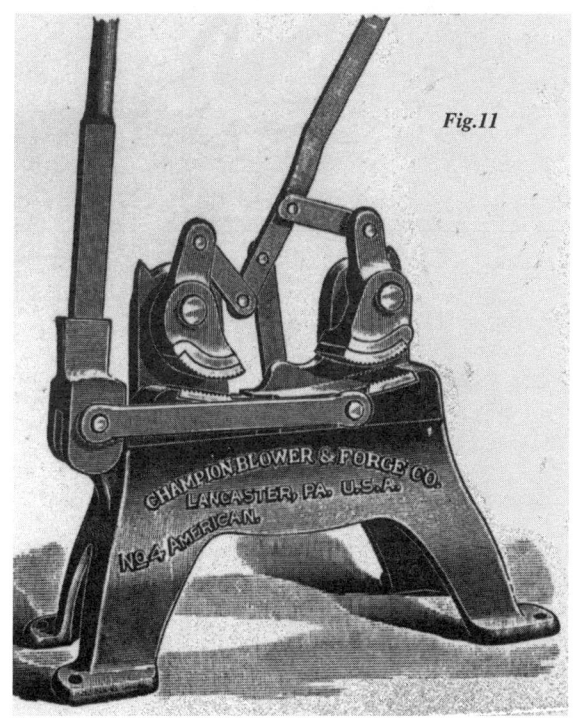

Fig.11

No. 2 Pattern.

Fig. 12

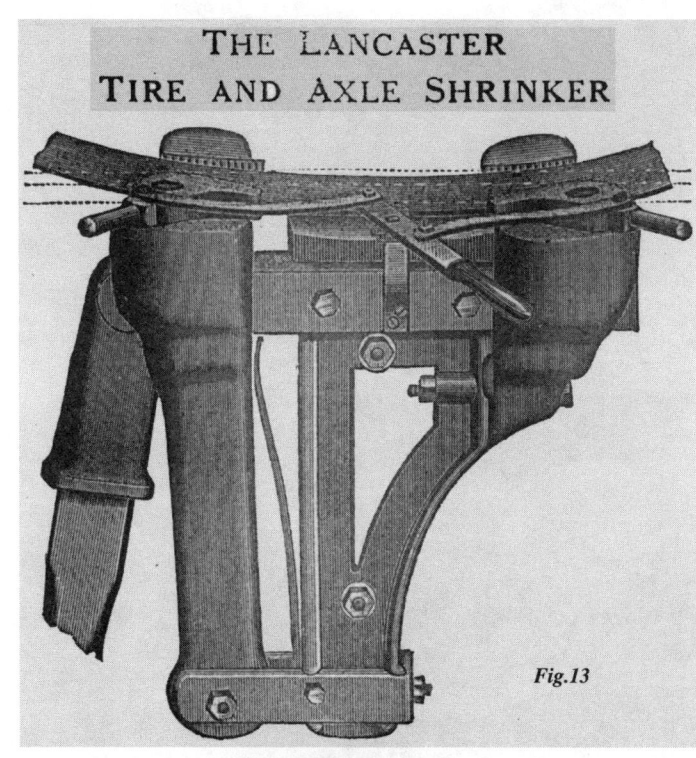

THE LANCASTER TIRE AND AXLE SHRINKER

Fig. 13

CHAMPION STODDARD TIRE SHRINKER

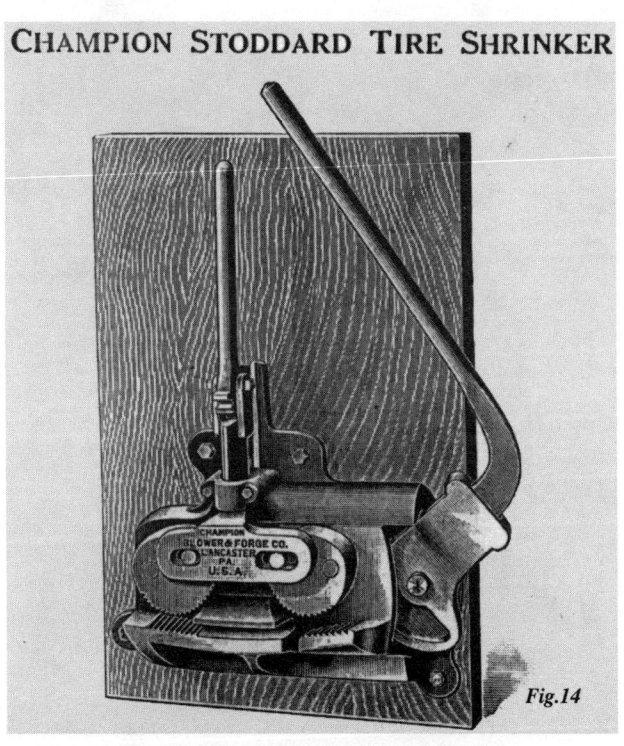

Fig. 14

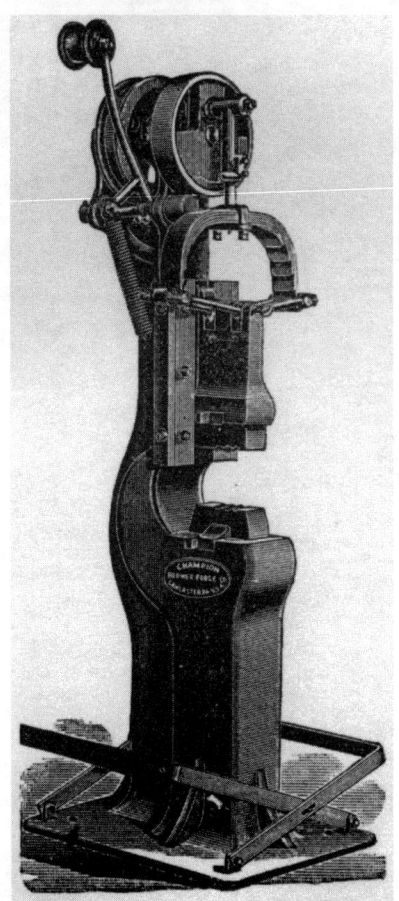

Fig. 15

Hercules "Patented" Power Hammer. Weight of Ram 65 lbs. The Hammer with the Flexibility in Stroke of a Hammer in a Mechanic's Hand.

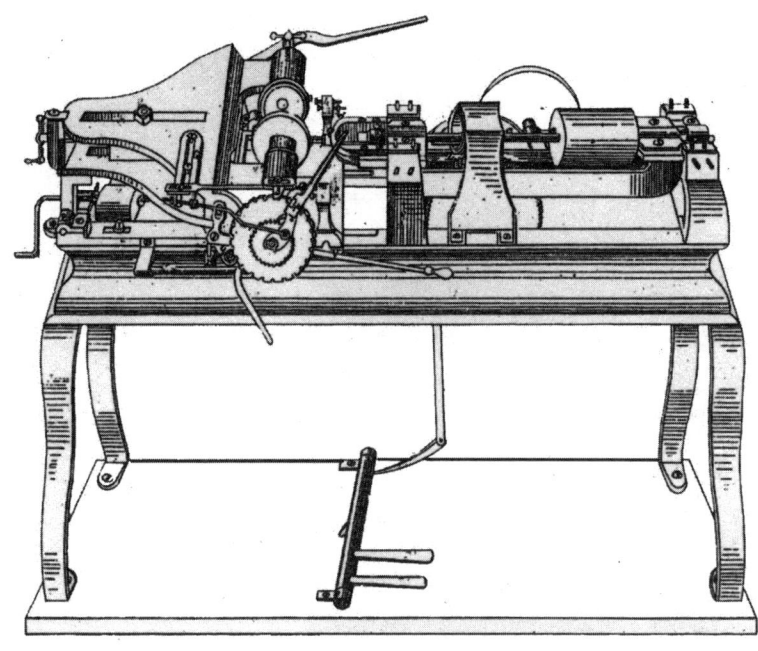

CHUBB, STEWART & LUTHER, Grand Rapids, MI

A maker of agricultural implements, the firm also made machinery for its own use and for sale to others. Production of wagon makers' machines included a horizontal hub mortising machine, patented October 17, 1871, by Peter Snyder, shown at right.

CINCINNATI TOOL CO., Cincinnati, OH

Formed in 1879 by Frank Martin and P.S. Anderson to make spokeshaves, scrapers and other woodworking tools. The firm incorporated in 1884 with Martin as president and E.H. Hargrave as secretary and treasurer. Hargrave was elected president in 1899 and reorganized the company as the Hargrave Tool Co. in 1925.

Products for carriage and wagon makers, offered in 1894, included spoke pointers made in two sizes (Fig.1), the No. 1 hollowauger, adjustable from 3/8" to 1" (Fig.2),and the No. 3 hollowauger, adjustable from 1/4" to 1 1/4" (Fig.3).

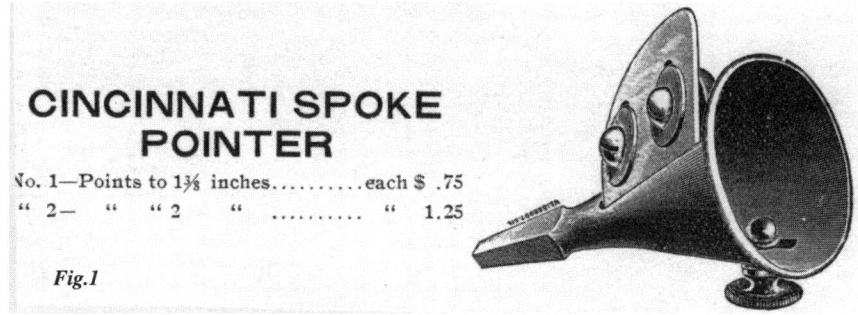

CINCINNATI SPOKE POINTER

No. 1—Points to 1⅜ inches..........each $ .75
" 2— " " 2 " .... " 1.25

Fig.1

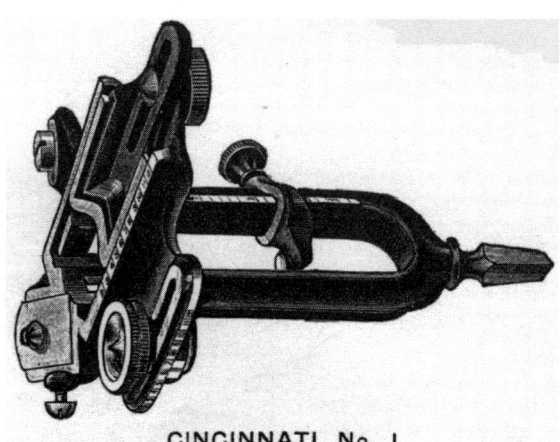

Fig.2

CINCINNATI, No. 1

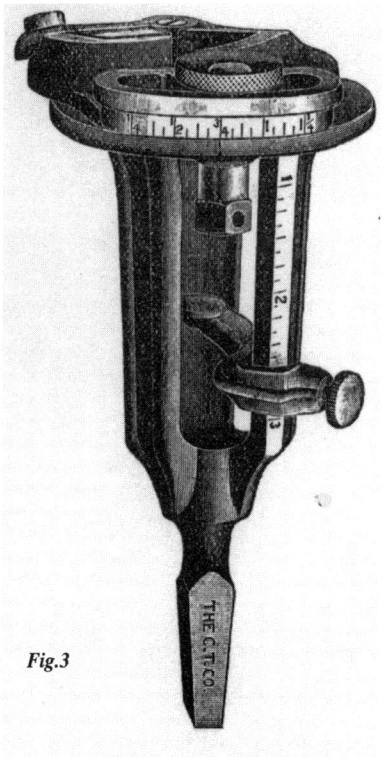

Fig.3

Adjustable Hollow Auger No. 3.

41

COE, CHARLES W., Fenton, MI

Maker, beginning about 1869, of tools for blacksmiths and wheelwrights. Early production included a post drill patented January 19, 1869.

By 1882, Coe had introduced a line of tire shrinkers and benders that eventually included the LITTLE GIANT, offered in two sizes (Fig.1); COE'S No. 1 (Fig.2); COE'S No. 2 (Fig.3); COE'S No. 3;and COE'S No. 4 (Fig.4). The tire benders were offered as late as 1906.

Fig.1

Little Giant.

No. 1—With Bench, Upsets Tires up to 2 in., . $12.00
Weight 100 Lbs.

No. 2—Without Bench, Upsets Tires up to 4 in., . 18.00
Weight 175 Lbs.

COE'S TIRE BENDER. *Fig.2*

NO. 1.

Will bend Tire 4 inches wide.................................... $12 00

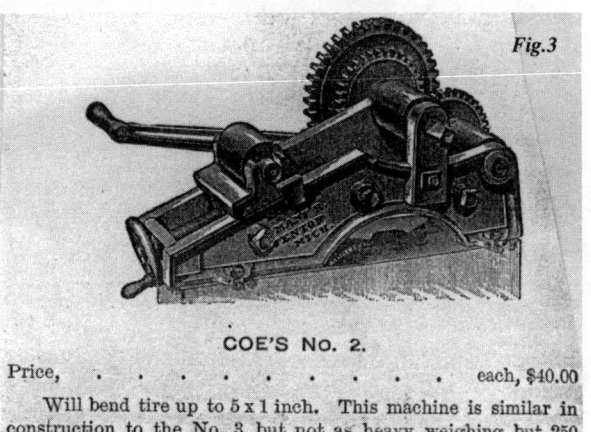

Fig.3

COE'S No. 2.

Price, ... each, $40.00

Will bend tire up to 5 x 1 inch. This machine is similar in construction to the No. 3, but not as heavy, weighing but 250 pounds. It is a wrought iron gib roller that can be removed to free the bended tire.

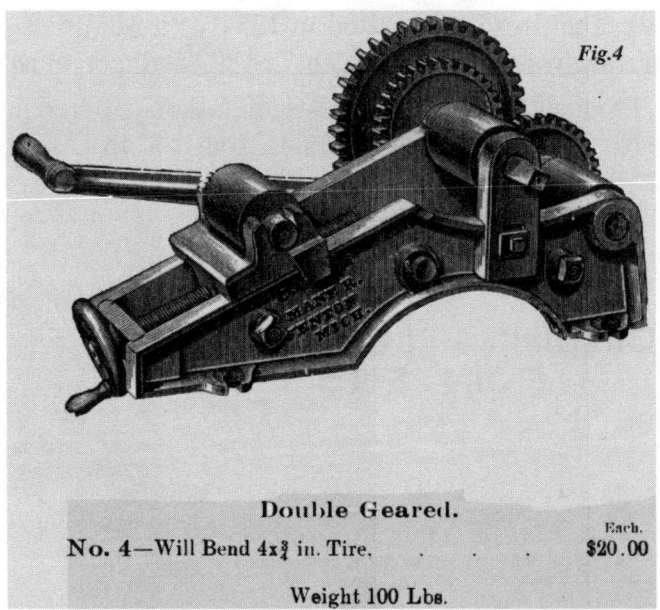

Fig.4

Double Geared.

No. 4—Will Bend 4x¾ in. Tire, . . . $20.00

Weight 100 Lbs.

COMBS & BAWDEN, Freehold, NJ

Maker, beginning in 1875, of Schou's improved tire-upsetting machine for shortening wagon tires (Fig.1). Iron wagon tires became loose as the wooden spokes and fellies shrank over time. The tire was removed, heated, and then clamped in the tire-upsetting machine where it was shortened. The machine was also used to fit tires on newly made wheels.

The tire machine, priced at $25.00, was offered in 1887 (Fig.2) and later. By 1906 the upsetter was a product of CHAMPION BLOWER & FORGE CO. and offered as its LANCASTER model. *(Illustrations next page)*

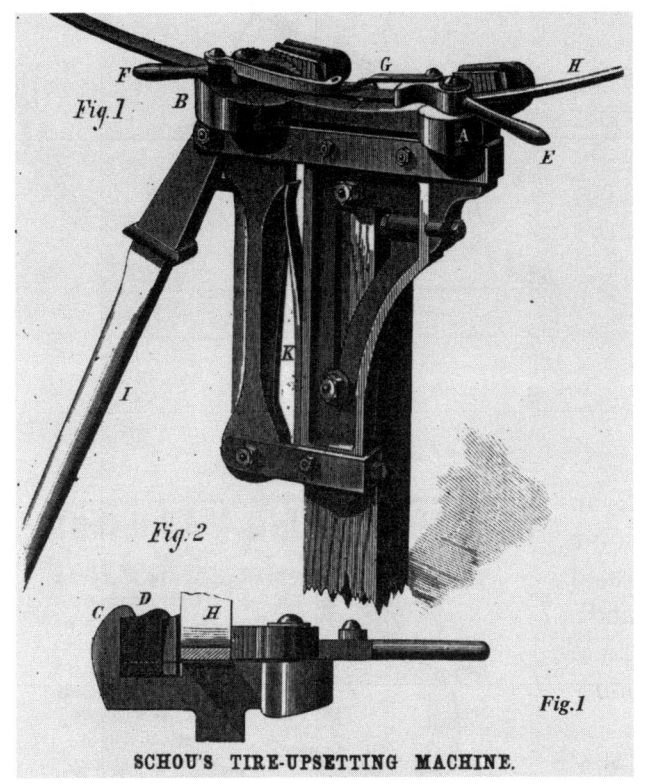

SCHOU'S TIRE-UPSETTING MACHINE.

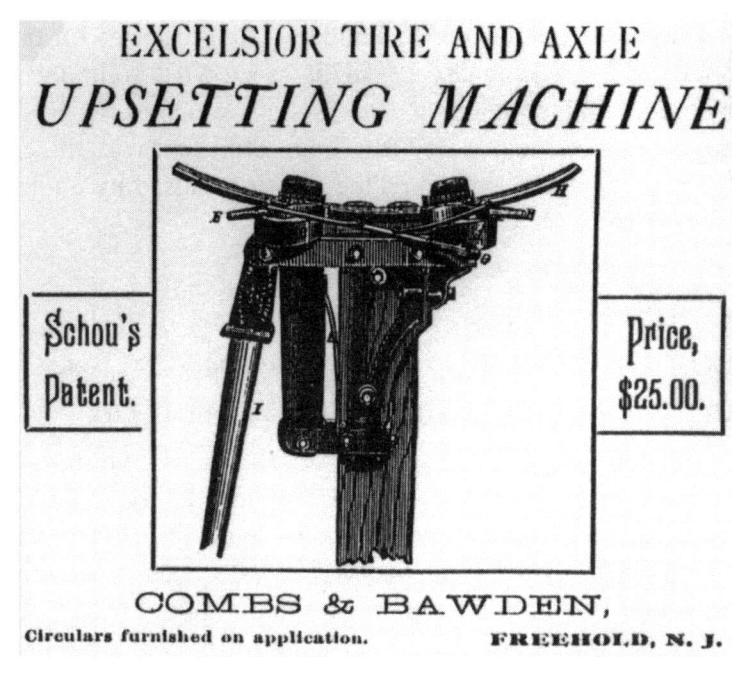

EXCELSIOR TIRE AND AXLE
UPSETTING MACHINE

Schou's Patent.

Price, $25.00.

COMBS & BAWDEN,
Circulars furnished on application. FREEHOLD, N. J.

Fig.2

COMMON SENSE TIRE REMOVER CO., Dowagiac, MI

Maker of the COMMON SENSE tire remover, patented February 27, 1900, by Myron Stark. A 1916 ad is reproduced at right.

COMMON SENSE TIRE REMOVER
The Best Machine on Earth for Removing Tires

For sale by the trade. If your dealer does not handle them, write to us at once for a descriptive circular.
Price, $20.00
Common Sense Tire Remover Co. - Dowagiac, Mich.

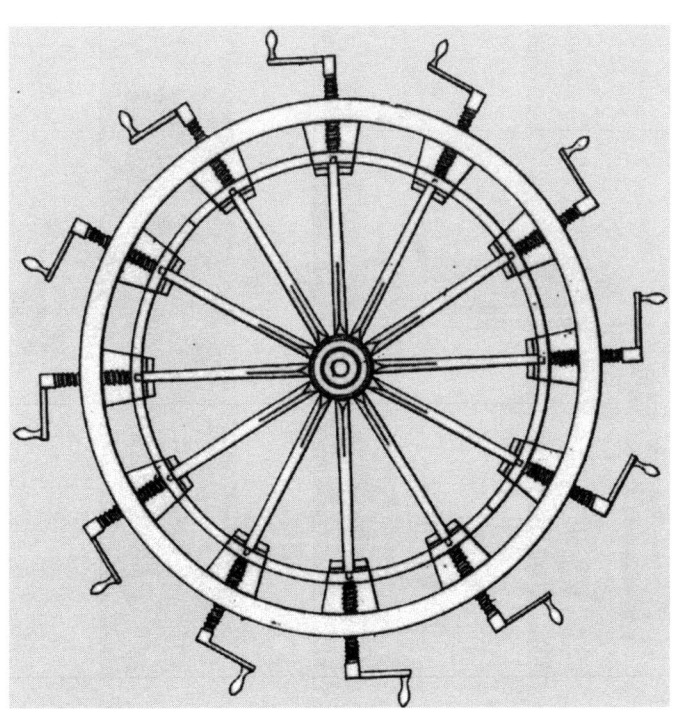

COOK & CO., G.& D., New Haven, CT

Carriage maker formed ca. 1858 by George and David Cook. By 1868, the firm employed 300 hands making carriages. The firm ceased operation by 1887and was succeeded by Henry Hooker & Co.

Cook & Co. also designed and built wheel machinery for their own use and for sale to others. Such machinery included a machine for compressing carriage wheels, patented July 21, 1863,and shown at left.

COON, PHILLIP, Canton, NY

Inventor and maker of a hand operated machine for tapering spokes, patented January 12, 1875. As shown at right, the design included a pair of guide pins that could be adjusted for the desired angle of taper. Coon noted that the machine cut with the grain of the wood and thus prevented the splitting caused by implements such as spokeshaves.

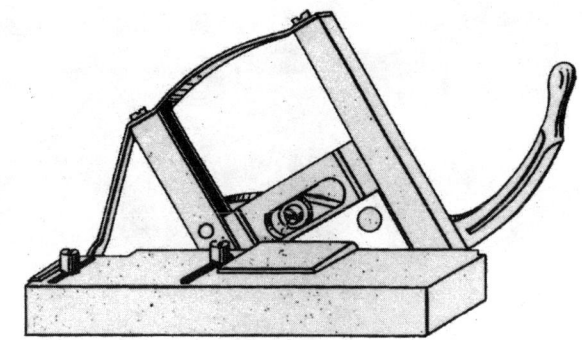

CORDESMAN, EGAN & CO., Cincinnati, OH, later
CORDESMAN & EGAN CO., Cincinnati, OH, later
CORDESMAN MACHINE CO., Cincinnati, OH

A partnership of Henry J. Cordesman and Thomas P. Egan formed in 1874 to make wood working machinery, including some machinery for carriage and wagon makers. The firm incorporated as the Cordesman & Egan Co. in 1881 with Egan as president and a capital of $150,000. In 1884 the company split into the Cordesman Machine Co. and the EGAN CO., both firms continuing production of wood working machinery.

Fig.2

A wheel hub boring machine (Fig.1), patented March 21, 1882, was offered in 1882. In 1884, the Cordesman Machine Co. advertised "wood working machinery for carriage and buggy shops" (Fig.2) and in 1891 an ad for a general line of wood working machinery appeared in Carriage Monthly magazine (Fig.3). 1892 production included a tire truing machine (Fig.4), which straightened tires by passing them between a set of rollers.

The Cordesman Machine Co. appears to have gone out of business in 1893, possibly being absorbed by the newly formed J.A. FAY & EGAN CO. *(Fig.3 on next page)*

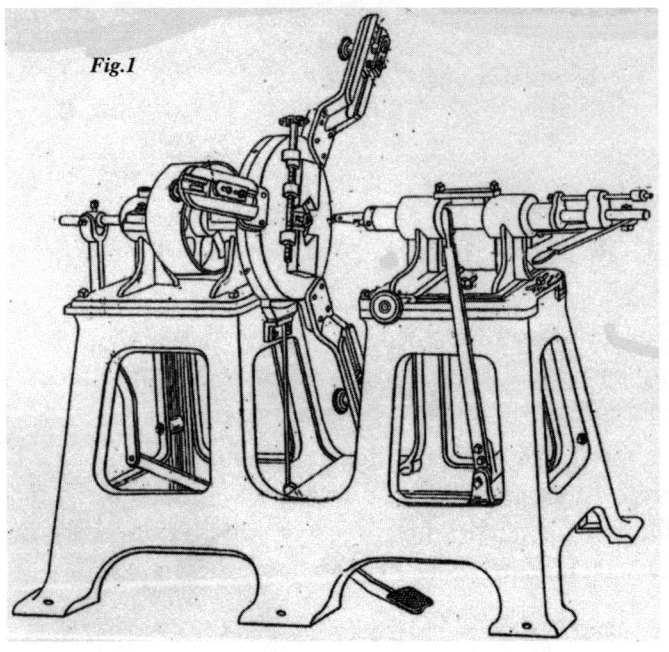

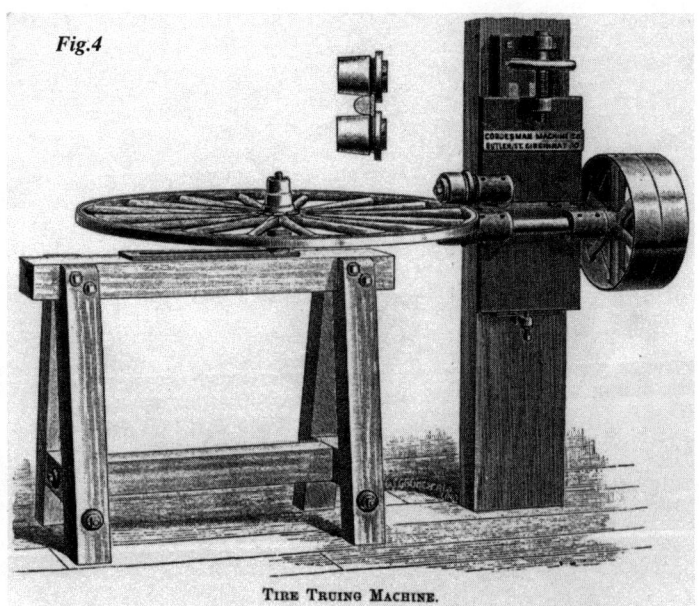

TIRE TRUING MACHINE.

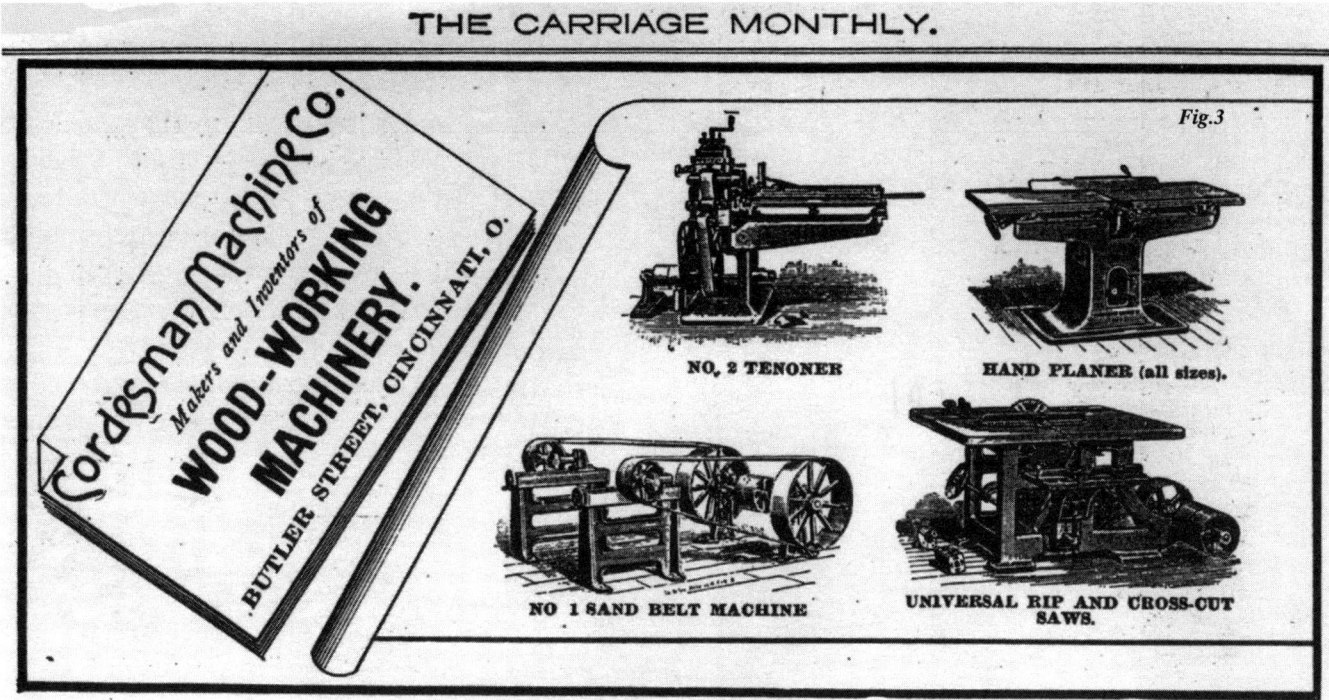

THE CARRIAGE MONTHLY.

Fig.3

NO. 2 TENONER   HAND PLANER (all sizes).

NO 1 SAND BELT MACHINE   UNIVERSAL RIP AND CROSS-CUT SAWS.

CORDESMAN, MEYER & CO., Cincinnati, OH

Woodworking machinery maker operating ca.1888-1905 or later. It advertised "machinery for carriage builders." This firm's relationship with the CORDESMAN MACHINE CO. is unclear.

COULTER & McKENZIE, Bridgeport, CT

A partnership of Thomas Coulter and Hector McKenzie, formed in 1876 to make a lathe jointly patented February 17, 1874. Designed to turn wagon and carriage axles, the machine was built with a wooden bed and a turret that carried tools for turning and threading the axle ends at the rate of 160 per ten-hour day. In later years Coulter claimed the machine was the first "large" turret lathe made.

The firm soon specialized in sheet metal presses and punches and operated until 1894.

THE FIRST LARGE TURRET LATHE.

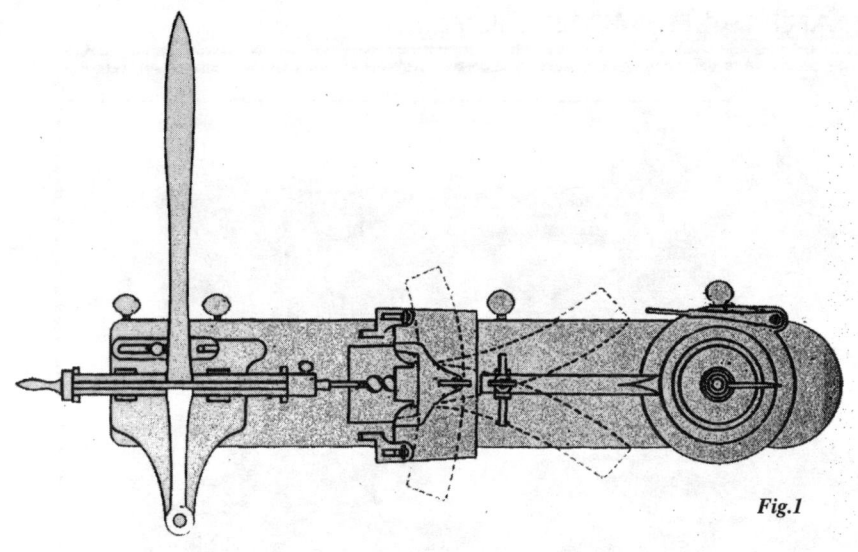

Fig.1

COWDRY & TOLLS, Ithaca, NY

Maker of a wheelwrights' machine, patented May 5, 1855, by Chauncey Cowdry, Orrin Tolls, and Chauncey C. Tolls. The machine was designed to bore spoke holes and dowel pin holes in felloes (Fig.1), cut round tenons on spoke ends (Fig.2),and bore a series of holes in hubs (Fig.3) which became mortises for the hub ends of spokes after opening with a chisel.

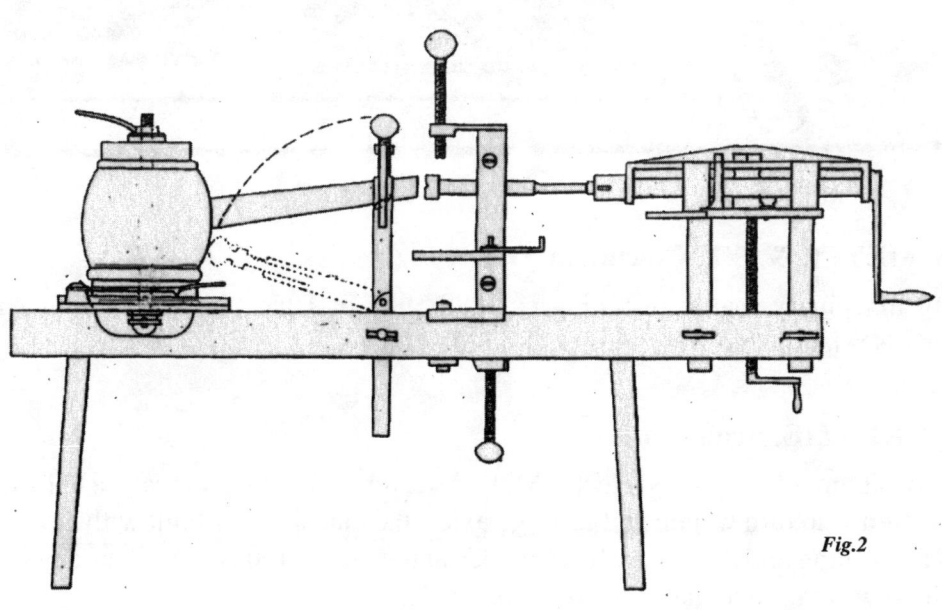

Fig.2

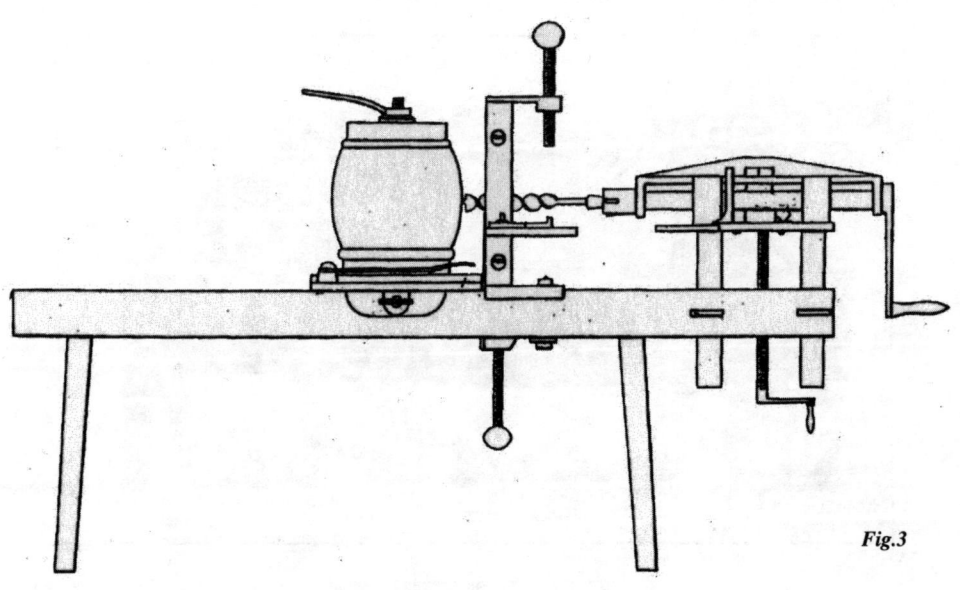

Fig.3

COX, THOMAS, Lancaster, PA

Inventor and maker of a felly bending machine, patented July 4, 1854. In operation, the fellies were bent around the mold B as it rotated past a flanged wheel M which bent the steamed wood to the shape of the mold. Each end of the felly was secured by dogs as shown in Fig. 4.

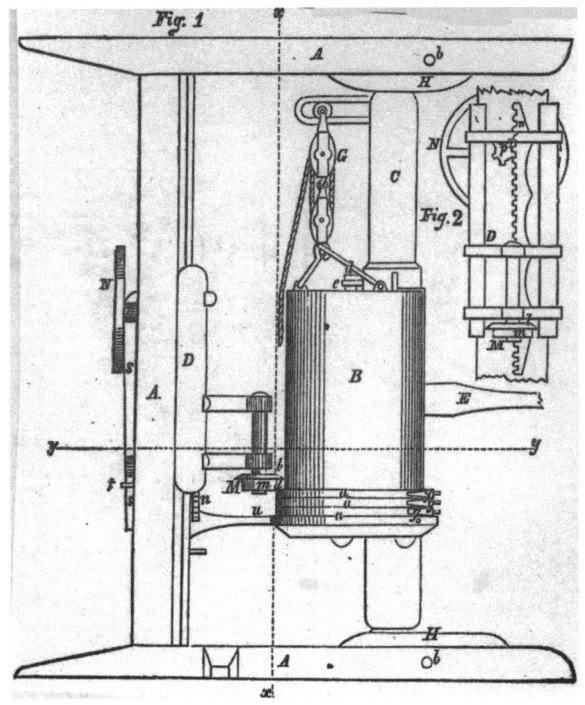

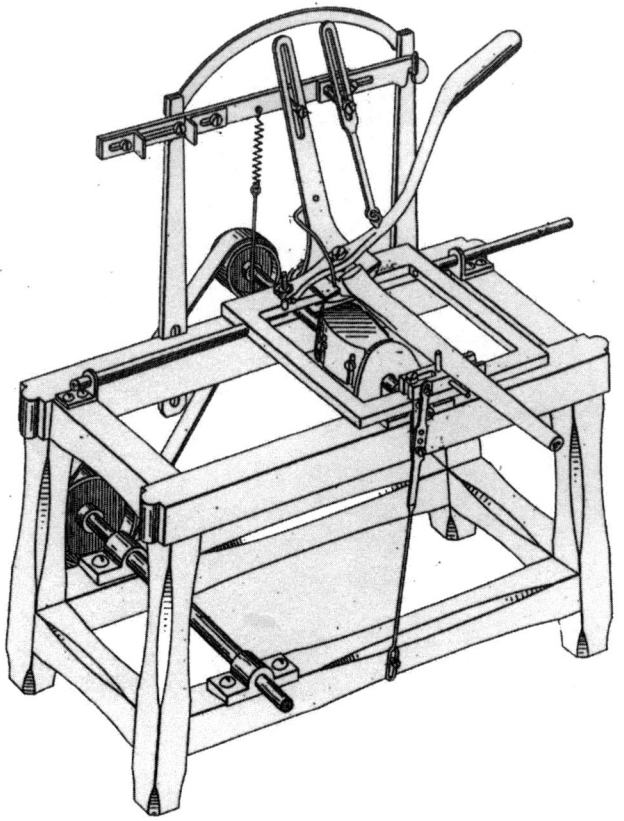

CRAMER, GEORGE R., Cincinnati, OH

Inventor and maker of a spoke throating machine, patented June 11, 1878. As shown below the cutter was power operated, but the feed of the spoke into the cutter was by hand.

CRUTCHFIELD & WHITTEN, Edgefield, SC

A partnership of J.P. Crutchfield and C.T. Whitten, formed in 1870 to make a spoke tenoning machine jointly patented January 11, 1870. In use, the hub was mounted on an iron plate D and the spokes inserted, the bars E adjusted to the desired length and the spokes manually rotated into position where the ends were tenoned by a hand driven cutter P.

CRUTCHFIELD AND WHITTEN'S SPOKE TENONING MACHINE.

CURTIS & CO., St. Louis, MO

Maker, in 1880, of a felloe sawing machine equipped with four concave saws mounted in two pairs. In use, the raw material was rotated past the rotating saws on a radius corresponding to the desired wheel radius. The machine was equipped with two sets of saws, configured to cut different radii; one for the front wheels and the other for the rear wheels.

Production was claimed to be 5,000 to 5,500 felloes per ten-hour day "with less than half the labor required to perform the same work on the old style machines."

In 1905, the firm was listed as a maker of barrel, keg, stave, carriage builders' and felly machines.

FELLOE SAWING MACHINE.

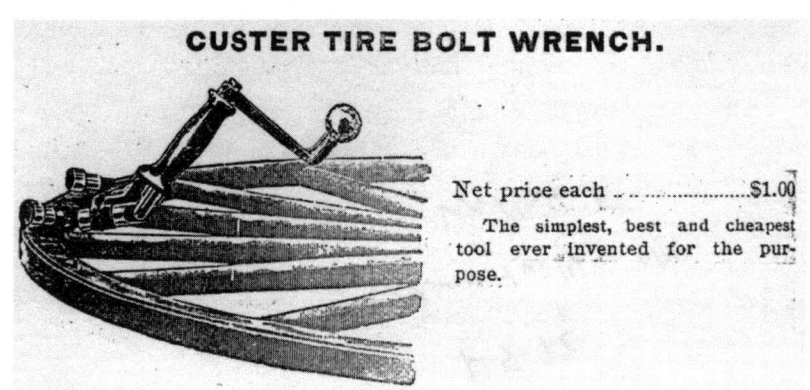

CUSTER TIRE BOLT WRENCH.

Net price each $1.00

The simplest, best and cheapest tool ever invented for the purpose.

CUSTER, WILLIAM F., Summitville, IN

Inventor and maker of a tire bolt wrench, patented January 5, 1892. The wrench was equipped with a universal joint which allowed use between the spokes.

DEFIANCE MACHINE WORKS, Defiance, OH

Formed in 1872 as the incorporation of KETTENRING, STRONG & LAUSTER. The company employed 15 hands making woodworking machinery, engines, boilers, shafting, plows, etc. in an 800 sq./ft. factory. Peter Kettenring (1836-1919) was president, William Lauster, treasurer.

The earliest machine made for wagon and carriage makers appears to have been an automatic hub mortising machine developed in 1868 (Fig.1). The machine was completely automatic, requiring the operator only to load and unload the hubs. Production was claimed to be 80 sets of hubs per ten-hour day. By 1880 an improved version of the machine (Fig.2) was offered, along with a hub turning machine, patented July 13, 1880, by Charles Seymour.

Kettenring's three sons, William A. (1861-1915), Ransom P. (1863-1929),and Charles H., joined the company in 1889. William became active head of the company in 1890, serving until his death in 1915.

Ca. 1890, the firm began to expand production of carriage and wagon makers' machinery. New products offered in the 1890s included a spoke and handle lathe (Fig.3), patented August 25, 1885, February 21, 1888,and June 10, 1890; an automatic spoke driving machine (Fig. 4), patented April 22, 1890; an automatic wheel boxing machine (Fig.5), patented January 19, 1892, and capable of boxing 600 wheels per day; a simple machine for bending shafts and poles (Fig.6); an automatic hub turning machine (Fig.7) made to turn hubs up to 20" diameter and 18" long at a rate of 600 per day; a 60 ton hydraulic press (Fig.8) for pressing boxes into wheels and forcing on hub bands; an improved 9" wood bending machine (Fig.9) for making bows, felloes, and other curved parts and a larger 12" version (Fig.10); an automatic double head axletree turning lathe (Fig.11), patented July 11, 1893; a larger automatic hub mortising machine (Fig.12) for making hubs up to 11 1/2" diameter at a rate of 400 per day; an automatic copying lathe (Fig.13) for making spokes, neck yokes, and other irregular shapes; a double drum felloe polishing machine (Fig.14); an automatic wagon axle skein setting and fitting machine (Fig.15), previously made by UNION FOUNDRY & MACHINE WORKS; an automatic tread sanding machine (Fig.16), patented August 30, 1898; an improved disc spoke facing and tapering machine (Fig.17); a spoke throating machine (Fig.18); a hub polishing machine (Fig.19) for hubs up to 20" diameter; and a felloe truing and polishing machine (Fig.20).

In 1899, the firm offered hub, spoke, wheel, bending, wagon, carriage, shaft, pole, neck-yoke, singletree, barrel hoop and handle machinery. Machine design was done by George A. Ensign and Charles Seymour.

Product development continued at a rapid pace through the early 1900s. New machines for wagon and carriage builders included an automatic hub turning and finishing machine (Fig.21), patented April 10, 1900; automatic spoke throat polishing machine (Fig.22), patented July 30, 1901; automatic double spoke facing and tapering machine (Fig.23), patented August 20, 1901; wheel tenoning and cutoff machine (Fig.24), patented November 12, 1901; automatic double spoke tenoning, mitering and pointing machine (Fig.25), patented November 26, 1901; automatic skein setting and fitting machine (Fig.26), patented January 7, 1902; automatic rim and felloe boring machine (Fig.27), patented January 14, 1902; automatic double spoke throating machine (Fig.28), patented January 28, 1902; automatic felloe boring and compressing machine (Fig.29), patented October 20, 1903; and automatic wheel rimming machine (Fig30), patented July 10, 1906.

A high water mark for the production of wagon and carriage machinery was reached ca. 1910 when catalog No. 200 was issued. It contained 533 pages of woodworking machinery, about a third of which were devoted to wagon and carriage makers' needs. Sixty six of these pages are reproduced following this entry.

By 1912, the firm employed 150 hands in a factory expanded to 25,000 sq/ft. In 1915 it claimed "for years past we have built practically all of the artillery wheel and military vehicle machinery used in government arsenals throughout the world. There is not an automobile or carriage wheel plant of any real consequence in either the eastern or western hemisphere that is not equipped with Defiance machines." Employment had grown to 275 hands by 1916.

Towards the end of World War I the firm began producing metal cutting machine tools which were in great demand. The added production, done in a large adjacent factory built by the U.S. Government, increased employment to 700 hands by 1921, but forced the firm into receivership due to over-extension.

In 1938, the company became the Defiance Division of the Toledo Scale Co. and expanded greatly during World War II. This second over-extension proved fatal; the company went out of business in March, 1949.

Fig 1

Automatic Hub Morticing Machine.

This is a double-chiseled Machine, and works automatic in all its parts, and all that is necessary for the operator to do is to place the Hub in the chuck and take it out. This Machine will mortice 80 sets of Lumber Hubs in ten hours with ease to the operator, and will mortice a staggered mortice as quick as a straight one. Specialty made and full line of Hub and Spoke Machinery kept constantly on hand. Address
DEFIANCE MACHINE WORKS, Defiance, O

Fig.2

DOUBLE-CHISEL AUTOMATIC HUB MORTISING MACHINE.

Fig.3

A COMBINED SPOKE AND HANDLE LATHE.

Fig.4

Fig. 10668.

Fig.5

AUTOMATIC WHEEL-BOXING MACHINE.

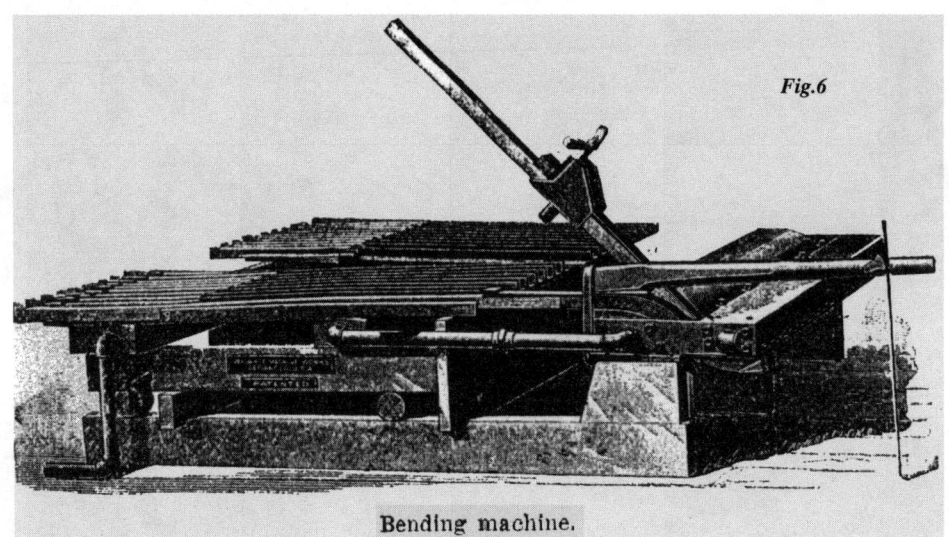

Fig.6

Bending machine.

Fig.7

NO. 1 PATENT, AUTOMATIC HUB TURNING MACHINE.

Fig.8

SIXTY-TON HYDRAULIC WHEEL PRESS.

Fig.9

Fig. 10 on
following page

AN IMPROVED WOOD BENDING MACHINE.

Fig.11

No. 1 Patent Automatic Double Head Axletree Turning Lathe.
Export Shipping Weight, 6,200 Pounds.

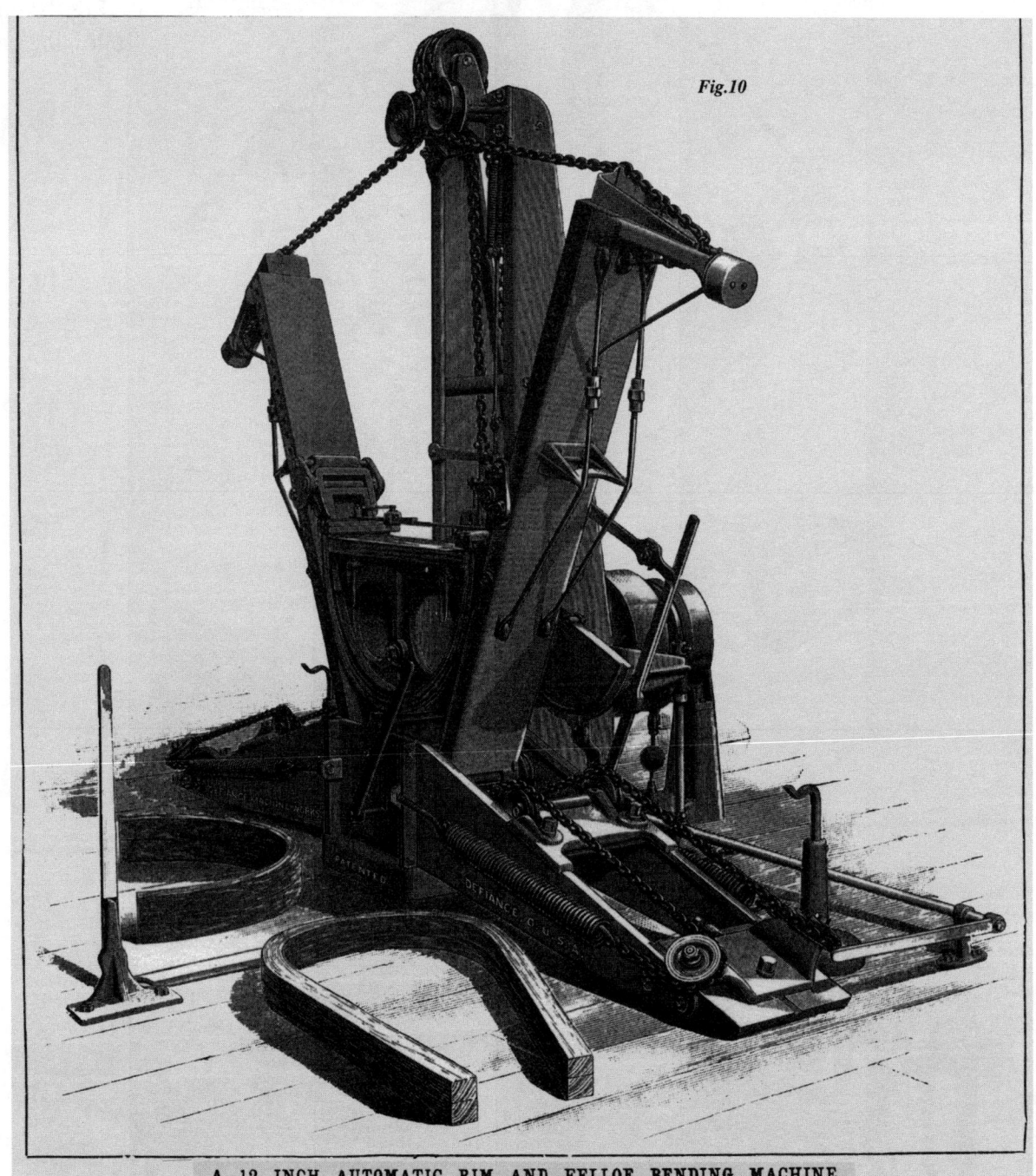

Fig.10

A 12 INCH AUTOMATIC RIM AND FELLOE BENDING MACHINE.

Fig.12

AN AUTOMATIC DOUBLE CHISEL MORTISING MACHINE.

Fig.13

PATENT AUTOMATIC COPYING LATHE WITH AUTOMATIC SCREW FEED.

Fig.14

PATENT DOUBLE DRUM FELLOE POLISHING MACHINE.

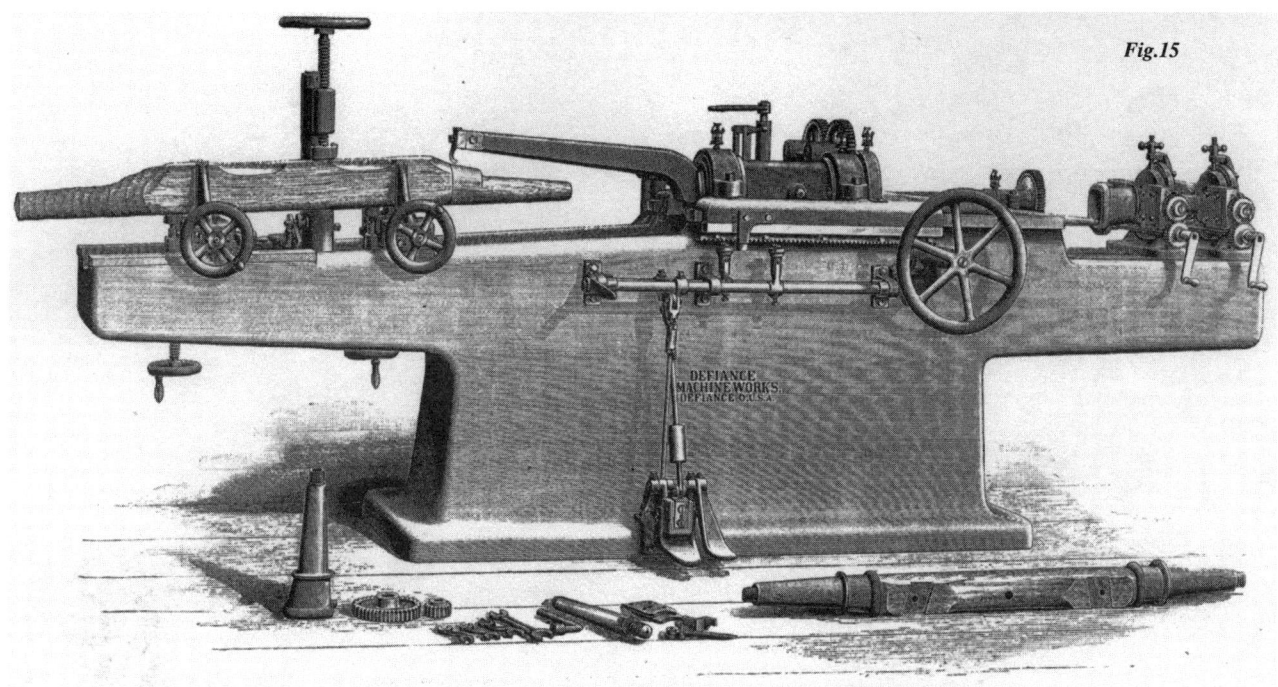

Fig.15

AN AUTOMATIC WAGON AXLE SKEIN SETTING AND FITTING MACHINE.

Fig.16

DOUBLE AUTOMATIC TREAD-SANDING MACHINE.

Fig.17

No. 1 Improved Disc Spoke Facing and Tapering Machine.

Fig.18

No. 0 Improved Spoke Throating Machine.

Fig.19

No. 1 Improved Hub Polishing Machine.

Fig.20

No. 0 Felloe Truing and Polishing Machine.

No. 0 Patent Automatic Hub Turning and Finishing Machine.

No. 3 Patent Automatic Double Spoke Facing and Tapering Machine.

No. 1 Patent Automatic Spoke Throat Polishing Machine.
Export Shipping Weight. 4.100 Pounds.

Fig.24

No. 2 Patent Heavy Wheel Tenoning and Cut-Off Machine.

Fig.25

No. 1 Patent Automatic Double Spoke Tenoning, Mitering, and
Pointing Machine.

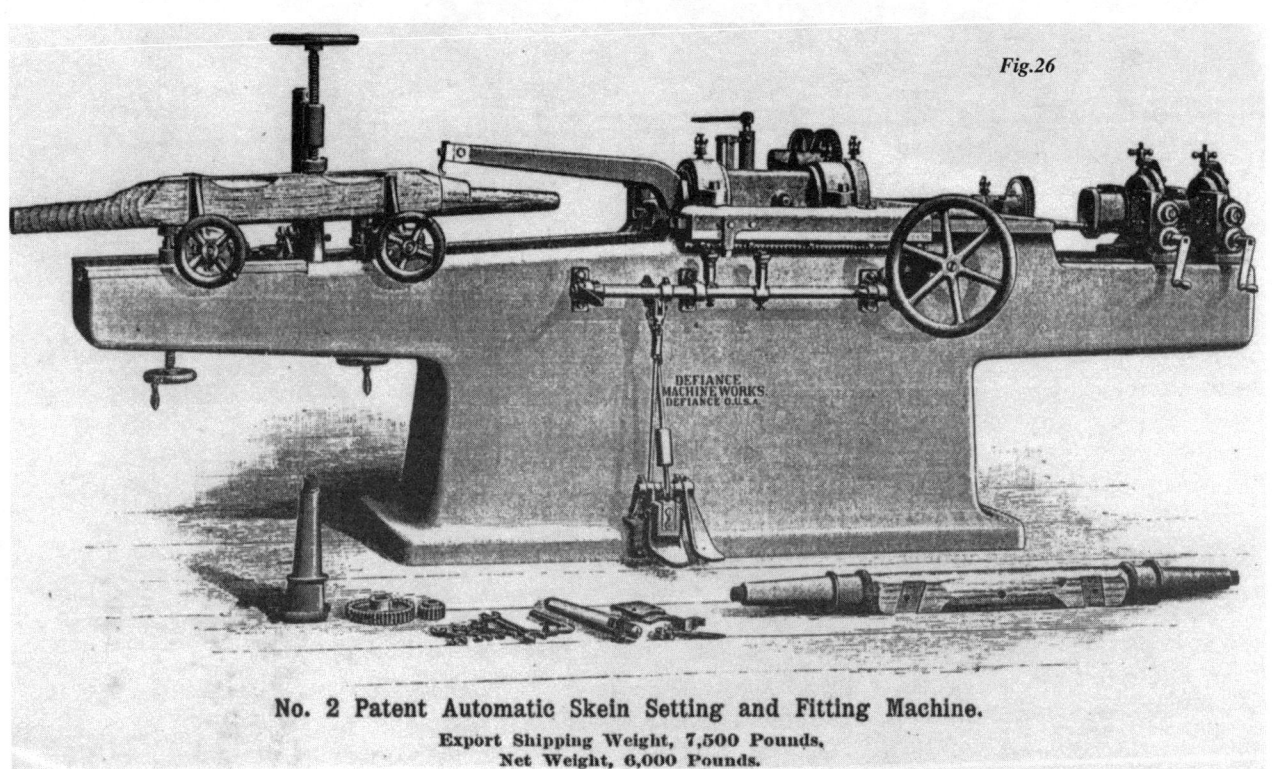

Fig.26

No. 2 Patent Automatic Skein Setting and Fitting Machine.
Export Shipping Weight, 7,500 Pounds,
Net Weight, 6,000 Pounds.

Fig.27

No. 1 Patent Rim and Felloe Boring Machine.

Fig.28

No. 1 Patent Automatic Double Spoke Throating Machine.

Fig.29

No. 3 Patent Automatic Felloe Boring and Compressing Machine.

Fig.30

No. 2 Patent Automatic Wheel Rimming Machine.

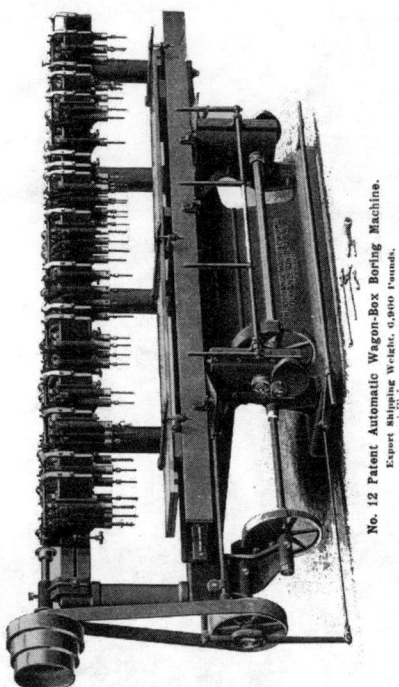

No. 12 Patent Automatic Wagon-Box Boring Machine.
Export Shipping Weight, 6,200 Pounds.

No. 2 Patent Rounding, Chamfering, and Cornering Machine.

Export Shipping Weight, 1,200 Pounds.
Net Weight, 800 Pounds.

No. 8 Patent Shaping, Cornering, and Planing Machine.

Export Shipping Weight, 1,200 Pounds.
Net Weight, 950 Pounds.

No. 2 Automatic Hub Block Boring Machine.
Export Shipping Weight, 3,700 Pounds.
Net Weight, 3,100 Pounds.

No. 1 Patent Automatic Double Chisel Hub Mortising Machine.
Export Shipping Weight, 3,900 Pounds.
Net Weight, 2,900 Pounds.

No. 2 Automatic Hub Block Roughing Machine.

Export Shipping Weight, 2,200 Pounds.
Net Weight, 1,700 Pounds.

No. 1 Improved Heavy Hub Boring Machine.
Export Shipping Weight, 2,100 Pounds.
Net Weight, 1,600 Pounds.

No. 2 Patent Automatic Double Chisel Hub Mortising Machine.
Export Shipping Weight, 6,300 Pounds.
Net Weight, 5,100 Pounds.

No. 1 Improved Hub Reaming Machine.

Export Shipping Weight, 1,300 Pounds.
Net Weight, 800 Pounds.

No. 5 Heavy Double Hub Equalizing Saw.

Export Shipping Weight, 1,600 Pounds.
Net Weight, 1,100 Pounds.

No. 1 Improved Spoke and Handle Blank Saw.

Export Shipping Weight, 1,700 Pounds.
Net Weight, 1,200 Pounds.

32" Patent Automatic Spoke Lathe.

Export Shipping Weight, 3,100 Pounds.
Net Weight, 2,450 Pounds.

No. 2 Heavy Double Spoke Tenoning Machine.

Export Shipping Weight, 2,100 Pounds.
Net Weight, 1,600 Pounds.

No. 3 Heavy Double Spoke Tenoning and Equalizing Machine.

Export Shipping Weight, 2,200 Pounds.
Net Weight, 1,550 Pounds.

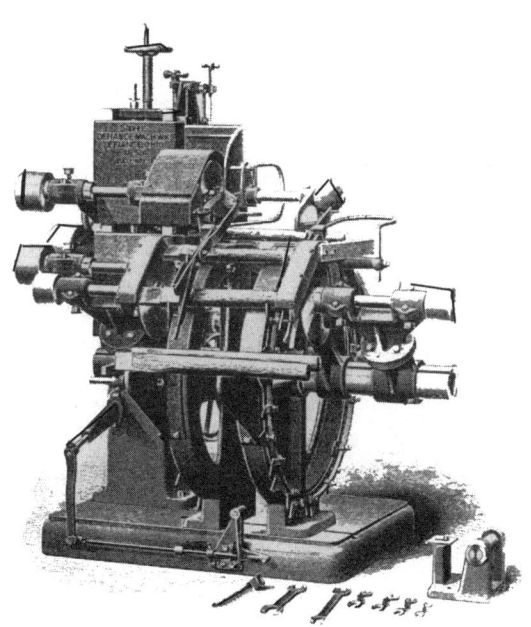

No. 4 Patent Automatic Double Spoke Tenoning and Equalizing Machine.

Export Shipping Weight, 4,800 Pounds.
Net Weight, 3,800 Pounds.

No. 1 Improved Spoke Sizing or Re-Tenoning Machine.

Export Shipping Weight, 1,000 Pounds.
Net Weight, 600 Pounds.

No. 2 Improved Rim Packing and Cut-Off Machine.

Export Shipping Weight, 1,700 Pounds.
Net Weight, 1,100 Pounds.

No. 0 Patent Spoke Facing and Tapering Machine.

Export Shipping Weight, 800 Pounds.
Net Weight, 500 Pounds.

No. 1 Improved Concave Felloe Sawing Machine.

Export Shipping Weight, 1,500 Pounds.
Net Weight, 1,070 Pounds.

No. 1 Patent Two-Side Felloe Planing Machine

Export Shipping Weight, 1,600 Pounds.
Net Weight, 1,200 Pounds.

No. 2 Patent Two-Side Felloe Planing Machine.

Export Shipping Weight, 2,300 Pounds.
Net Weight, 1,800 Pounds.

No. 3 Patent Two-Side Felloe Planing Machine.

Export Shipping Weight, 2,300 Pounds.
Net Weight, 1,800 Pounds.

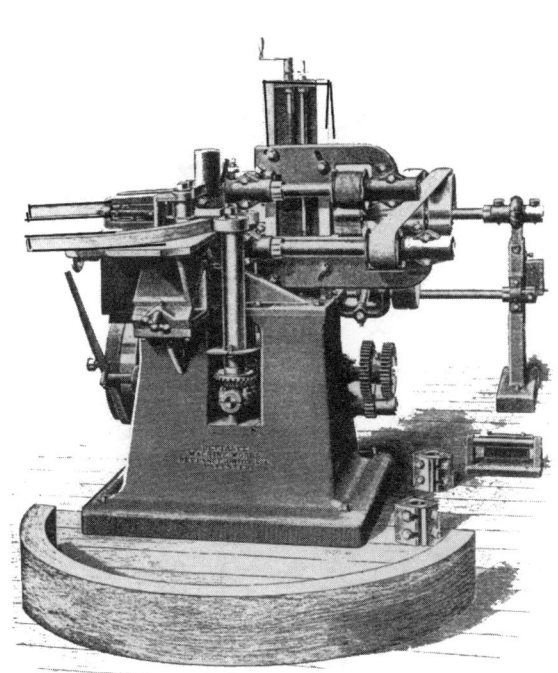

No. 4 Patent Two-Side Felloe Planing Machine.

Export Shipping Weight, 2,750 Pounds.
Net Weight, 2,150 Pounds.

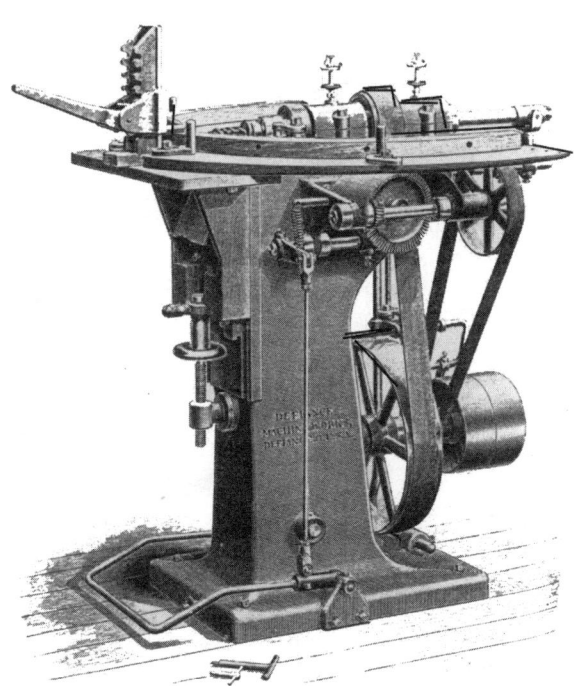

No. 2 Patent Automatic Rim and Felloe Boring Machine.

Export Shipping Weight, 1,100 Pounds.
Net Weight, 800 Pounds.

No. 1 Patent Felloe Dowel Hole Boring Machine.

Export Shipping Weight, 900 Pounds.
Net Weight, 600 Pounds.

No. 2 Patent Automatic Felloe Dowel Hole Boring Machine
Export Shipping Weight, 1,100 Pounds.
Net Weight, 900 Pounds.

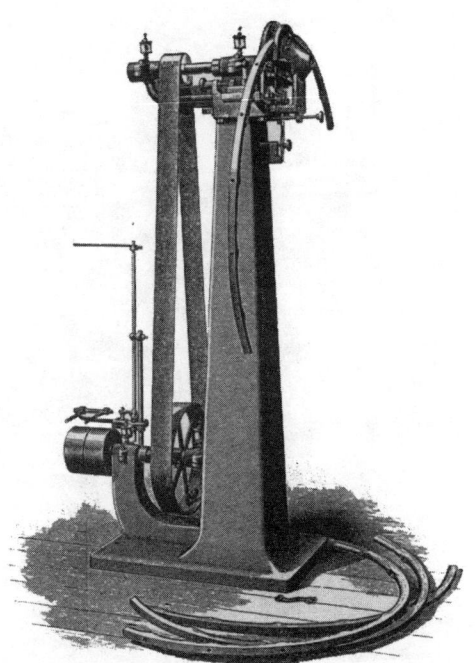

No. 3 Patent Rim and Felloe Rounding Machine.

Export Shipping Weight, 1,000 Pounds.
Net Weight, 800 Pounds.

No. 0 Rim and Felloe Cut-Off Machine.

Export Shipping Weight, 800 Pounds.
Net Weight, 500 Pounds.

No. 1 Felloe Cut-Off and Doweling Machine.

Export Shipping Weight, 1,250 Pounds.
Net Weight, 750 Pounds.

No. 3 Improved Hub Equalizing Saw.

Export Shipping Weight, 1,200 Pounds.
Net Weight, 700 Pounds.

No. 3 Hub Reaming and Boring Machine.

Export Shipping Weight, 1,300 Pounds.
Net Weight, 800 Pounds.

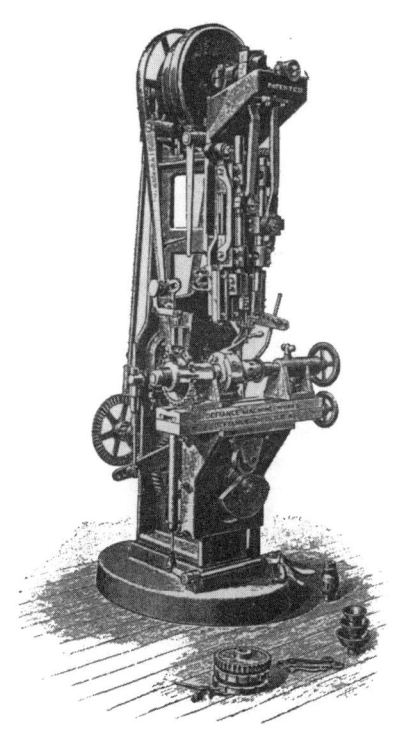

No. 0 Patent Automatic Double Chisel Hub Mortising Machine.

Export Shipping Weight, 3,300 Pounds.
Net Weight, 2,300 Pounds.

No. 0 Patent Pneumatic Spoke Driving Machine.

Export Shipping Weight, 1,600 Pounds.
Net Weight, 1,200 Pounds.

No. 1 Patent Automatic Spoke Driving Machine.
Export Shipping Weight, 3,400 Pounds.
Net Weight, 2,600 Pounds.

No. 2 Patent Automatic Spoke Driving Machine.

Export Shipping Weight, 3,800 Pounds.
Net Weight, 3,000 Pounds.

No. 1 Patent Combination Wheel and Spoke Tenoning Machine.
Export Shipping Weight, 1,500 Pounds.
Net Weight, 1,100 Pounds.

No. 1 Wheel Rimming and Finishing Stand.

Export Shipping Weight, 300 Pounds.
Net Weight, 200 Pounds.

No. 2 Patent Automatic Heavy Wheel Tenoning and Cut-Off Machine.

No. 4 Patent Automatic Wheel Rimming Machine.
Export Shipping Weight, 6,100 Pounds.
Net Weight, 5,400 Pounds.

No. 3 Patent Automatic Wheel Rimming Machine.

No. 1 Heavy Sarven Wheel Riveting Stand.

Export Shipping Weight, 300 Pounds.

Net Weight, 200 Pounds.

Model K Vehicle Wheel Tread Sander.
Export Shipping Weight, 3,000 Pounds.
Net Weight, 2,400 Pounds.

No. 0 Sarven Wheel Flange Seat Facing Machine.

Export Shipping Weight, 1,000 Pounds.

Net Weight, 700 Pounds.

No. 0 Spoke Tenon Compress.

Export Shipping Weight, 1,500 Pounds.

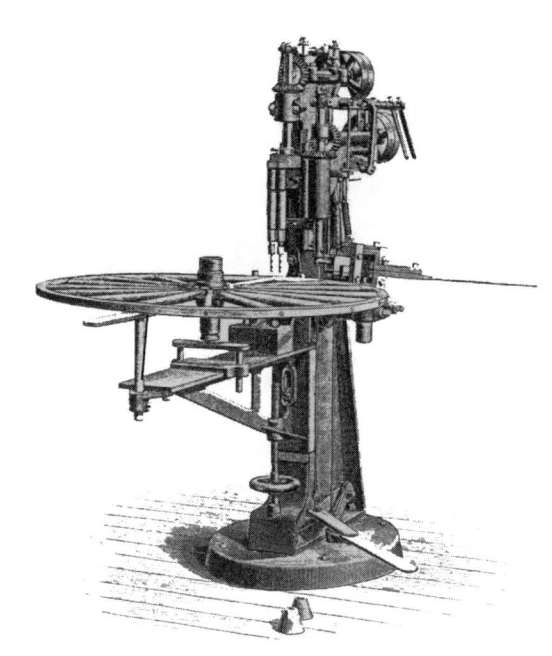

No. 0 Wheel Boring, Screwing, and Cut-Off Machine.

Export Shipping Weight, 1,200 Pounds.
Net Weight, 700 Pounds.

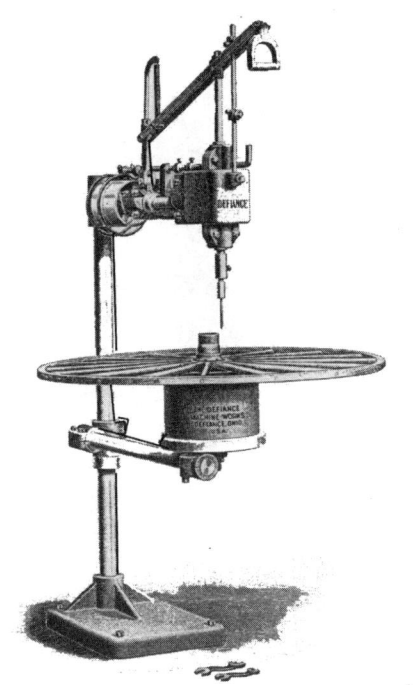

No. 18 Improved Sarven Wheel Rivet Drilling Machine.

Export Shipping Weight, 700 Pounds.
Net Weight, 525 Pounds.

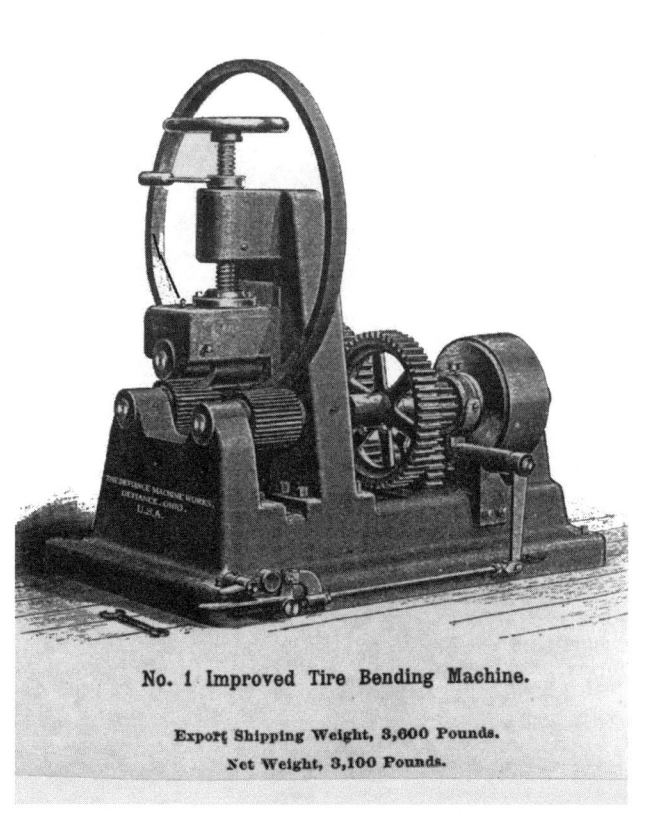

No. 1 Improved Tire Bending Machine.

Export Shipping Weight, 3,600 Pounds.
Net Weight, 3,100 Pounds.

No. 1 Patent Automatic Wheel Rim Finishing Machine.
Export Shipping Weight, 4,400 Pounds.
Net Weight, 3,700 Pounds.

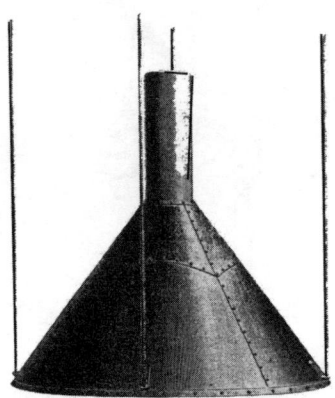

No. 1 Improved Tire Heater.

Export Shipping Weight, 1,480 Pounds.
Net Weight, 1,280 Pounds.

Patent Tire Setting and Cooling Machine.

No. 1 MACHINE.

Export Shipping Weight, 1,700 Pounds.
Net Weight, 1,200 Pounds.
Cubic Measurement, 42 Feet.
Cable Word, TOWER.

No. 2 MACHINE.

Export Shipping Weight, 2,200 Pounds.
Net Weight, 1,500 Pounds.
Cubic Measurement, 47 Feet.
Cable Word, THAMES.

No. 3 MACHINE.

Export Shipping Weight, 2,600 Pounds.
Net Weight, 1,700 Pounds.

No. 00 Patent Automatic Wheel Boxing Machine.

Export Shipping Weight, 3,800 Pounds.
Net Weight, 2,800 Pounds.

No. 1 Automatic Wheel Boxing Machine.

Export Shipping Weight, 6,000 Pounds.
Net Weight, 4,700 Pounds.

No. 3 Automatic Wheel Boxing Machine.

Export Shipping Weight, 7,000 Pounds.
Net Weight, 5,000 Pounds.

No. 2 Automatic Wheel Boxing Machine.

Export Shipping Weight, 6,750 Pounds.
Net Weight, 5,250 Pounds.

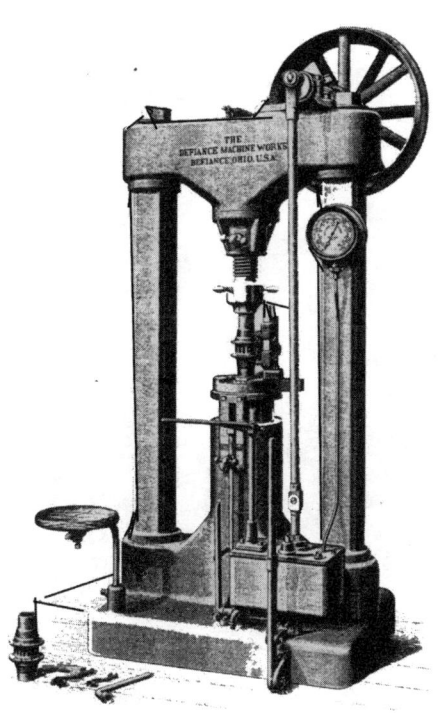

No. 0 Patent 60-Ton Hydraulic Hub Band and Flange Press.

Export Shipping Weight, 3,600 Pounds.
Net Weight, 3,000 Pounds.

No. 1 Improved Iron Frame Power Pressing Machine.

Export Shipping Weight, 4,800 Pounds.
Net Weight, 4,100 Pounds.

No. 3 Patent 80-Ton, Low Down, Iron Frame, Hydraulic Wheel Press.

Export Shipping Weight, 6,000 Pounds.

Net Weight, 5,000 Pounds.

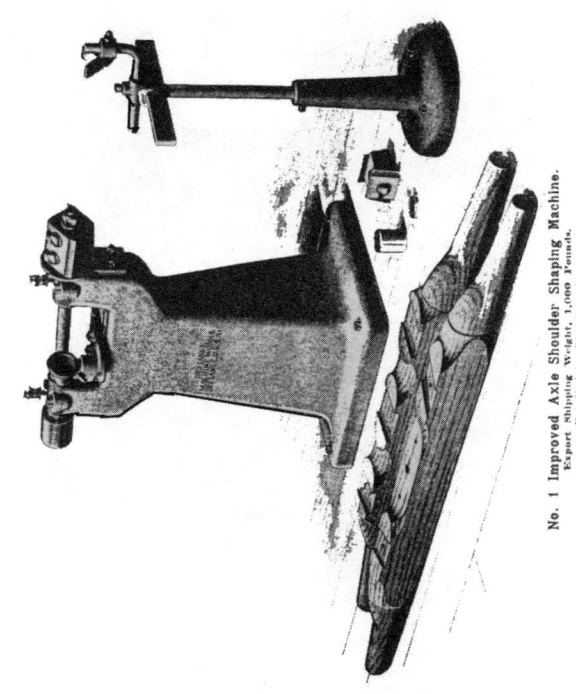

No. 1 Improved Axle Shoulder Shaping Machine.
Export Shipping Weight, 1,000 Pounds.
Net Weight, 700 Pounds.

No. 1 Improved Lag Screw Boring and Driving Machine.
Export Shipping Weight, 1,600 Pounds.
Net Weight, 1,100 Pounds.

No. 2 Double Spindle Axle Shoulder Shaping Machine.
Export Shipping Weight, 1,800 Pounds.
Net Weight, 1,100 Pounds.

No. 1 Patent 48″ Neck-Yoke and Single-Tree Turning Lathe.

Export Shipping Weight, 3,400 Pounds.
Net Weight, 2,800 Pounds.
Cubic Measurement, 105 Feet.
Cable Word, LIVERY.

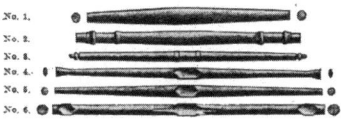

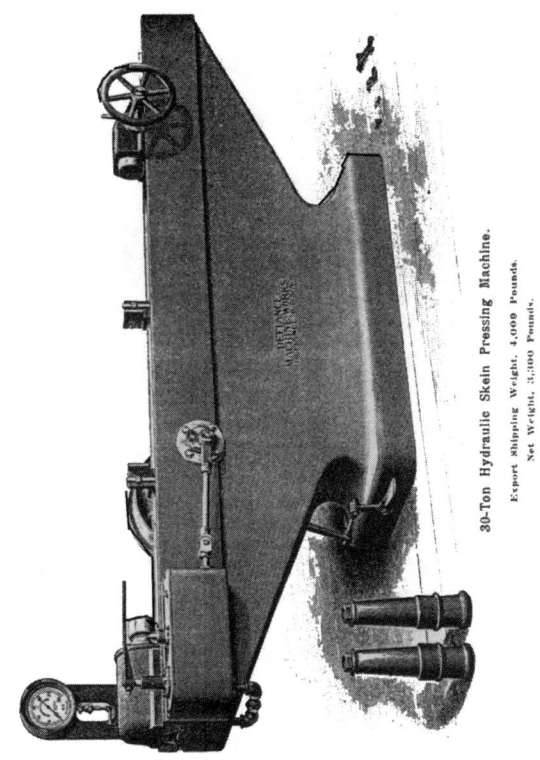

30-Ton Hydraulic Skein Pressing Machine.

Export Shipping Weight, 4,000 Pounds.
Net Weight, 3,300 Pounds.

No. 3 Single-Tree Dressing and Pointing Machine.

Export Shipping Weight, 1,000 Pounds
Net Weight, 700 Pounds.

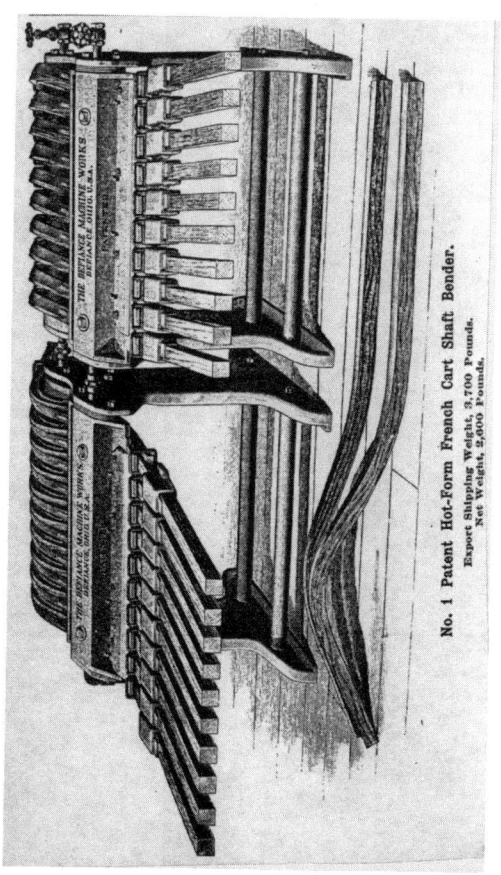

No. 1 Patent Hot-Form French Cart Shaft Bender.

Export Shipping Weight, 3,700 Pounds.
Net Weight, 2,800 Pounds.

No. 3 Patent Hot Form Shaft and Pole Bending Machine.
Export Shipping Weight, 2,000 Pounds.
Net Weight, 1,800 Pounds.

No. 2 Patent Hot-Form Shaft and Pole Bending Machine.
Export Shipping Weight, 5,000 Pounds.
Net Weight, 4,500 Pounds.

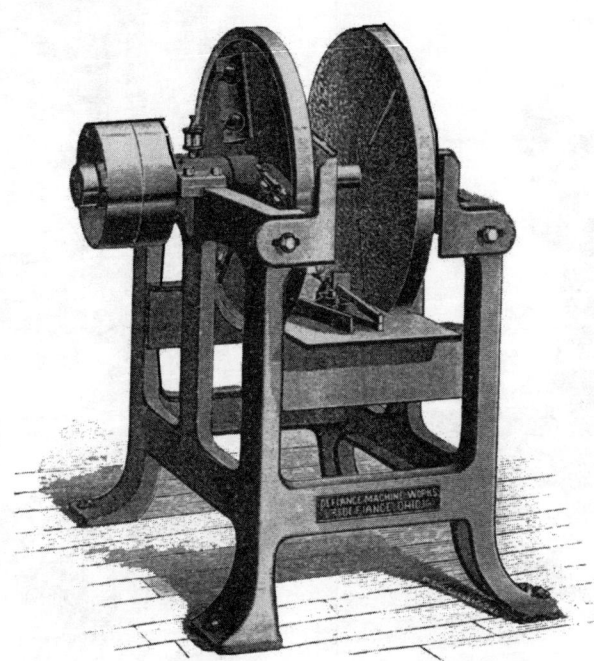

30″ Improved Shaft and Pole Heel Tapering Machine.
Export Shipping Weight, 1,350 Pounds.
Net Weight, 950 Pounds.

DIENELT, EISENHARDT & CO. , Philadelphia, PA

A partnership of Herman Dienelt (1836-1905) and George T. Eisenhardt formed in July, 1874. Dienelt bought Eisenhardt's share in 1897and incorporated the firm in 1903.

The firm made a variety of machines including a line of dead stroke power hammers taken over from the original maker, PHILLIP S. JUSTICE, in 1881. The hammers were made in seven sizes from 5 to 250 pounds and were produced as late as 1915.

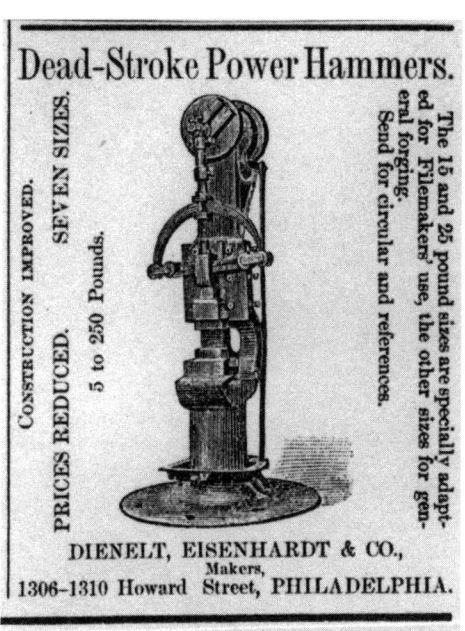

DOANE, SETH C. , Chicago, IL

Inventor and maker of an axle gauge, patented February 26, 1895. The gauge was used to check and set the proper pitch to the axle arms so that the wheels would run with the desired "set" and "gather." The gauge, which was fitted with a ball and socket joint, appears to be one of the best designs noted among axle gauges.

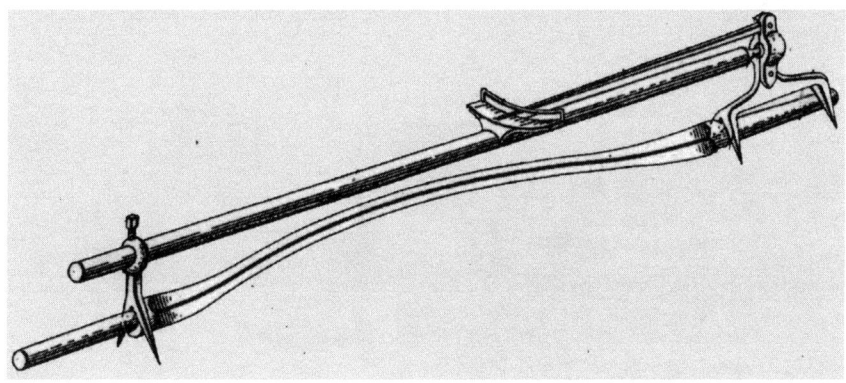

DOLE & SILVER , Salem, OH, later
DOLE, SILVER & DEMING , Salem, OH

A partnership of Levi A. Dole and Albert R. Silver (1823- 1900) formed in 1854 to make a hub boring machine (Fig.1) patented July 25, 1854, by Dole. The firm reorganized as Dole, Silver & Deming when John Deming (1817-1894) became a partner in 1866.

Other products included an improved tenoning machine, actually a hollow auger, (Fig.2) patented by Dole, January 10, 1860; spoke tenoning machines fitted with the hollow auger (Figs.3-4), introduced in 1863; and a tire upsetter (Fig.5), patented January 12, 1864, by Dole. An improved version of the spoke tenoning machine (Fig.6), patented October 31, 1865,and now fitted with a felly boring attachment (Fig.7), was introduced in 1866. Dole's patent self-centering arm hub-boxing machine (Fig.8), patented March 13, 1866, was introduced in 1866and offered as late as 1887 by Silver & Deming.

Albert Silver and John Deming reorganized the firm as SILVER & DEMING when Dole died in 1868.

Fig.1

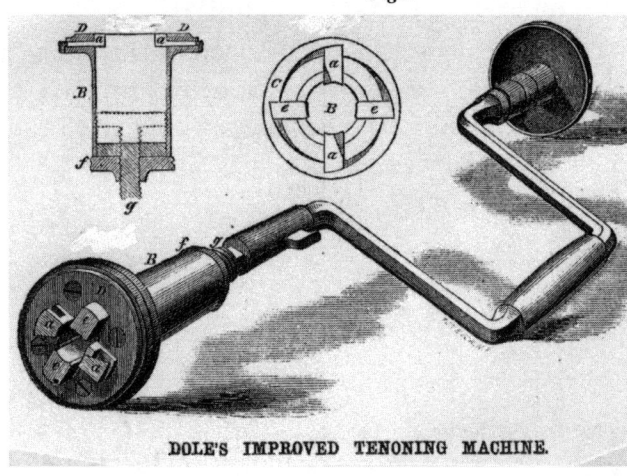

Fig.2

DOLE'S IMPROVED TENONING MACHINE.

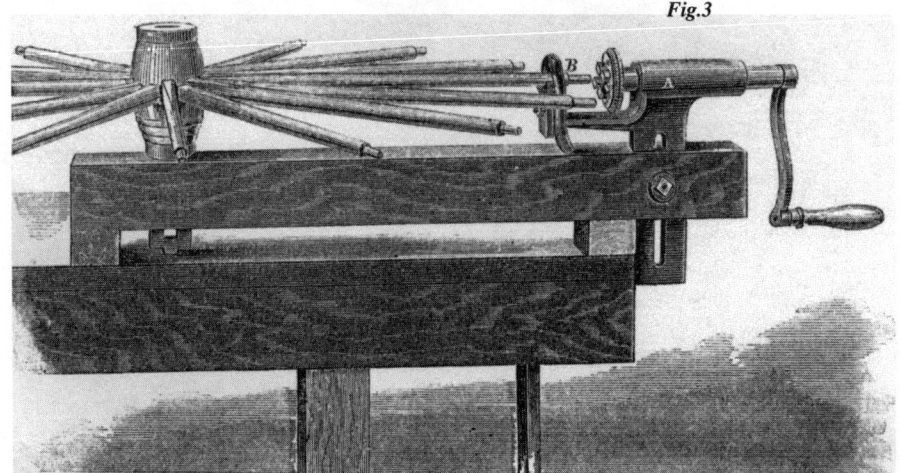

Fig.3

Fig.4

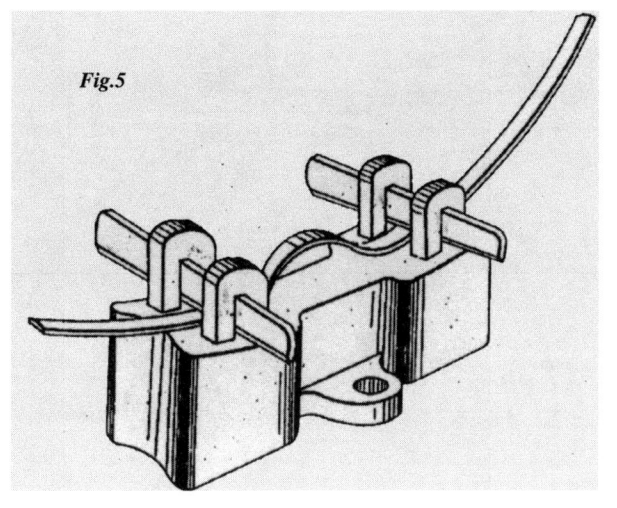

Fig.5

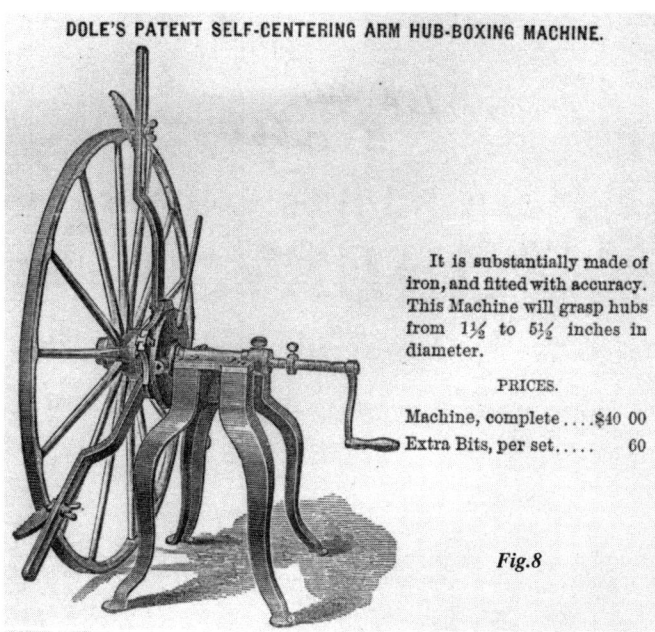

DOLE'S PATENT SELF-CENTERING ARM HUB-BOXING MACHINE.

It is substantially made of iron, and fitted with accuracy. This Machine will grasp hubs from 1½ to 5½ inches in diameter.

PRICES.

Machine, complete....$40 00
Extra Bits, per set..... 60

Fig.8

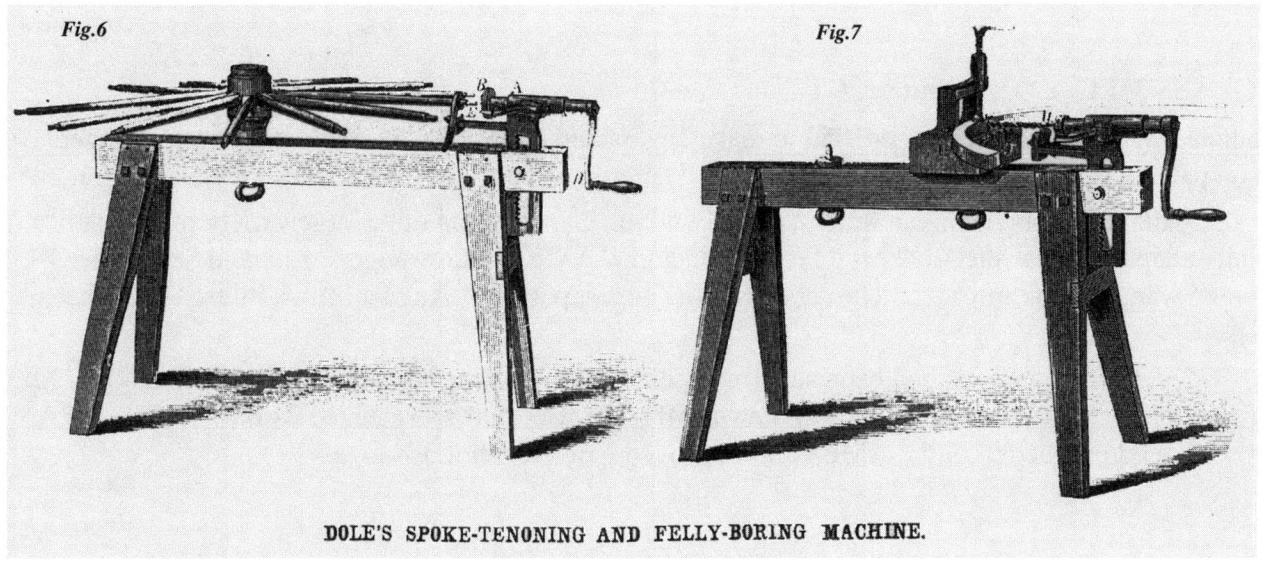

Fig.6

Fig.7

DOLE'S SPOKE-TENONING AND FELLY-BORING MACHINE.

DOTY MFG. CO. , Janesville, WI

Formed in 1868 when Ellis Doty (1838-1874) and his brother Ezra P. Doty combined their washing machine firm with the Badger State Mfg. Co. The new firm concentrated on punching and shearing machinery (Fig.1).

Products offered included plain tire upsetters priced at $30 and a combination tire upsetter, punch and shear for tires up to 3/8" priced at $50. The latter (Fig.2) was patented January 22, 1869, by J.C. Jordan and Ellis Doty and was designed to shear the tire to length, punch the bolt holes, and upset the tire to size.

By 1888, when the firm reorganized as the New Doty Mfg. Co., products appear to have been exclusively power punching and shearing machinery.

(Illustrations on next page)

Fig.1

Fig.2

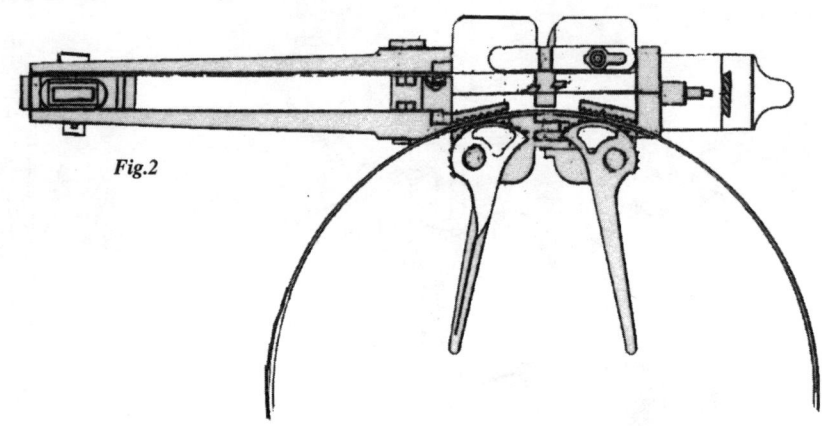

DOUGLASS MFG. CO. , Seymour, CT

Founded by Charles Douglass in 1856 to make augers and edge tools. Production of hollow augers (Fig.1), based on patents issued February 25, 1862, to A.B. Hendryx and July 21, 1863, to R. Gaylord, began in 1865.

In 1873, the firm bought Oliver Ames & Son, continuing production of "a large variety of mechanics' tools, especially adapted for carriage-makers." Products included AMES hollow augers, patented September 19, 1871, by James Swan, and the Improved Universal hollow auger, patented August 30, 1870, byAustin F. Cushman (Fig.2).

In 1877, James Swan, who had been superintendent of Oliver Ames & Son. bought the Douglass Mfg. Co. with financial backing from the Russell & Erwin Mfg. Co. He then reorganized as the JAMES SWAN CO., which continued production of the AMES and Improved Universal hollow augers.

Fig.1

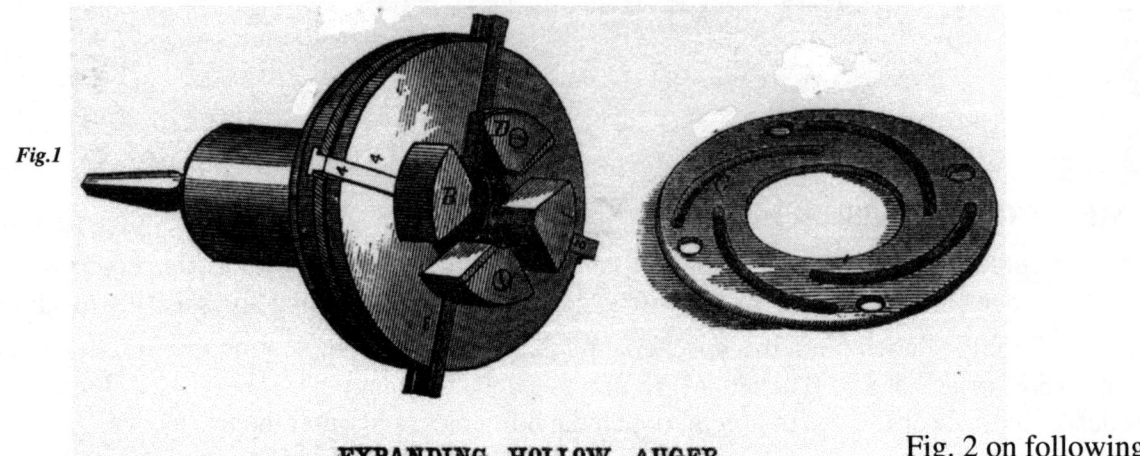

EXPANDING HOLLOW AUGER.

Fig. 2 on following page

Fig.2

DUPONT MFG. CO. , St. Johnsbury, VT

Formed in 1892 to make the Dupont power hammer used by carriage and wagon makers. In 1902 the hammer line was sold to E.& T. Fairbanks Co.

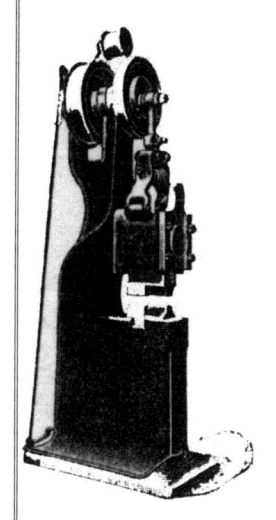

The Dupont Power Hammer.

ITS POINTS OF SUPERIORITY.

No. 3. ECONOMY OF POWER.

" Does not take any more power than a sewing machine," is what everybody says who sees it run. It is, in fact, a phenomenon in the amount of power used, a one hundred pound Hammer having been run on regular work with a one-inch belt. Where steam is used power means money, and this is one of the strongest recommendations for this Hammer.

DUPONT MANUFACTURING COMPANY,

ST. JOHNSBURY, VT.

EAMES, LOVETT , Kalamazoo, MI

Operator of a sawmill beginning in 1844, Eames branched out into hub and spoke production in the 1850s. He soon began to offer hub machinery of his invention, including a hub turning machine (Fig.1), patented June 9, 1857, and a hub mortising machine (Fig.2) patented May 11, 1858.

The hub turning machine was operated by mounting the rough hub between centers and, by use of hand crank C moving the slide B, the workpiece was moved into a set of revolving planer cutters and saw blades which shaped and grooved the body of the hub as it was rotated by a second hand crank.

The hub mortising machine was designed to supplement the turning machine, cutting the required mortises for the spokes. In operation, the hub was mounted between centers. The mortises were cut by a hollow chisel tool E with a rotating cutter inside. One of the centers Q was a stop wheel with a spring stop fitting into holes on its periphery and thus locating the hub to the proper radial location for the mortises. A moveable plate M was located by a pattern of holes n and pin h to give the hub the proper angle to the cutting tool; feed motion was supplied by the crank F.

EAMES' MACHINE FOR TURNING HUBS.

Fig.1

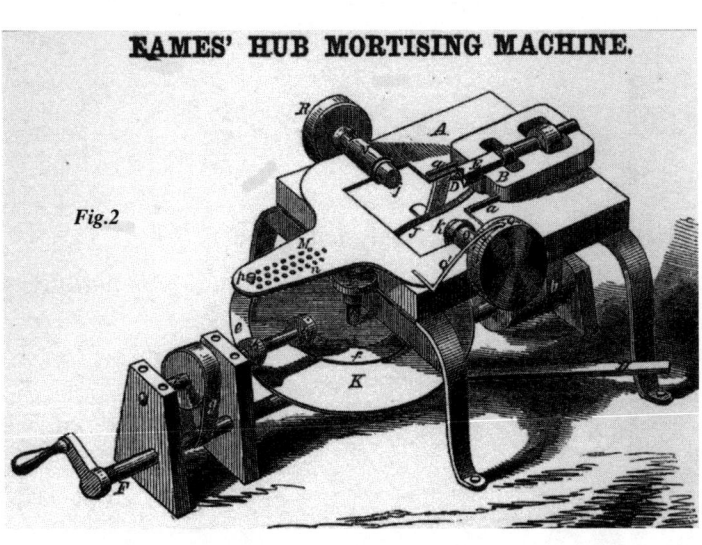

EAMES' HUB MORTISING MACHINE.

Fig.2

ECKMAN & MIKKELSON , Granite Falls, MN

A partnership of Andrew Eckman and Hans A. Mikkelson formed ca. 1880. Products included a hand operated spoke trimming machine patented December 12, 1882, by Eckman. The machine was designed to dress and finish the foot and shoulders of carriage and wagon spokes before insertion in the hub mortises.

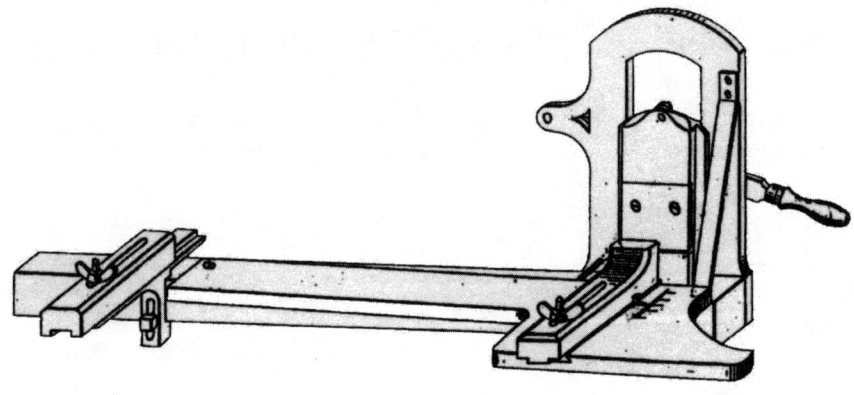

EDWARDS & MORLAN , Salem, OH, later
EDWARDS, GROVE & WATSON , Salem, OH, later
EDWARDS CO., M.L. , Salem, OH

Founded in 1872 by Martin L. Edwards who had been employed by DOLE & SILVER from 1854 to 1872. Edwards' first product appears to have been a hollow auger (Fig.1), patented December 3, 1872. In 1883, the firm became Edwards, Grove & Watson and offered hand and power meat choppers, lard presses, butchers' supplies, blacksmith drills, hub boxing machines (Fig.2), Edwards' patent adjustable hollow augers, and spoke tenoning machines.

By 1892, the firm had reorganized as the M.L. Edwards Co., which continued in business as late as 1905.

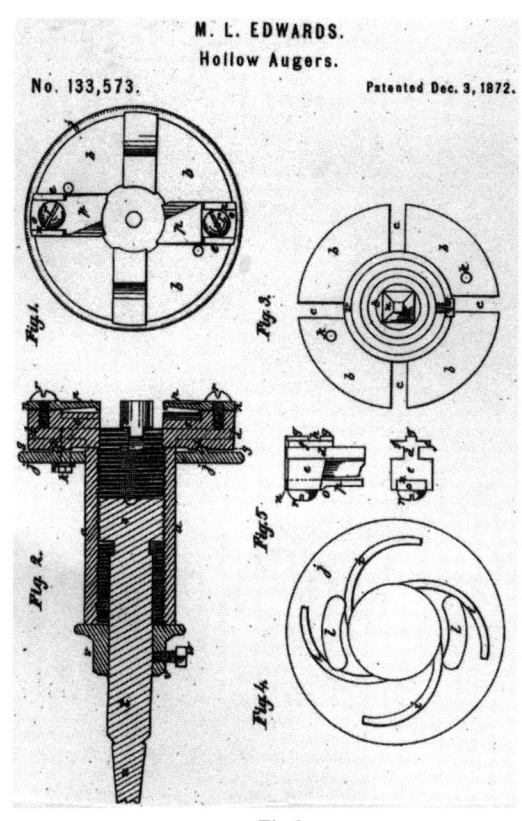

M. L. EDWARDS.
Hollow Augers.

No. 133,573.

Patented Dec. 3, 1872.

Fig.1

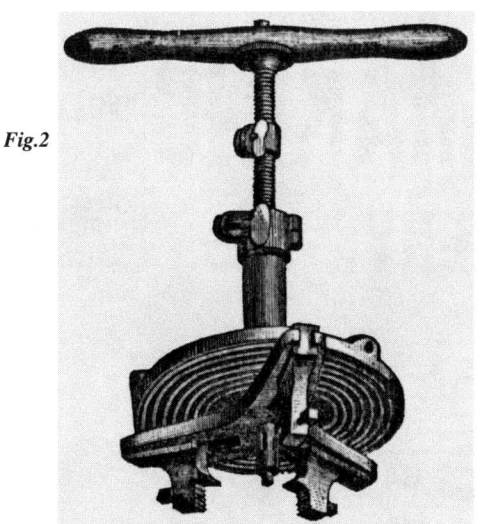

Fig.2

EGAN CO. , Cincinnati, OH

Formed in 1884 when the CORDESMAN & EGAN CO. split into the CORDESMAN MACHINE CO. and the EGAN CO. Cordesman and Egan had been founded in 1874 by Henry J. Cordesman and Thomas P. Egan (1847-1922) to make wood working machinery, including machinery for carriage and wagon makers. In 1893, the Egan Co. merged with J.A. FAY & CO. to form the J.A. FAY & EGAN CO. Thomas Egan was elected president of the new company, serving until his death in 1922.

In 1885, the firm advertised "woodworking machinery for planing mills, furniture and chair factories, car and agricultural works, carriage and buggy shops, and general wood workers." Its 1891 ad in Carriage Monthly magazine (Fig.1) claimed that they were "builders of the largest line of the latest improved carriage making machinery."

Products offered in 1889 included an automatic spoke lathe (Fig.2) of the Blanchard type, patented September 4, 1888, for which Egan claimed a production of 2,400 to 2,700 spokes per day. 1892 production included a hub mortising and boring machine (Fig.3) with a chuck spaced to mortise 10, 12, 14, 16, or 18 spokes, either in line or staggered; a spoke tenoner for round tenons (Fig.4) equipped with a dished circular saw for cutting the spokes to length;and a felloe boring machine (Fig.5).

1892 production included a felloe sanding machine (Fig.6), "capable of finishing spokes, handles, etc."

(Illustrations on next two pages)

Fig.2

AUTOMATIC SPOKE LATHE.

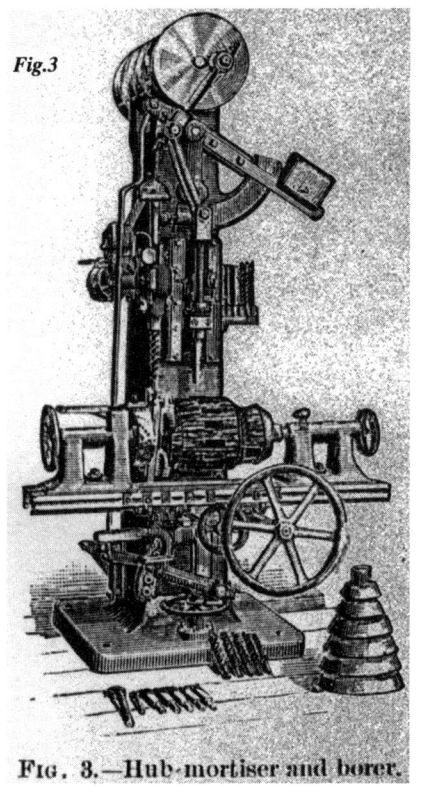

Fig.3

FIG. 3.—Hub-mortiser and borer.

Fig.4

IMPROVED SPOKE TENONER FOR ROUND TENONS.

Fig.5

FELLOE BORING MACHINE.

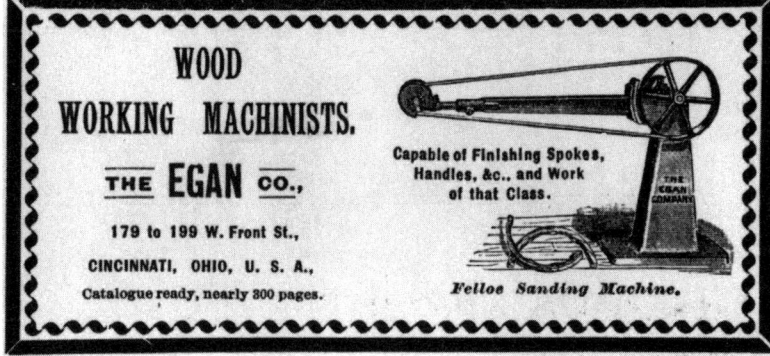

WOOD
WORKING MACHINISTS.
THE EGAN CO.,
179 to 199 W. Front St.,
CINCINNATI, OHIO, U. S. A.,
Catalogue ready, nearly 300 pages.

Capable of Finishing Spokes,
Handles, &c., and Work
of that Class.

Felloe Sanding Machine.

Fig.6

EMERSON & FISHER CO. , Cincinnati, OH

Formed in 1872 by Lowe Emerson (1837-1916) to make buggies and other horse drawn vehicles. Emerson gained a reputation as the first to build buggies by machinery. That may have beenban overstatement, but the firm did develop a number of machines for producing horse drawn vehicles, including a hub boring machine patented September 14, 1880.

EMPIRE MACHINE WORKS , Mount Morris, NY

Maker of a spoke polishing machine, patented September 25, 1877, by Oscar Allen (Fig.1). As shown below, the machine mounted two spokes, one each side of center, which were polished by rotating "quartz belts" on each end of the machine as they were traversed out from the center while slowly rotating.

Allen patented a spoke throating and tapering machine on August 10, 1880. An improved version (Fig.2), patented October 11, 1881, June 12, 1883, and August 23, 1887, was offered by 1889. The spokes, fed by a rotary feeding device, passed between two cutter-heads, the outer or felloe end guided partially around each head by two spring pressure guides. The tenon end moved in a horizontal plane. The firm claimed that the machine would throat both sides complete at a rate of 15,000 per day.

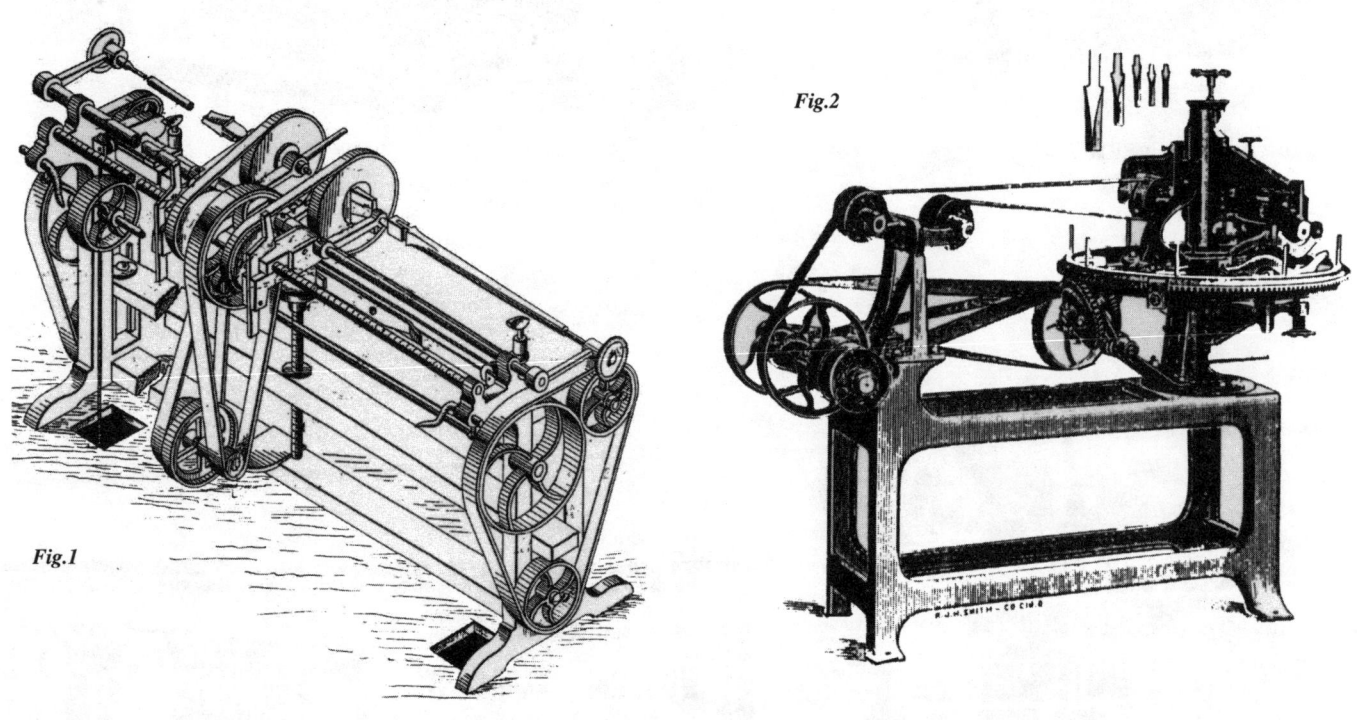

Fig.2

Fig.1

EXETER MACHINE WORKS , Exeter, NH

Founded ca.1860 by William Burlingame. Products included steam engines, machine tools and wheel machinery.

An 1867 ad offered "spoke lathes, hub mortising, boring and shaping machines. Also improved tenoning machines, made entirely of iron, easily adjusted to any size. Price $75."

The firm operated into the 1880's.

FAY & CO., J.A., Keene, NH , Worcester, MA, Norwich, CT, and Cincinnati, OH, later

FAY & EGAN CO., J.A. , Cincinnati, OH

Founded by George Page and Jerub A. Fay (1808-1854) ca. 1830 as Page & Co., Keene, NH. The firm made wood working machinery patented by Page and Fay, primarily machinery for cutting mortises and tenons. In 1836, Edward Joslin (1810-1901) joined with Fay to buy out Page and, in 1841, form J.A. Fay & Co.

Early production of wagon and carriage makers' machinery included mortising machines with a hub attachment, (Fig.1) patented by Fay January 17, 1842, and a spoke lathe (Fig.2) offered by 1850.

A branch factory was established in Norwich, CT, in 1848 with C.B. Rogers as the resident partner. In 1853, the partners bought the small woodworking machinery business of Childs & Tainter in Worcester, MA, operating it as a branch of J.A. Fay & Co., with Ephraim C. Tainter as resident partner. Another branch factory was opened in Cincinnati, OH, in 1852 with John Cheney and E. Reed as the resident partners.

Fay's widow and the other partners continued operation of the firm after Fay's death April 25, 1854, but the firm began to break up in 1861.

The Norwich, CT, factory was sold to C.B. Rogers in 1861 and continued in operation as the C.B. ROGERS CO. The Worcester operation was closed in 1861 and the factory sold to E.C. Tainter in 1862. Tainter, as late as 1866, continued to advertise as E.C. TAINTER, SUCCEEDING PARTNER to J.A. FAY & CO. The Keene factory was closed in 1863. *(continued on following pages)*

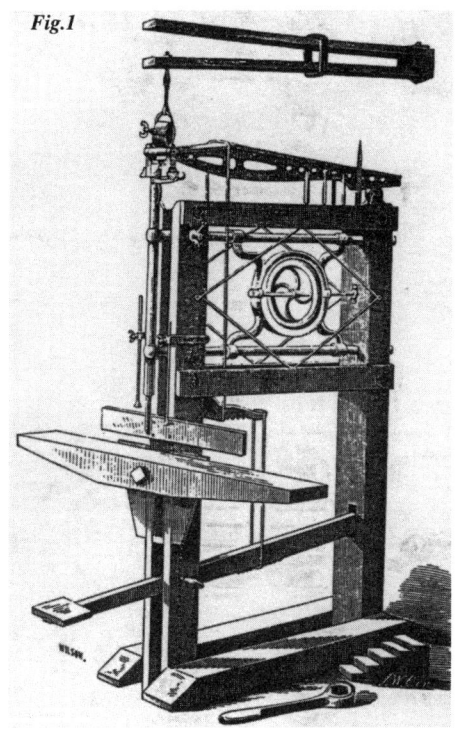

Fig.1

Fig.2

SPOKE LATHE.

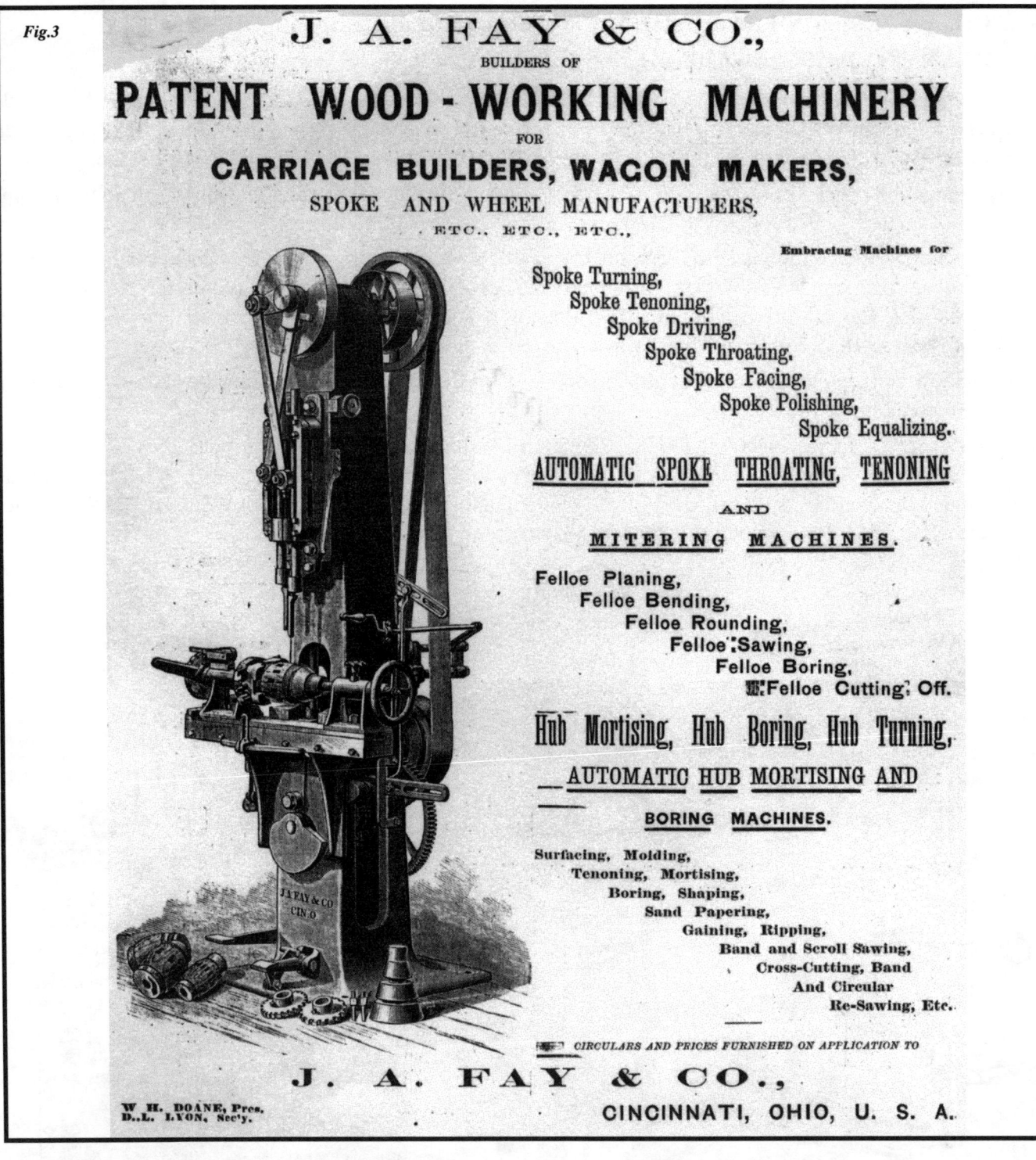

Fig.3

J. A. FAY & CO.,
BUILDERS OF

PATENT WOOD-WORKING MACHINERY

FOR

CARRIAGE BUILDERS, WAGON MAKERS,

SPOKE AND WHEEL MANUFACTURERS,
ETC., ETC., ETC.,

Embracing Machines for

Spoke Turning,
Spoke Tenoning,
Spoke Driving,
Spoke Throating,
Spoke Facing,
Spoke Polishing,
Spoke Equalizing.

AUTOMATIC SPOKE THROATING, TENONING

AND

MITERING MACHINES.

Felloe Planing,
Felloe Bending,
Felloe Rounding,
Felloe Sawing,
Felloe Boring,
Felloe Cutting Off.

Hub Mortising, Hub Boring, Hub Turning,

AUTOMATIC HUB MORTISING AND

BORING MACHINES.

Surfacing, Molding,
Tenoning, Mortising,
Boring, Shaping,
Sand Papering,
Gaining, Ripping,
Band and Scroll Sawing,
Cross-Cutting, Band
And Circular
Re-Sawing, Etc.

CIRCULARS AND PRICES FURNISHED ON APPLICATION TO

J. A. FAY & CO.,

W. H. DOANE, Pres.
D. L. LYON, Sec'y.

CINCINNATI, OHIO, U. S. A.

J. A. FAY & CO
CIN. O

W.H. Doane took over management of the Cincinnati works in 1861 and, by 1882, employed over 400 hands. Its 1883 ad (Fig.3) illustrated its new hub mortising machine and offered a variety of other machines for wagon and carriage makers. These included the Hosler spoke driving machine (Fig.4), patented September 10, 1867, and made by HOSLER, MILES & CO. until taken over by Fay in 1873; a wheelwright machine (Fig.5), patented November 1, 1881; spoke throating machines, patented March 9, 1880, (Fig.6); and a felly planer (Fig.7), patented September 25, 1883. Later production included an improved spoke lathe (Fig.8), patented July 7, 1885; and a double wheel sanding machine (Fig.9) offered in 1887.

Fig.4

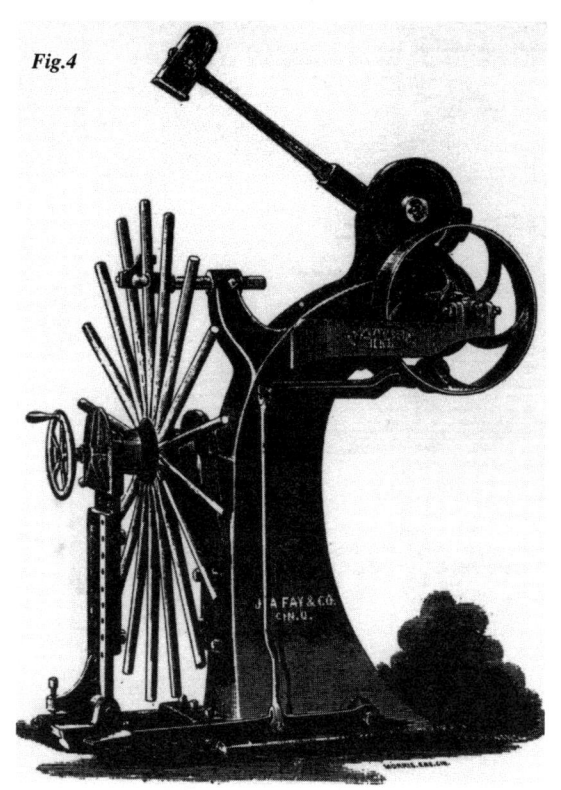

Fig.5

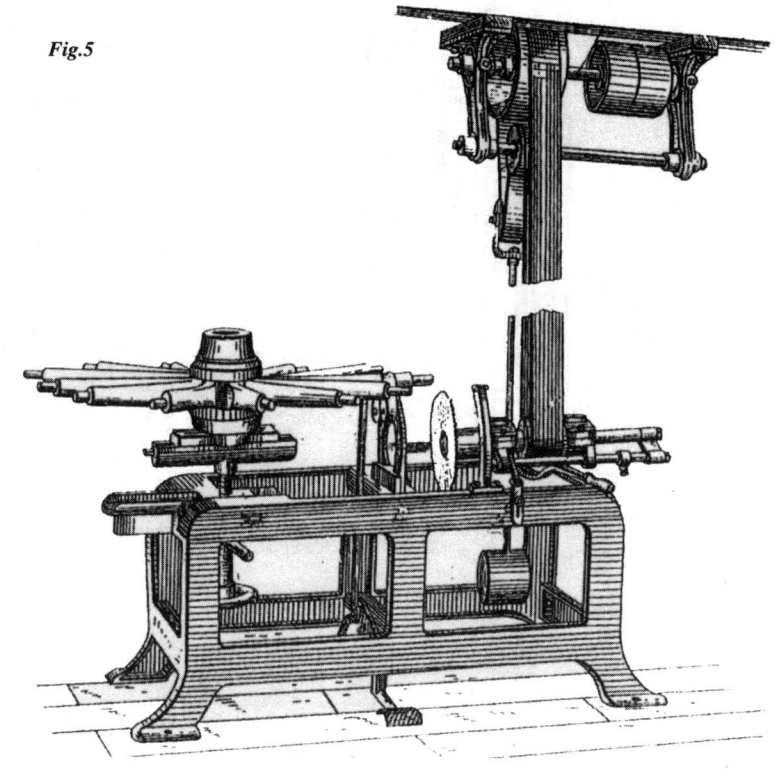

Fig.6

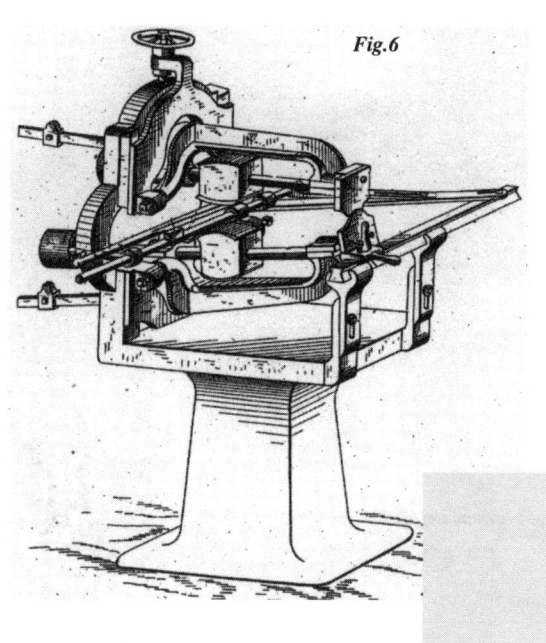

Fig.7

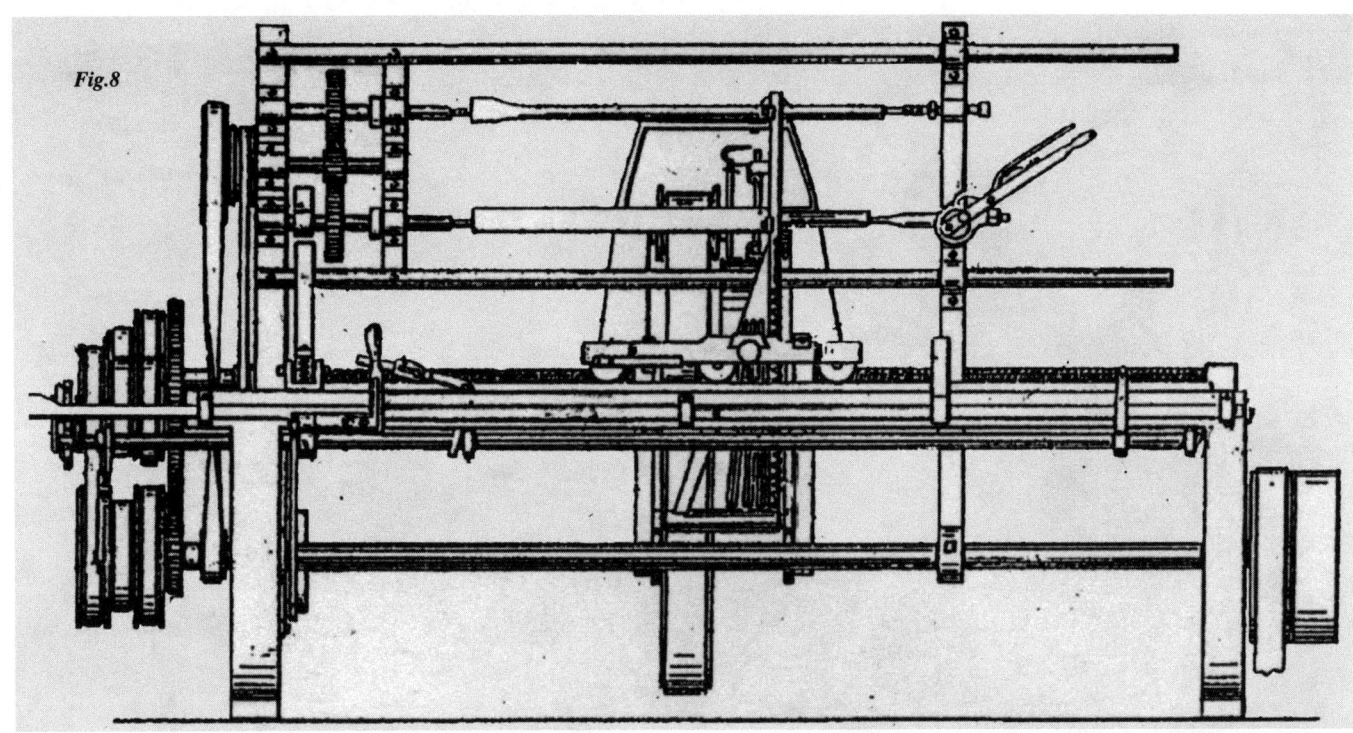

Fay's 1890 catalog offered an improved hub mortising machine (Fig.10); patent automatic spoke throating, tenoning and mitering machine (Fig.11); patent hand feed spoke tenoning and mitering machine (Fig.12); new improved spoke polishing machine (Fig.13); improved Hosler's patent spoke driving machine (Fig.14); Corr's patent automatic wheel machine (Fig.15), patented August 6, 1878, by Columbus W. Corr, equipped with his February 25, 1873, patent hollow augers (Fig.16); a patent oval spoke tenoning machine (Fig.17), patented May 11, 1869, by C.W. Cotton and previously made by Cotton; Morris patent wood bending machine (Fig.18), patented March 11, 1856, by John C. Morris; improved felloe rounding machine (Fig.19), patented December 6, 1859,and previously made by MILLER & DENNISON; double spindle hub boring machine (Fig.20); improved carriage wheel boxing machine (Fig.21); patent universal wheel finishing machine (Fig.22);and a wheel screwing machine (Fig.23) which had been made as early as 1874.

In 1893, the firm merged with the EGAN CO. to form the J.A. Fay & Egan Co. Production of wagon and carriage makers' machinery continued until at least 1929 when its catalog offered strip and felloe planers (Fig.24),Automatic spoke and handle lathes (Fig.25), patented March 2, 1909, and automatic benders (Fig.26).

Fig.10

Fig.11

PATENT AUTOMATIC

Spoke Throating, Tenoning, and Mitering Machine.

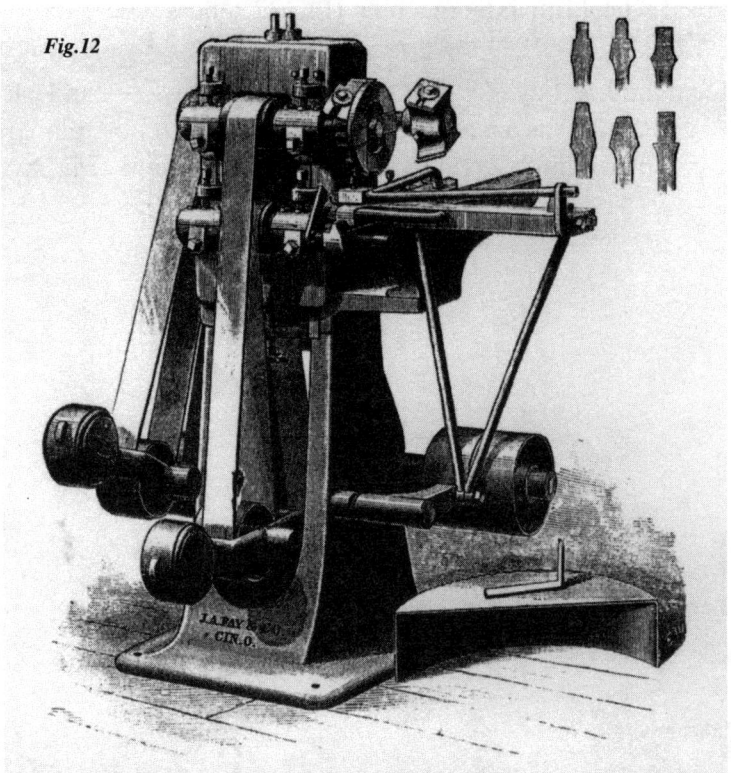

Patent Hand Feed Spoke Tenoning and Mitering Machine.

Hosler's Patent Spoke Driving Machine.

New Improved Spoke Polishing Machine.

Corr's Patent Automatic Wheel Machine.

Corr's Improved Hollow Auger.

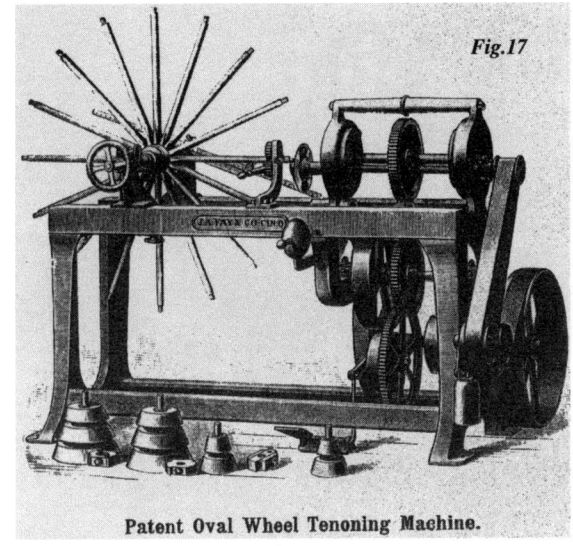

Patent Oval Wheel Tenoning Machine.

Improved Felloe Rounding Machine.

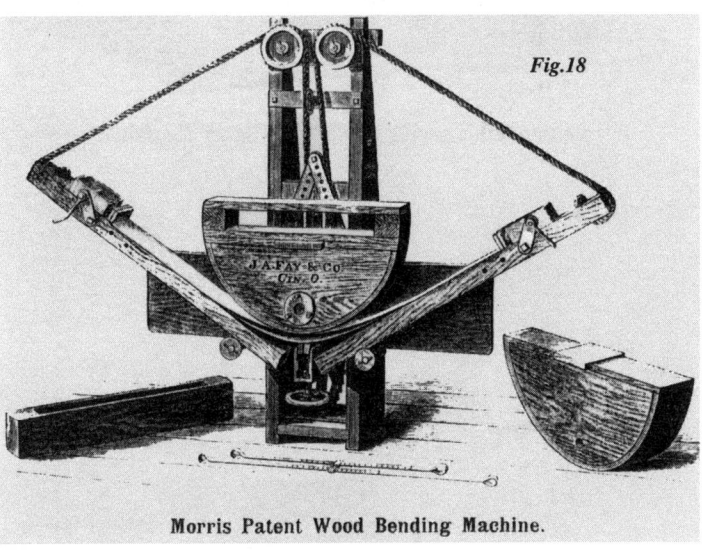

Morris Patent Wood Bending Machine.

Double Spindle Hub Boring Machine.

95

Fig.21

Improved Carriage Wheel Boxing Machine.

Fig.23

Wheel Screwing Machine.

Fig.22

Patent Universal Wheel Finishing Machine.

Fig.24

No. 5—Strip and Felloe Planer

DESIGNED for planing up felloe stock, shafts, carriage bows, etc. Owing to the sectional pressure roll, several strips of varying thickness can be planed at the same time It can also be used for regular surfacing, either light or heavy, and will perform the work very satisfactorily Planes material up to 24″ wide and 8″ thick. Motor, 10 to 15 h. p., belted to cylinder.

Fig.25

No. 222—Patented
Automatic Spoke and Handle Lathe

DESIGNED to meet the highest requirements in spoke and wheel factories where large output and finest quality of spoke turning is required.   It is also well adapted to the rapid turning of pick, sledge and double edge axe handles, neck yokes, swingletrees, etc Rapid and easy in operation. The stock is first placed between the centers, then the operator throws in the tail center with the eccentric lever at the right. He then drops his hand on the starting lever, lifting the vibrator frame and bringing the stock into the cut. At the same time the carriage starts forward at a fast speed; when it reaches the throat of the spoke it automatically changes to a slower speed to turn the square end. When the end of the spoke is reached, the carriage automatically and quickly returns to its original position, where it is brought to a standstill by an automatic brake, which prevents it from overrunning.

CAPACITY: This machine is made in three sizes to turn 36″, 42″ and 48″ in length, and up to 4″ in diameter. A first class operator can turn from 2,500 to 3,000 spokes of medium size in a single day.

No. 165—Automatic Benders

Fig.26

DESIGNED for bending felloes, hames, chair and wagon material, etc. A very powerful machine. Will bend material up to 9″, 12″ or 14″ wide and 3″ thick. Felloes for wheels from 30″ to 72″ in diameter may be formed on this machine. Bending arms are solid.

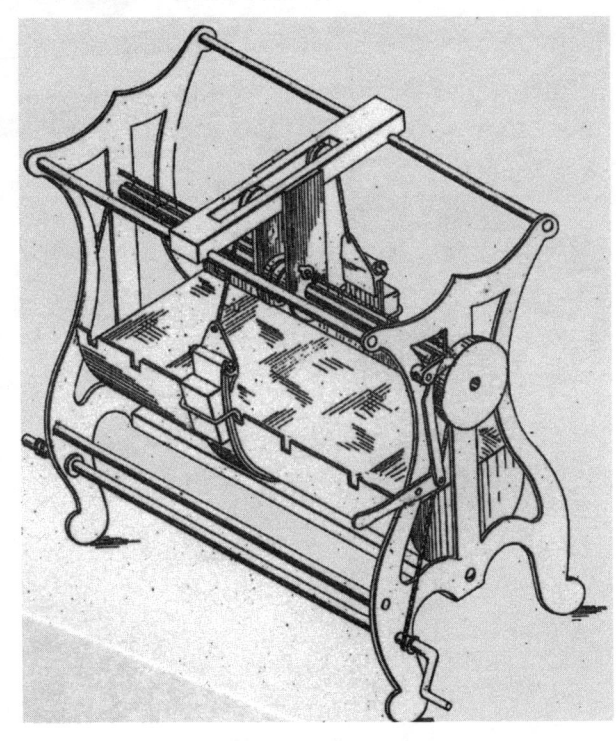

FINDLAY CARRIAGE BENT WORKS , Findlay, OH

Formed in 1879 as a partnership of Charles Wright and Yeatman Bickham. Within a few years, the firm employed 25 hands and was processing 250,000 feet of hickory annually into bent work such as fellies.

Products also included a felly bending machine, shown at right, patented February 17, 1880, by Charles Wright.

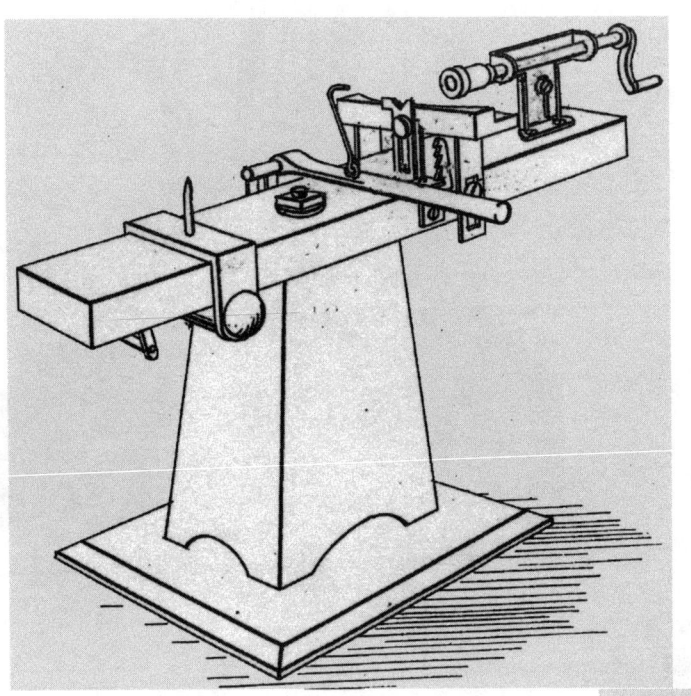

FINDLAY CARRIAGE CO. , Findlay, OH

Founded ca. 1879 by Oliver J. Dougherty and Parlee C. Tritch. Dougherty was a carriage maker; Tritch was the county coroner and operated a harness making firm.

Products included a spoke tenoning and felly boring machine, shown at left, jointly patented February 4, 1879, by the partners.

FLICKINGER WHEEL CO. , Galion, OH

Primarily a wheel maker, the firm also made spoke finishing machines, patented May 9, 1899, by Frederick Unkrich. The machine, shown at right, was equipped with automatic feed in both left/right and in/out directions.

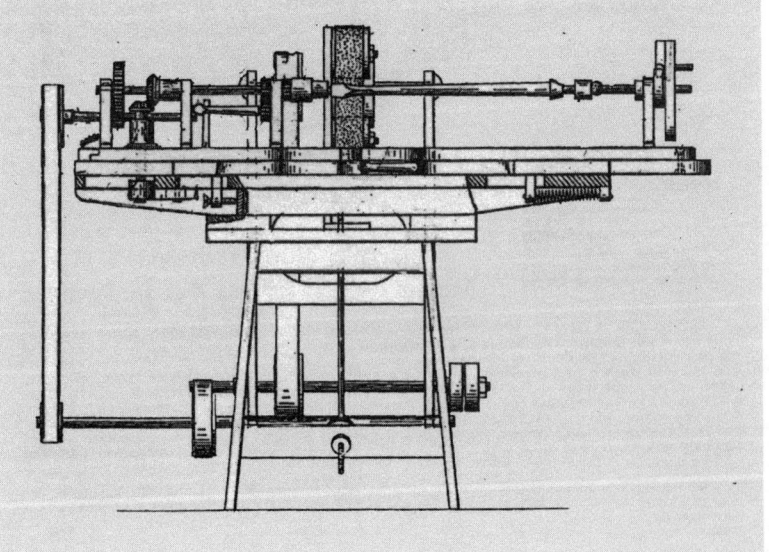

FULTON IRON & ENGINE WORKS , Detroit, MI

Founded in 1851 by J.B. Wayne. By 1878, 80 hands were employed making vises, anvils and other blacksmiths' tools. CHAMPION tire benders (Fig.1) were offered by 1882 and DETROIT tire benders (Fig.2), in six styles, by 1897.

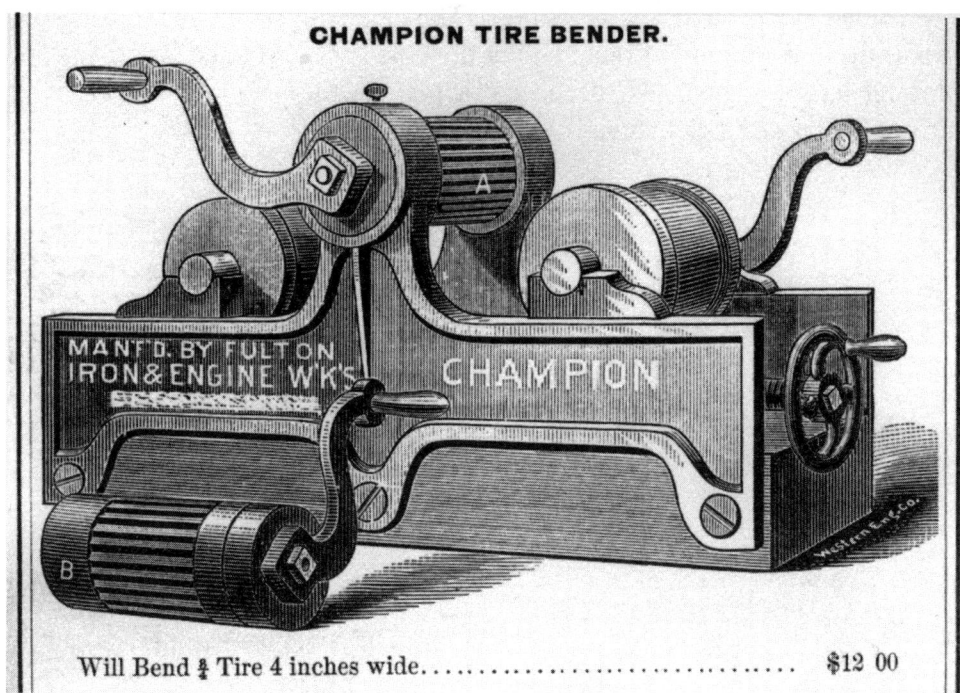

CHAMPION TIRE BENDER.

Fig.1

MANF'D. BY FULTON IRON & ENGINE WK'S

CHAMPION

Will Bend ¼ Tire 4 inches wide.................................. $12 00

THE DETROIT PERFECTED TIRE BENDER.

The great advantage which this machine offers is that the Center Top Roll is removable, and a heavy tire can be taken out after bending, without springing the ends apart.

The body of machine consists of one solid piece without bolt or nut. The rolls are TURNED TRUE, and are adjusted by a screw as shown in cut. The size of circle ranges from 12 inches to 12 feet. Tires can be trued up after welding. This Bender is not to be classed with the numerous low-priced machines in the market, and as one will last a life-time the additional expense is well invested.

PRICES.

No. 21 will take 4 x ½ inch tire, not geared $12.00
  " 22 " 4 x ⅞ " is geared 19.00
  " 23 " 6 x ¾ or 4 x 1 in. tire, is geared. 26.00
  " 24, same as No. 23, with counter-shaft and
     pulleys................... ... 35.00
  " 25 will take 6 x 1 inch tire, doubled geared,
     extra heavy bed................... 55.00
  " 26, same as No. 25, with counter-shaft and
     pulleys........................... 65.00

Fig.2

GAGE, IRA B. , Constantine, MI

Maker, in 1867, of a hand operated hub-boring machine (right) "intended for wheelwrights and carriage makers who do not have stationary machinery or power to assist them in their business." The machine was designed to produce the taper bore required for the iron box fitted in wagon and carriage hubs. The taper was bored by "setting the cutters one half the diameter of the small end of the hole gaged from center of the shaft and bore through the hub. Then move the eccentric plate by the set screw, D, to half the taper required and bore through again."

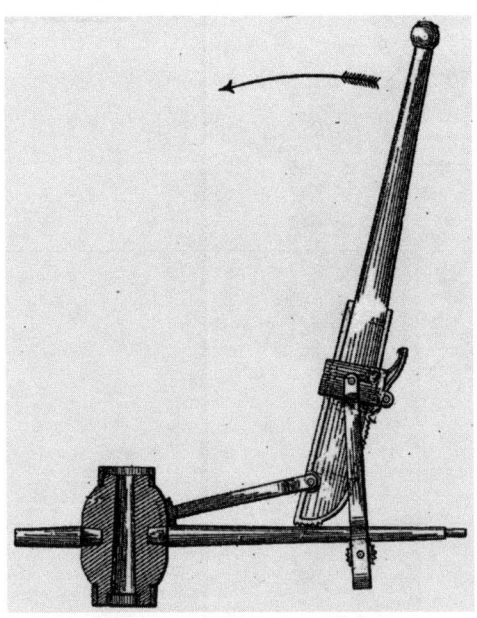

GERMANN , JOHN M. , New York, NY

Inventor and maker of a spoke puller, shown left, patented April 24, 1888.

GILCHRIST'S IMPROVED SPOKE MACHINE.

GILCHRIST, JOHN , Berlin, WI

Inventor and maker of a spoke lathe, patented October 23, 1860 (right). The machine was equipped with a rotating cutter the full length of the spoke that cut as the spoke was fed in and slowly rotated in front of it. Feed motion was caused by hand operation of lever H that applied force through a heavy spring G.

GILMAN, F.B. , Springfield, VT, later
GILMAN & TOWNSEND , Springfield, VT, later
GILMAN & SON , Springfield, VT

Founded by F.B. Gilman in 1854 to make last and spoke lathes. Gilman was joined by F.V.A. Townsend in 1861 and the firm became Gilman & Townsend, which continued production of lathes for turning spokes and other irregular forms.

Townsend retired in April, 1892; W.F. Gilman was admitted to the firm which now became Gilman & Son. Sixteen hands were employed in 1895 making lathes for markets in the U.S., England, France and Germany.

GLEASON, J. , Philadelphia, PA, later
GLEASON'S SONS, JOHN , Philadelphia, PA

Maker, in 1866, of a spoke turning lathe. The lathe was a modified Blanchard design which utilized a pattern piece A in the illustration at right. The workpiece is mounted between centers E and rotated slowly and at the same rate as the pattern. The cutter assembly F is moved in and out by the pattern as it moves along the length of the workpiece.

By 1893, the firm had become John Gleason's Sons "manufacturers of latest improved wheel machinery," including a slightly improved model of the 1866 spoke turning lathe.

GLEASON'S SPOKE-TURNING LATHE.

GOGEL MFG. CO. , Toledo, OH

Maker, in 1916, of tire heaters fired by oil, natural gas and gasoline. Also tire coolers, fifth wheels and other iron wagon fittings.

GOODMAN, ALLEN , Dana, MA

Inventor and maker of a variety of woodworking machinery in the 1840s and 1850s. Products included a spoke lathe, patented December 19, 1848. The design was unique in using a rotating cam and follower to control the motion of a cutter bar. This allowed multiple workpieces to be machined by a single elongated cutter as the carriage holding the workpieces was traversed.

An 1851 ad mentioned machines that "turn four spokes at a time or 50 per hour leaving them better to finish than any other machine."

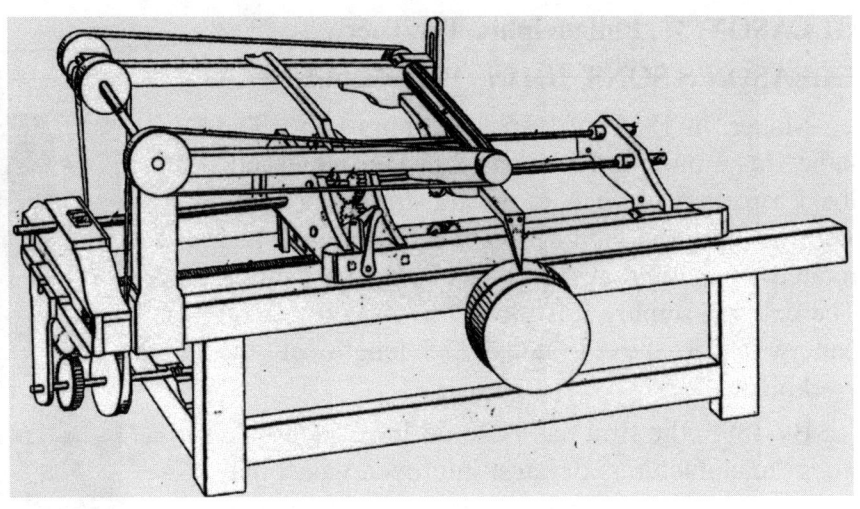

GOODYEAR, ANDREW , Albion, MI

Listed in the 1870 U.S. census as a hub maker, Andrew Goodyear (1819-1897) was also the inventor and maker of hub making machinery. Products included a lathe, patented August 23, 1864, that used form tools operated by levers (Fig.1); automatic hub lathes, patented June 25, 1867, (Fig.2) and August 31, 1869, (Fig.3); and a hub shaping machine (Fig.4) patented August 31, 1869, in which a rotating block was fed into a wheel-like set of cutters rotating at 90 degrees to the axis of the hub.

Goodyear was listed in the 1880 census as a mechanic, with no reference to any firm.

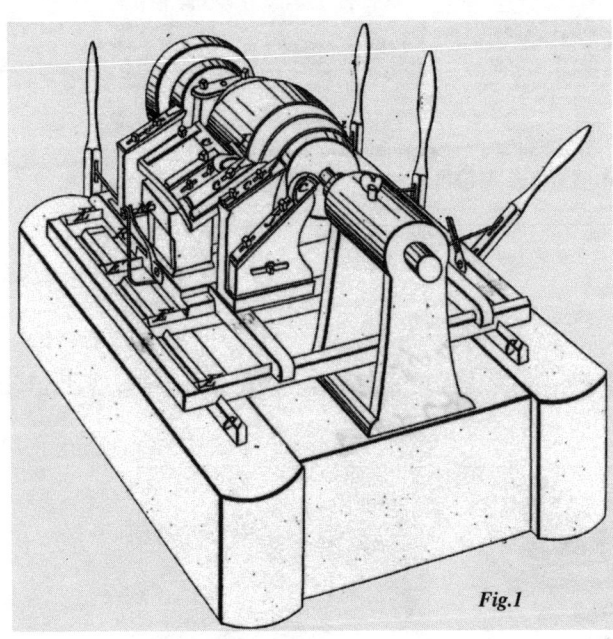

Fig.1

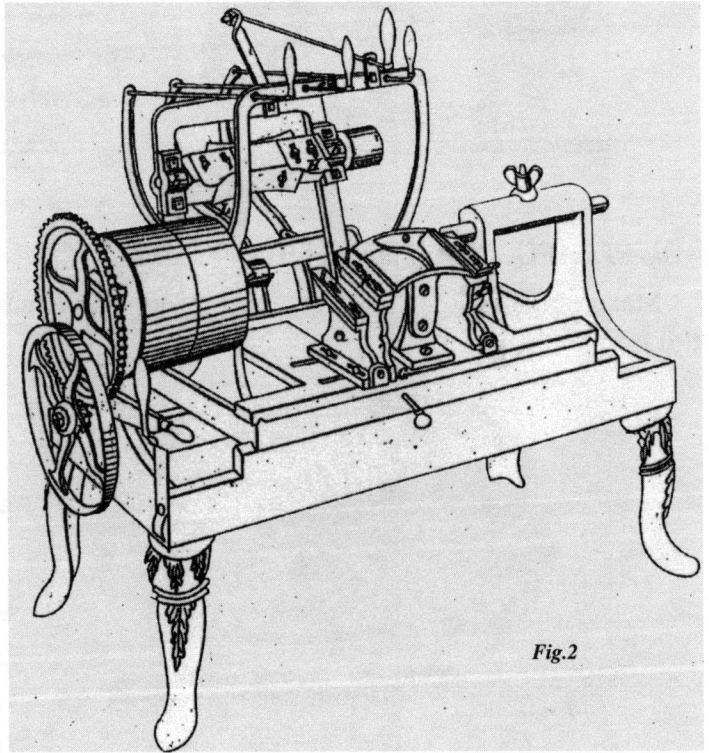

Fig.2

(continued next page)

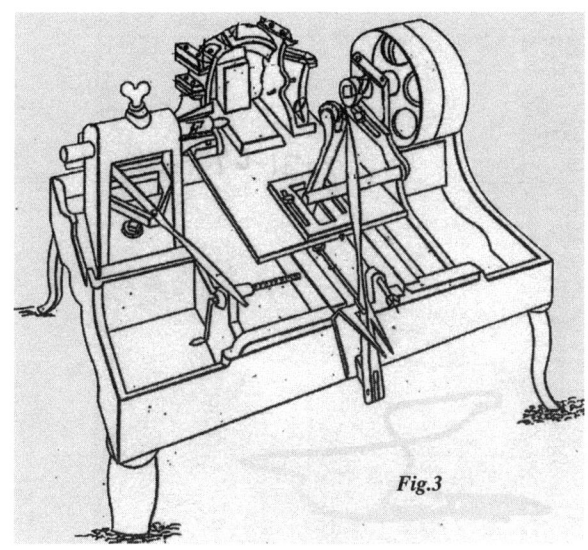

Fig.3

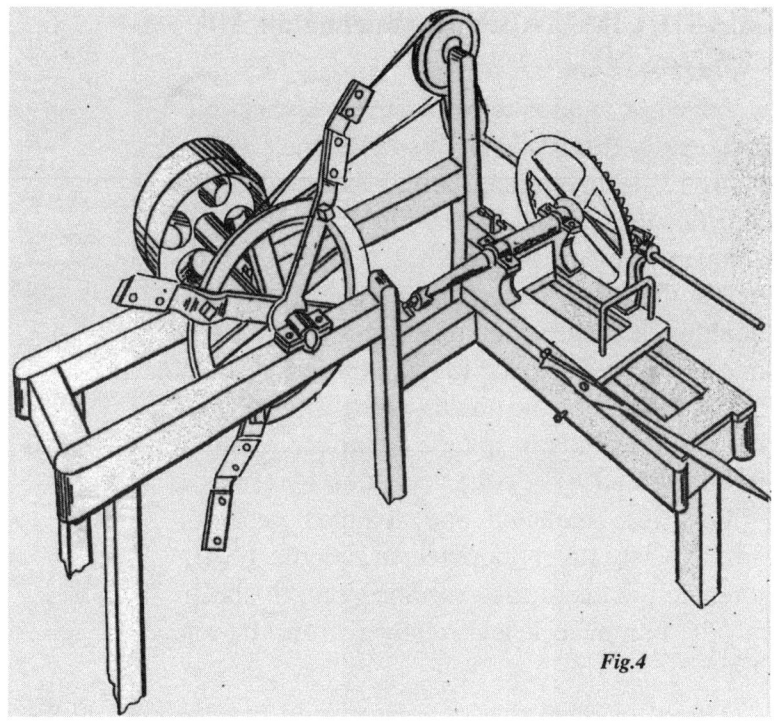

Fig.4

GORTON, JOHN , Providence, RI

Inventor and maker of an axle-setting machine, patented July 25, 1865. Most axles used by small carriage and wagon makers were bought from large factories, which furnished the end pieces only. The buyer then welded them onto a center piece to get the desired length. The assembly then had to be "set" so that the wheels would run true.

The axle was mounted on the machine as shown in Fig.1 and a gauge G, which had to be set to the hub bore taper as shown in Fig.2, used to ascertain that the axle end was square with the tapered bore of the hub. The axle was then turned end for end and the operation repeated.

Fig. 1

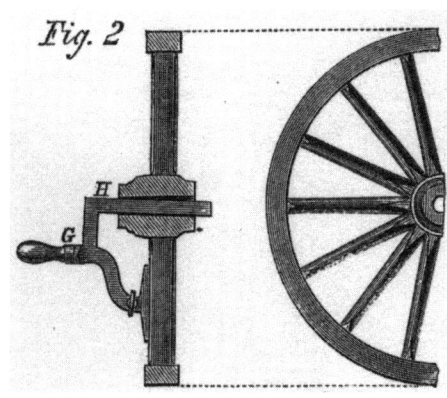

Fig. 2

GORTON'S AXLE-SETTING MACHINE.

GUARD, CHAUNCEY H. , Burlington, VT, later **Troy, NY**

Inventor and maker of a carriage wheel machine, patented September 7, 1852, and October 20, 1857. In operation, the hub is mounted between centers D and located by a self centering clamp operated by a hand wheel K. The outer surface of the hub was bored and mortised by tools mounted in a sliding spindle F. The spokes were then installed and sized to length using gauge n. The outer end of the spokes were tenoned by a tool now mounted in spindle F, and the center of the hub bored by a cutter operated by crank k. Fellies were mounted and clamped on, hand bored by an auger mounted in spindle F. The bored fellies were then installed on the spokes and the complete wheel removed from the machine.

Guard claimed that one man could produce three sets of wheels, six large and six small, in six or seven hours.

On February 4, 1862, Guard, then operating in Troy, NY, was granted a patent for further improvements on the machine.

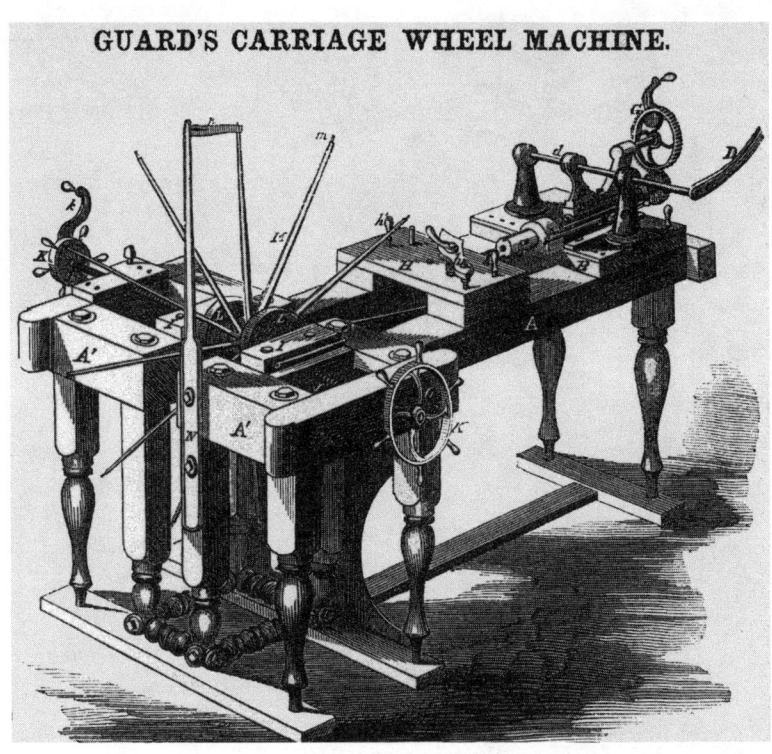

GUARD'S CARRIAGE WHEEL MACHINE.

GUE, ALBERT F. , Eastmanville, MI

Inventor and maker of a hand operated spoke tenoning machine, patented June 21, 1870, (Fig.1). The machine was designed to cut and bevel the hub end tenons. A later design, patented February 13, 1872, (Fig.2) was also capable of sizing spokes.

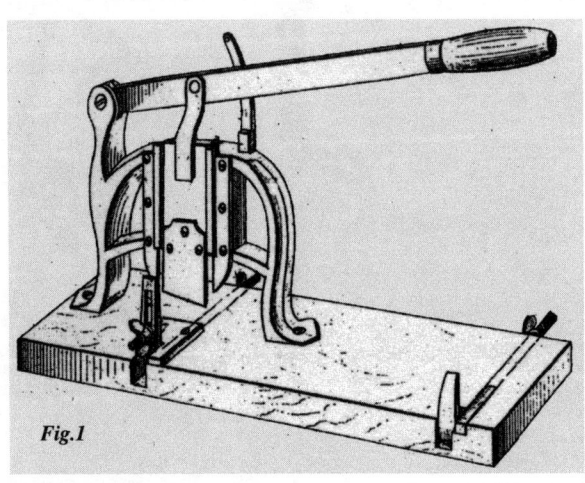

Fig.1

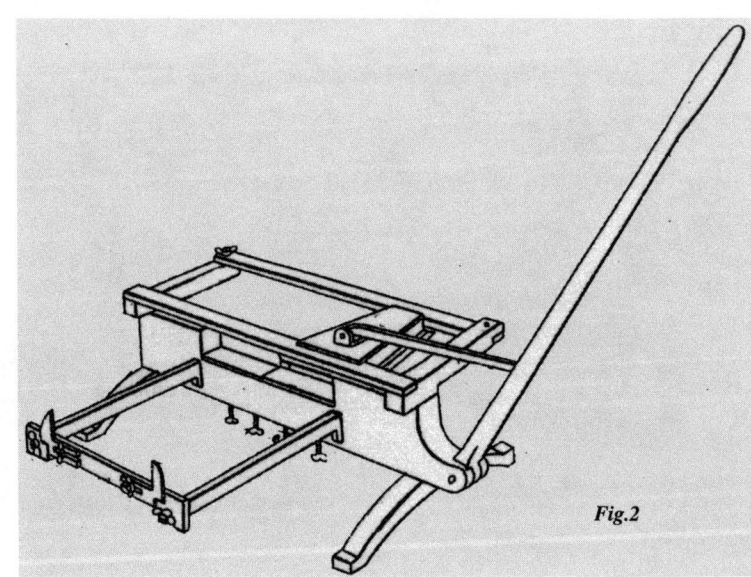

Fig.2

HACKNEY HAMMER CO. , Cleveland, OH

Formed in 1891 to make power hammers. The hammers were offered in two sizes; a 50 pound size striking 350 blows per minute as shown in the left of the illustration below and a 300 pound size striking 200 blows per minute shown on the right.

TO BUILDERS OF FINE VEHICLES.
THE HACKNEY HAMMER CO.
OF CLEVELAND, OHIO,
MANUFACTURE THE MOST SUCCESSFUL
POWER HAMMER
THAT HAS YET BEEN OFFERED TO THE TRADE.
THOROUGHLY & PRACTICALLY TESTED FOR TWO YEARS
BEFORE BEING PUT ON THE MARKET.
NOW ENDORSED BY SOME OF
THE BEST FIRMS IN THE COUNTRY.
WRITE FOR CATALOGUE AND ALL INFORMATION.
GUARANTEED EXACTLY AS RECOMMENDED, OR NO SALE.

HALL & BROWN , St. Louis, MO, later

HALL & BROWN WOODWORKING MACHINE CO. , St. Louis, MO

Founded in 1877 by Gorham O. Hall (1833-1896). The firm incorporated as the Hall & Brown Woodworking Machine Co. in 1888.

Products offered in 1889 included a spoke and handle lathe (Fig.1) with a capacity of 200 to 600 spokes per day and priced at $220. 1904 production included an improved version of the spoke lathe (Fig.2), a hollow chisel mortising machine "designed especially for wagon and carriage builders' use" (Fig.3), and a carriage shop sand-papering machine "especially adapted for use in carriage, buggy and wagon factories" (Fig.4).

Improved Lathe.

Fig.1

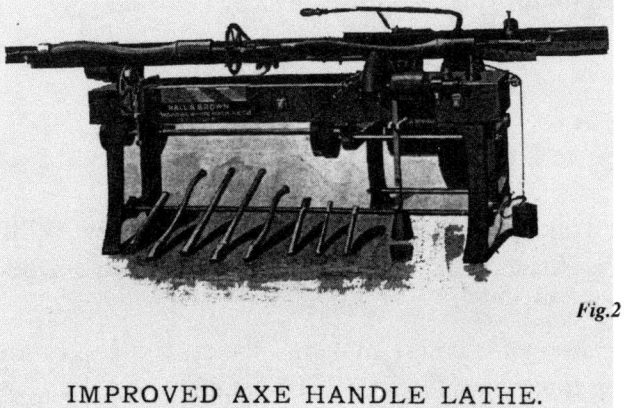

Fig.2

IMPROVED AXE HANDLE LATHE.

(continued next page)

No. 10. HOLLOW-CHISEL MORTISING MACHINE.
Table Can be Set on Horizontal Angles.

No. 2. CARRIAGE-SHOP SAND-PAPERING MACHINE.

HALLAWELL, JAMES , North Vernon, IN

Maker, in 1891, of hub block machinery, including boring machines that bored from both sides at the same time at a rate of 3,000 pieces per day. Hallawell also offered a hub roughing machine which "will more than keep up with the Boring Machine."

HAMMACHER, SCHLEMMER & CO. , New York, NY

A large hardware dealer established in 1848 by William Tollner. Tollner was joined by his nephew William Schlemmer in 1853 and by Alfred Hammacher in 1859. After Tollner's death the firm reorganized as Hammacher, Schlemmer & Co.

It offered nearly every variety of tool, including a selection of carriage makers' planes, routers, beaders, moulding tools, and spokeshaves, as shown on the following four pages from its 1904 catalog.

CARRIAGE MAKERS' IRON "T" PLANES

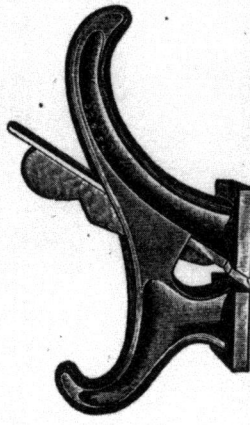
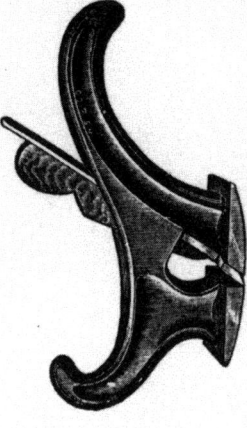

No. 2. Straight. 3½ in., 1½ in. cutter, will cut 7/8 in. deep .... Each, $1.35

No. 4. Round. 3 in., 1½ in. cutter, will cut 7/8 in. deep .... Each, $1.35

CARRIAGE MAKERS' PANEL ROUTERS

No. 5. For 5/16 and 3/8 in. moulding. Made especially for heavy work .... Each, $6.00

See Discount Sheet

CARRIAGE MAKERS' PANEL ROUTERS

No. 6. Double. 7/8 in. cutter. Can be set to cut groove from 1/16 to 1 in.; gauge can be adjusted either right or left hand .... Each, $3.00

SINGLE-HANDED BEADER

For beading, reeding or fluting diagonal lines, etc.

No. 69. Nickel-plated, with six steel cutters and one blank. Each $0.75

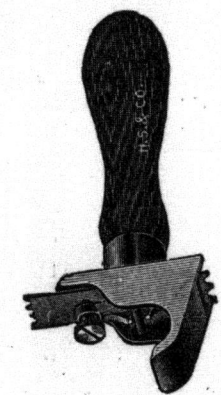

UNIVERSAL HAND BEADER

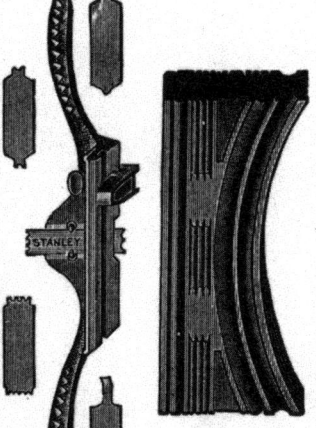

For beading, reeding, or fluting straight or irregular surfaces, and for all kinds of light routering. With square gauge for straight and an oval gauge for curved work.

Seven steel cutters, sharpened on both ends, go four sets of beads, with each tool, embracing six ordinary sizes of beads, two fluters and a double router iron (⅛ and ¼ in.).

No. 66. Nickel-plated .... Each, $1.00

See Discount Sheet

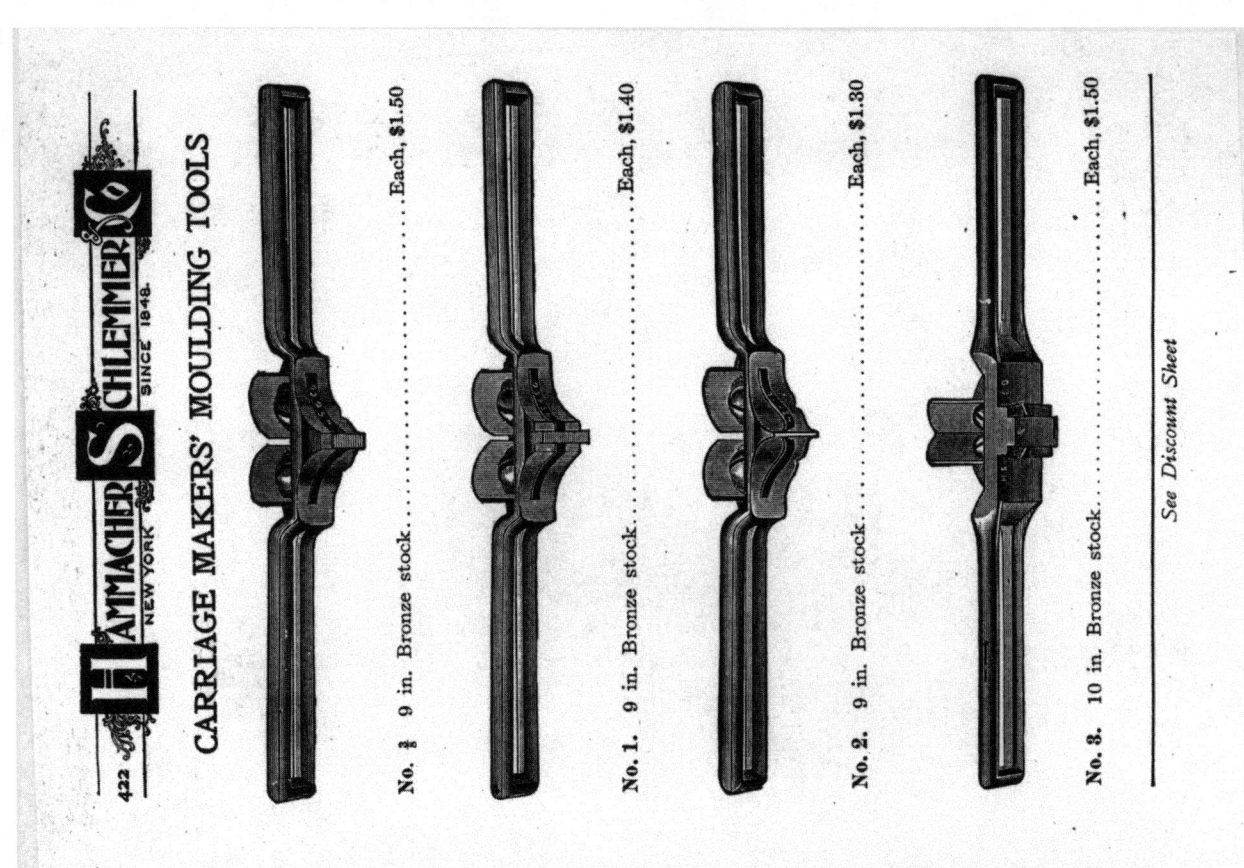

422 HAMMACHER SCHLEMMER Co NEW YORK SINCE 1848

CARRIAGE MAKERS' MOULDING TOOLS

No. ½ 9 in. Bronze stock.........................Each, $1.50

No. 1. 9 in. Bronze stock.........................Each, $1.40

No. 2. 9 in. Bronze stock.........................Each, $1.30

No. 3. 10 in. Bronze stock.........................Each, $1.50

See Discount Sheet

423 HAMMACHER SCHLEMMER Co NEW YORK SINCE 1848

CARRIAGE MAKERS' SPOKESHAVES

No. 4. 2 in. cutter.........................Each, $2.00

CARRIAGE MAKERS' PANEL SPOKESHAVES

No. 7. 2⅜ in. cutter, cuts ⅜ in. rabbet.........................Each, $1.50

No. 8. 1¾ in. cutter, cuts 1⅝ in. rabbet.........................Each, $1.35

No. 9. 2 in. cutter, cuts ¼ in. rabbet.........................Each, $0.75

See Discount Sheet

HARLOW & CO., C.C. ,Bridgewater, MA

Maker, in 1877, of DAMAN standard hollow augers, spoke & dowel trimmers, metallic combination plow planes, and other hardware items.

HARPER, HENRY , Butler, IL

Inventor and maker of an axle gauge (below), patented November 18, 1862. The gauge was designed to give the proper pitch to the axle arms so that the wheels ran true with the desired "set" and "gather." In typical 19th century fashion, Harper claimed that its use made axles "run easier than the previously supposed fundamental laws of science will admit that mechanical power can make the most delicate machinery capable of running" (whatever that means).

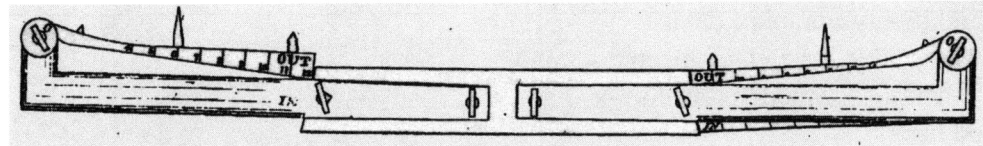

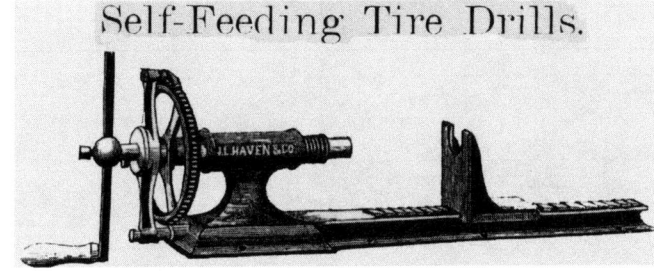

Self-Feeding Tire Drills.

HAVEN & CO., J.L. , Cincinnati, OH

Founded in 1856, the firm made a great variety of cast iron goods, including the self-feeding tire drill, shown at left, offered in 1883. The business closed in 1891.

HAWKEYE MFG. CO. , Cedar Rapids, IA

Maker of helve hammers beginning in 1904. By 1916, the hammers were offered in two sizes; No. 1 (Fig.1) and No. 2 (Fig.2).

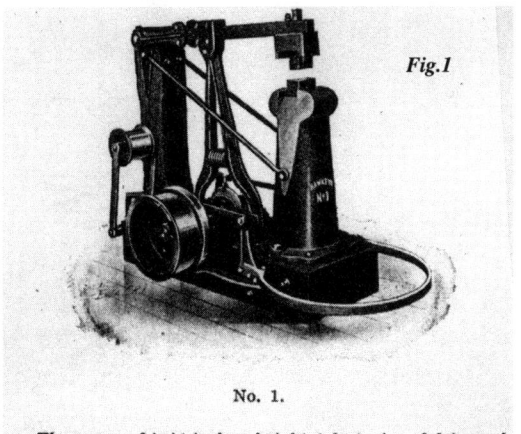

Fig.1

No. 1.

Floor space 24x44 inches, height 4 feet, size of drive pulley 12x4 inches, weight 700 pounds.

Fig.2

No. 2.

Floor space 28x44 inches, height 4 feet, size of drive pulley 14x5 inches, weight 850 pounds.

HAYES, WOODRUFF & CO. , Quincy, IL

A carriage maker, the firm also offered a hub mortising machine, patented September 2, 1856, by Henry Hayes. The hub to be machined was mounted vertically on an indexing plate which positioned the hub radially before a boring head and a separate mortising head, mounted at 90 degrees offset. Hayes claimed that a hub could be bored and mortised in one and one-half minutes.

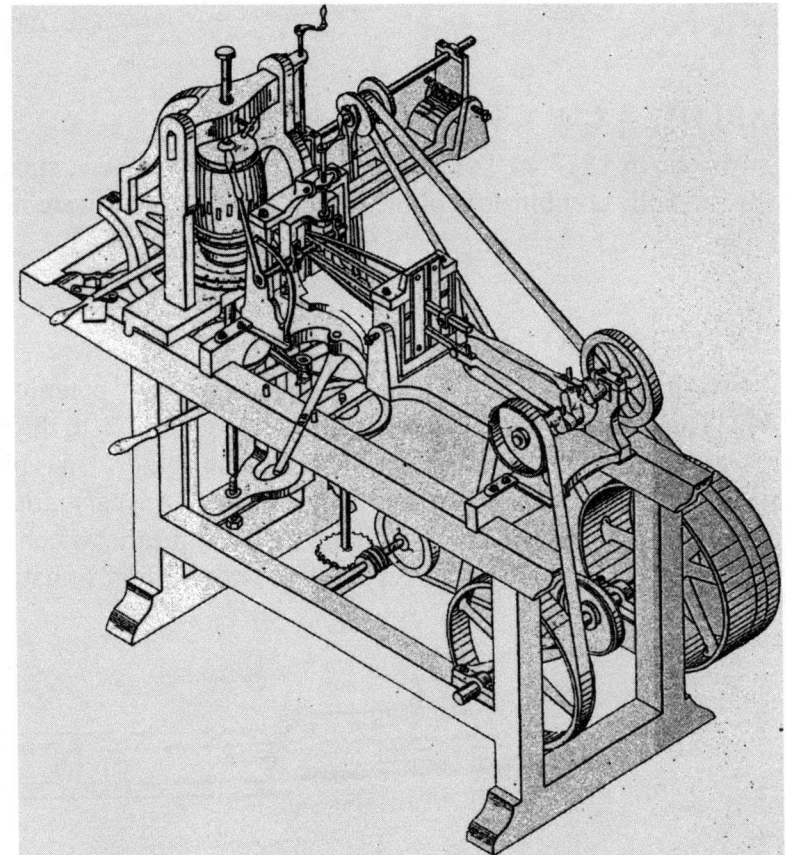

HAZEN & GIBBS , Homer, MI

Maker of a tire upsetter, jointly patented July 7, 1857. A relatively complex device, it used a wedge, moved by a hand crank and screw, to move a set of jaws which in turn compressed the heated tire.

This is an early and probably unsuccessful design; only one older patent (1855) has been noted.

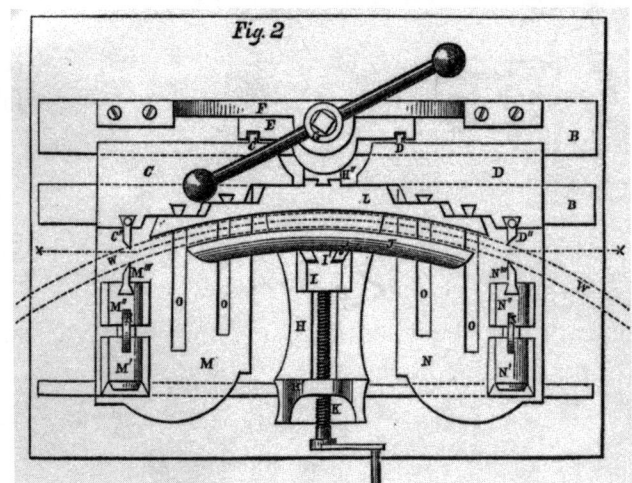

HAZEN & GIBBS' DEVICE FOR UPSETTING TIRES.

HEARTLEY, GEO., W. , Toledo, OH, later
HEARTLEY MACHINE, VARIETY, IRON & TOOL WORKS , Toledo, OH

Founded in 1881 as a blacksmith and machine shop. In 1885, Heartley introduced a line of metal wheel and band tools for carriage and wagon makers. Products offered in 1896 included a machine for rolling and welding rims (Fig.1) and tire stretchers (Fig.2) which used an expanding mandrel for increasing tire diameter.

In 1916, the firm offered the LITTLE GIANT axle box press (Fig.3). *(illustrations on next page)*

Fig.1

Fig.2

HENDERER & CO., E. , Wilmington, DE, later
HENDERER'S SONS , Wilmington, DE

Maker, in 1884, of hand and power drilling machines, tire benders and other machinery for blacksmiths and wagon builders. By 1902 the firm was operating as Henderer's Sons.

HENDERSON & LOURIE , Keokuk, IA

Maker of a cold tire setter, patented March 11, 1902, by Henry T. Henderson. As shown below, it was offered in six sizes.

HENDERSON'S COLD TIRE SETTER.
HAND POWER.

No. 1 —Setting, 1¼ x ¾ inches and less, on wheels 32 to 48 inches diameter,	each,	$135.00
No. 2 —Setting, 2 x ¾ inches and less on wheels 33 to 56 inches diameter,	"	160.00
No. 2½—Setting, 2½ x ¾ inches and less, on wheels 33 to 56 inches diameter,	"	200.00
No. 3 —Setting, 3 x ¾ inches and less, on wheels 33 to 56 inches diameter,	"	230.00
No. 3½—Setting, 3½ x ¾ inches and less, on wheels 33 to 56 inches diameter,	"	260.00
No. 4 —Setting, 4 x ¾ inches and less, on wheels 33 to 56 inches diameter,	"	290.00

Consists of a circular bed-plate about six feet in diameter, with a raised rim through which sixteen powerful screws are placed to operate against a series of cast blocks which press against the tire of the wheel. Proper sized nuts are placed in recesses on inside of cast rim. The outer end of screws, or bolts, are provided with cranks to be used in turning bolts in or out quickly, and heads are also made on bolts, to which wrenches are applied when setting tires. There are six circles of heavy cast presser blocks made to fit different diameters of wheels. These blocks or segments are easily and quickly removed or put in place for different sized wheels. In resetting old tires it is unnecessary to remove the bolts.

HENNESSY, JAMES F. , Winona, MN

Inventor and maker of an axle setting machine, patented January 3, 1888,and shown below. A simple device, it was made of heavy timbers that clamped and supported the axle as a heavy screw was turned to bend the axle ends. A separate axle gauge would be used to find when the axle was set to the desired "pitch"and "gather" of the wheels.

HERTZLER & ROGERS , Lawrence, KS

Makers of a tire bolting machine, patented March 9, 1897, by John F. Hertzler and Frank Rogers. As can be seen at right, the tool could be either bench mounted or hand held.

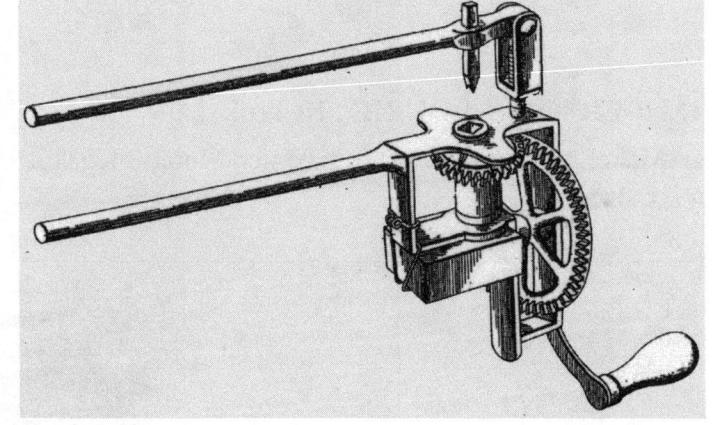

Hibbard's Improved Adjustable Hollow Auger.

HIBBARD MFG. CO., C.B. , Grand Rapids, MI

Maker, in 1901, of a hollow auger (left) adjustable from 1/4" to 1 1/2". It was furnished with a graduated scale and a malleable iron depth stop.

HILBERT-FREIBERG MACHINE CO. , Cincinnati, OH

Formed in 1899 by Charles and Edward Hilbert and Harry A. Freiberg with a capital of $75,000.

Products included a power post hammer, shown at right, with a 50 pound head mounted on a four by one inch slide.

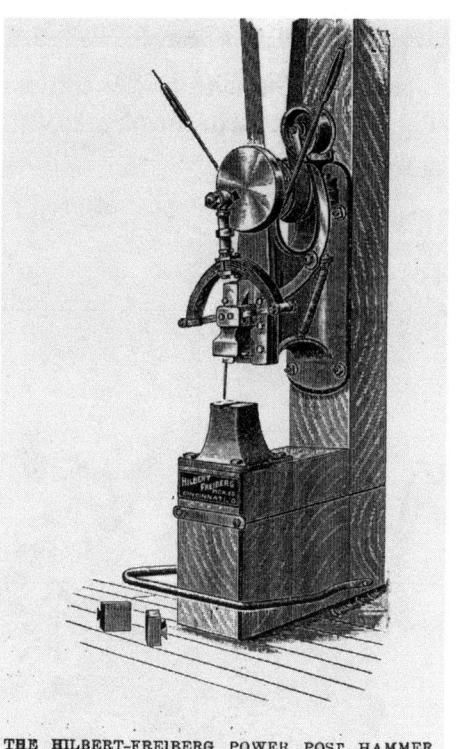

THE HILBERT-FREIBERG POWER POST HAMMER.

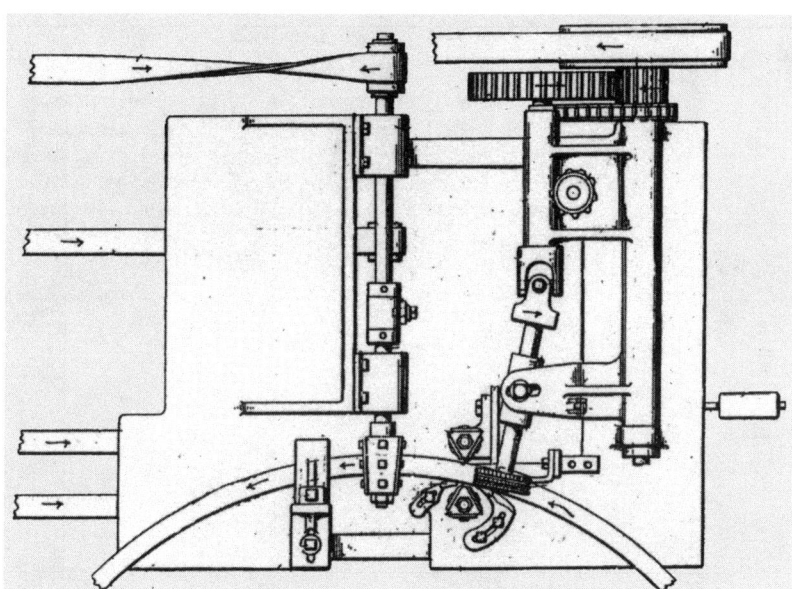

HOOPES BRO. & DARLINGTON , Chester, PA

Maker of wheel rim trimming machines, at left, patented October 25, 1892, by Russell Hoopes. The machine was fitted with four rotating cutters, in two sets of two each, which smoothed and formed all four sides of the rim in one pass.

HOSLER, MILES & CO. , Michigan City, IN

Maker of a spoke driving machine, right, patented September 10, 1867, by G.W. Miles. Note the simple design and construction. By 1873, the machine was a product of J.A. FAY & CO.

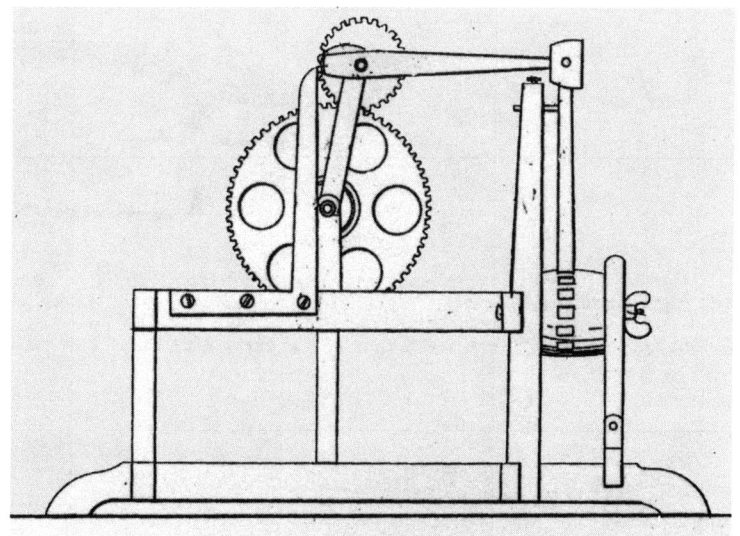

HOUSE COLD TIRE SETTER CO. , St. Louis, MO

Maker of a hand power cold tire setter, patented January 7, 1902,and June 6, 1905, by Samuel N. House (Fig.1). Designed to shrink tires while still mounted on the wheel, the machine was made in two sizes and offered as late as 1916.

By 1916, the firm also offered the EVER READY spoke auger (Fig.2) for cutting tenons on the felloe end of spokes.

Fig.1

THE HOUSE COLD TIRE SETTER.
HAND POWER, STEEL CASTINGS.

No. 1—Will shrink 2 x ¾ inch tires and less, weight 750 pounds, ... each, $145.00

No. 2—Will shrink 3½ x ⅞ inch tires and less, weight 1300 pounds, ... each, 250.00

With this machine you are able to set tires without removing bolts from wheels and also control the amount of dish required. The tires are gripped by keys with toothed edges, preventing slipping, and the machine heads are forced together by the use of a heavy compound lever. Each machine furnished with three sets of grip keys, one each for buggy, hack and wagon tires. The clamp holding felloe firmly against the machine prevents kinking or bulking so that it is impossible to set tire imperfectly. A well made satisfactory machine.

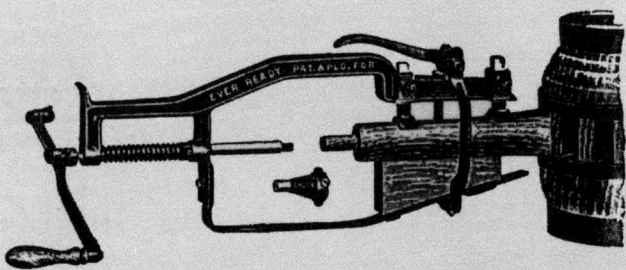

SPOKE AUGER MACHINE

EVER READY.

Fig.2

It is self-feeding, easy running, light and handy. Quickly adjusted to all size spokes up to 4 inches. Holds on firm and rigid, insuring accuracy. Cuts tenons either on line of spoke or with face of wheel. It actually makes the hardest work easy. No more crushing your wind out boring hard spokes. Arranged to use practically all makes of spoke augers. Chuck not required where brace shank in auger screws out. The prices of these machines do not include spoke augers.

HOWE, J.M. , Portland, OR

Inventor and maker of a wheel-wrights' machine, patented July 11, 1865. Shown in plan view at left, the machine was designed for boring fellies, sawing fellies to length, tenoning spokes on both ends, cutting spokes to length, and simultaneously planing fellies on three sides.

HUBER, JOS. H. , Lancaster, PA

Maker, in 1881, of HUBER'S Adjustable Axle Box reamer as shown below. The reamer was a simple adaptation of adjustable taper reamers long in use by machinists.

ILLINOIS IRON & BOLT CO., Carpentersville, IL

Formed ca. 1878 to make tools and equipment for blacksmiths, wagon makers, and carriage makers. Products offered in 1882 included No. 1 tire benders (Fig.1), No. 2 tire benders (Fig.2), MAGIC tire shrinkers (Fig.3),and the OLMSTEAD & DINSMORE tire shrinker and punch (Fig.4).

1893 offerings included updated versions of the OLMSTEAD & DINSMORE tire shrinker and punch (Fig.5), the MAGIC tire shrinker (Fig.6),and the No. 2 tire bender (Fig.7). A No. 3 tire bender (Fig.8) had been added to the line. Other 1893 products included hydraulic presses (Fig.9) for pressing boxes into hubs, and pressing on hub bands for farm and freight wagons; and carriage makers' vises (Fig.10).

In 1906, the firm offered improved STODDARD tire shrinkers (Fig.11) in five styles, and improved MOLE tire shrinkers (Fig.12) in four styles. Both the STODDARD and MOLE were older designs and were also manufactured by other makers.

Nearly all the above products were still available in 1918, most under the trade name VULCAN. New products offered in 1918 included the VULCAN tire and axle shrinker (Fig.13) for tires 4" wide and smaller and axles up to 1 1/4", and the I.I.&B. tire shrinker (Fig.14) for tires 4" wide and smaller. *(continued next two pages)*

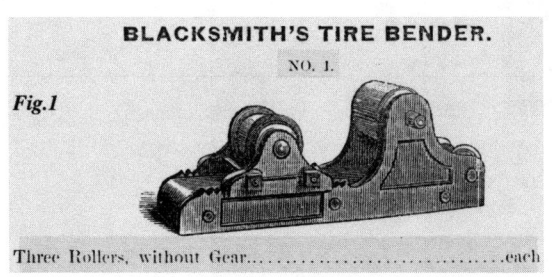

BLACKSMITH'S TIRE BENDER.
NO. 1.
Fig.1
Three Rollers, without Gear...............................each

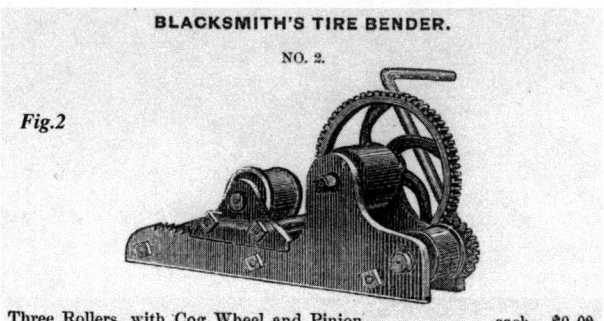

BLACKSMITH'S TIRE BENDER.
NO. 2.
Fig.2
Three Rollers, with Cog Wheel and Pinion................each $9 00

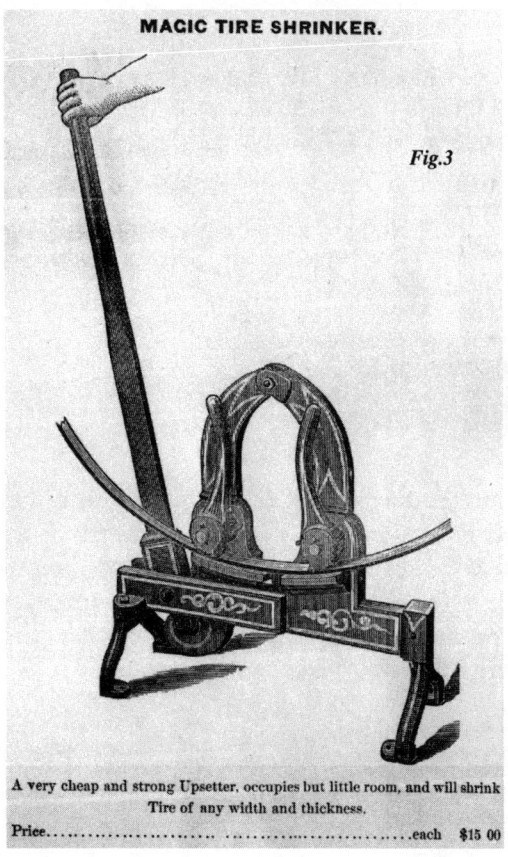

MAGIC TIRE SHRINKER.
Fig.3
A very cheap and strong Upsetter, occupies but little room, and will shrink Tire of any width and thickness.
Price...each $15 00

TIRE SHRINKER AND PUNCH.
OLMSTEAD & DINSMORE.
Fig.4

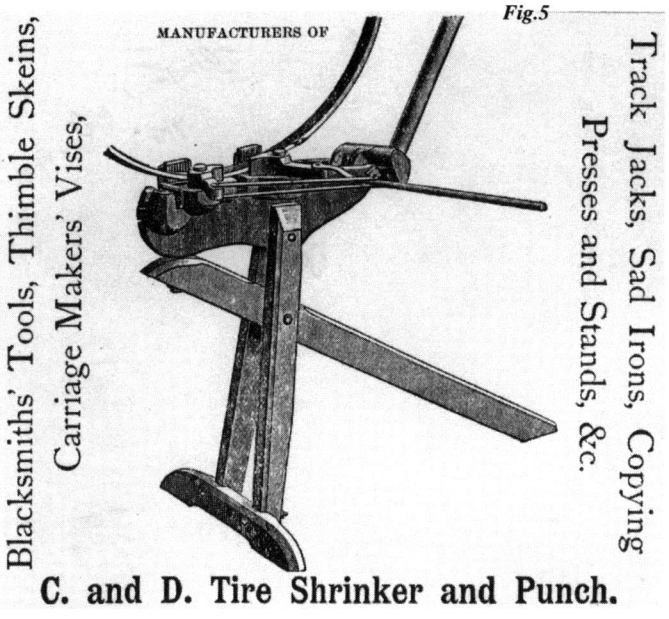

MANUFACTURERS OF

Fig.5

Blacksmiths' Tools, Thimble Skeins, Carriage Makers' Vises,

Track Jacks, Sad Irons, Copying Presses and Stands, &c.

C. and D. Tire Shrinker and Punch.

MANUFACTURERS OF

Fig.6

Blacksmiths' Tools, Thimble Skeins,

Track Jacks, Carriage Makers' Vises,

Magic Tire Shrinker,

SAD IRONS, COPYING PRESSES AND STANDS, &c.

MANUFACTURERS OF

Fig.7

Blacksmiths' Tools,

Thimble Skeins,

Tire Bender No. 2,

MANUFACTURERS OF THE

Fig.8

THIMBLE SKEINS.

BLACKSMITHS' TOOLS

TIRE BENDER, No. 3.

Fig.9

MANUFACTURERS OF

Hydraulic Presses

For pressing Boxes into Hubs, and for pressing on Hub Bands for Farm and Freight Wagons.

It will raise 6 inches. Weighs 490 pounds. Can be operated by Hand or Power. Write for particulars and prices

Press of 50-Ton Capacity.

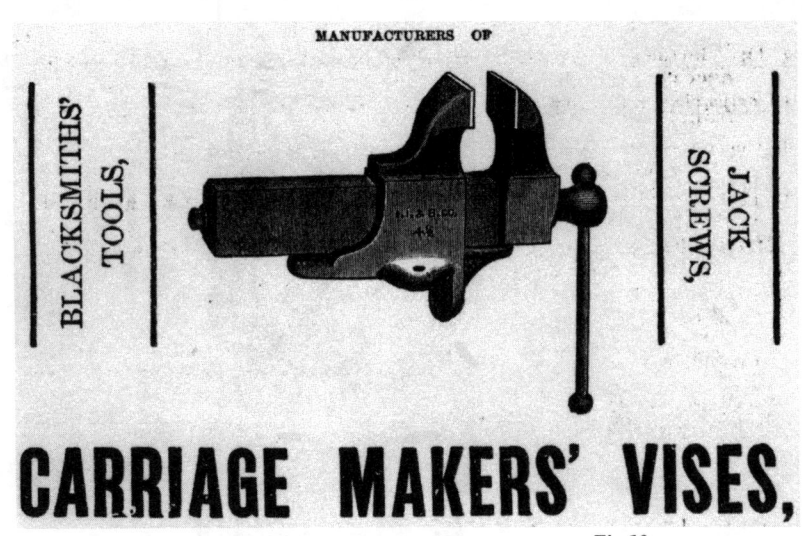

MANUFACTURERS OF

BLACKSMITHS' TOOLS, JACK SCREWS,

CARRIAGE MAKERS' VISES,

Fig.10

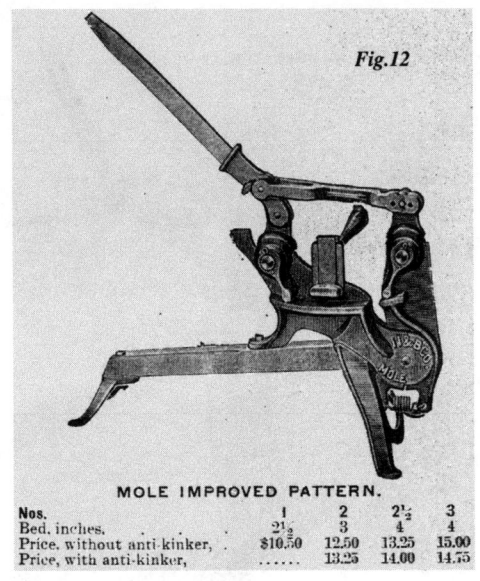

Fig.12

MOLE IMPROVED PATTERN.

Nos.	1	2	2½	3
Bed, inches,	2½	3	4	4
Price, without anti-kinker,	$10.50	12.50	13.25	15.00
Price, with anti-kinker,	......	13.25	14.00	14.75

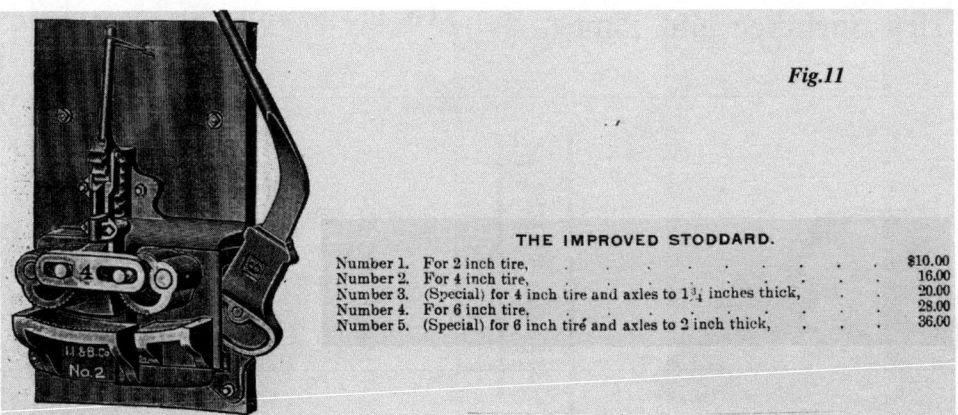

Fig.11

THE IMPROVED STODDARD.

Number 1.	For 2 inch tire,	$10.00
Number 2.	For 4 inch tire,	16.00
Number 3.	(Special) for 4 inch tire and axles to 1¾ inches thick,	20.00
Number 4.	For 6 inch tire,	28.00
Number 5.	(Special) for 6 inch tire and axles to 2 inch thick,	36.00

"Vulcan" Tire and Axle Shrinkers

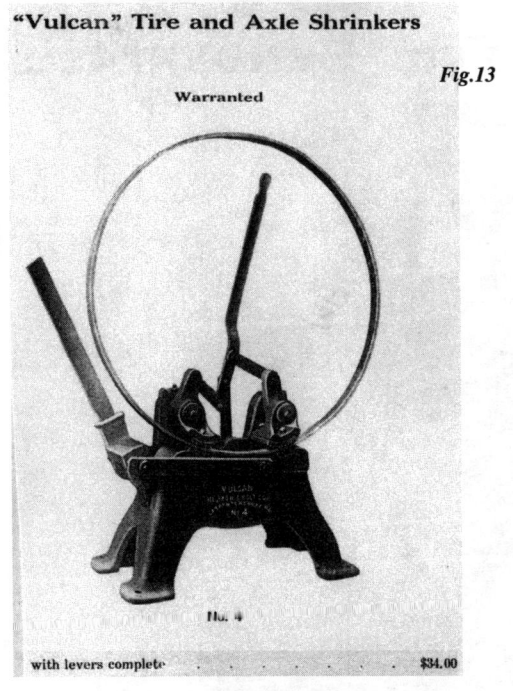

Fig.13

Warranted

No. 4

with levers complete $34.00

I. I. & B. Tire Shrinker

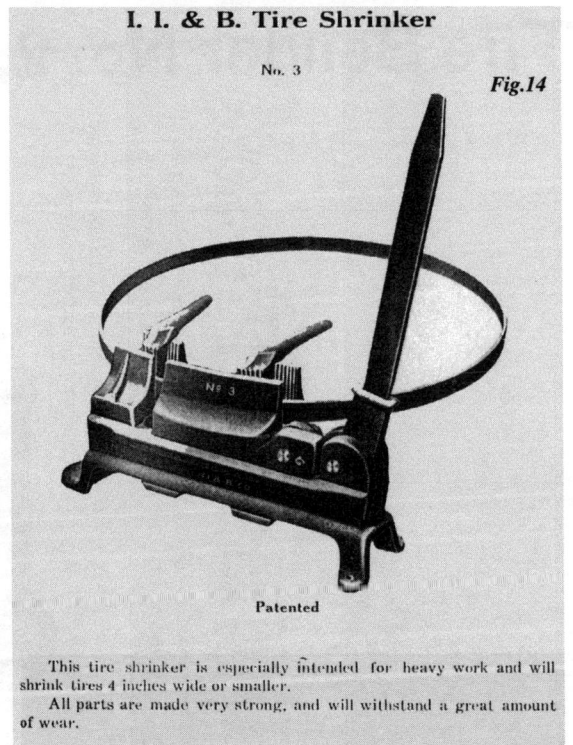

No. 3

Fig.14

Patented

This tire shrinker is especially intended for heavy work and will shrink tires 4 inches wide or smaller.

All parts are made very strong, and will withstand a great amount of wear.

Price, with lever as shown $15.00

IMPERIAL BIT & SNAP CO. , Racine, WI

Maker, in 1899, of the LIGHTNING tire setter and repair outfit shown right. In use, the turnbuckle jack assembly was put in the place of a broken spoke, and turned up until a new spoke could be sprung in place. It could also be used to reset a loose tire; or dished wheels could be straightened "all without taking the wheel from the axle or cutting the tire and welding it."

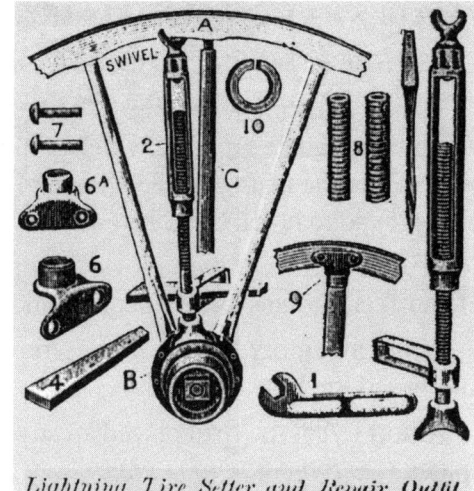

Lightning Tire Setter and Repair Outfit.

IVES & CO., W.A. , Hamden, CT

Formed in March, 1863, as a reorganization of the Hamden Auger Co. William A. Ives served as president until his death in 1888. The firm was absorbed by the Hamden Mfg. Co. on May 11, 1889. It manufactured a variety of wheelwrights' tools, including adjustable hollow augers patented October 13, 1868, (Fig.1), fixed hollow augers patented June 9, 1874, (Fig.2), and spoke pointers (Fig.3) offered in 1883.

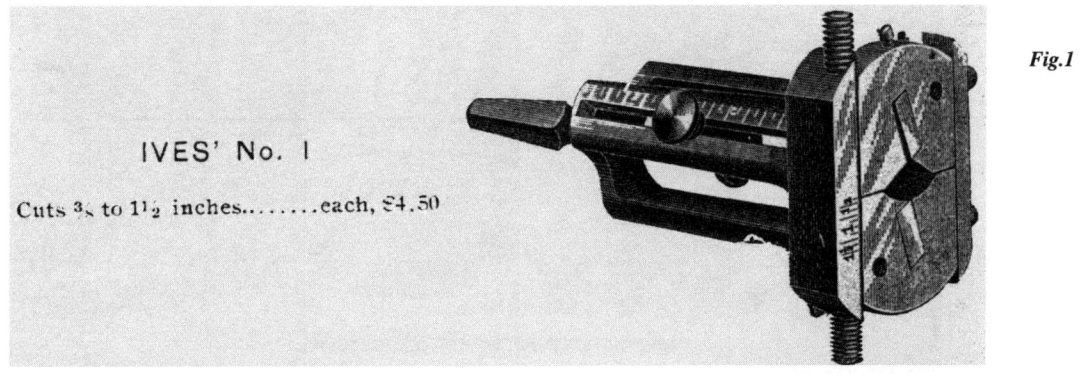

IVES' No. 1

Cuts ⅜ to 1½ inches........each, $4.50

Fig.1

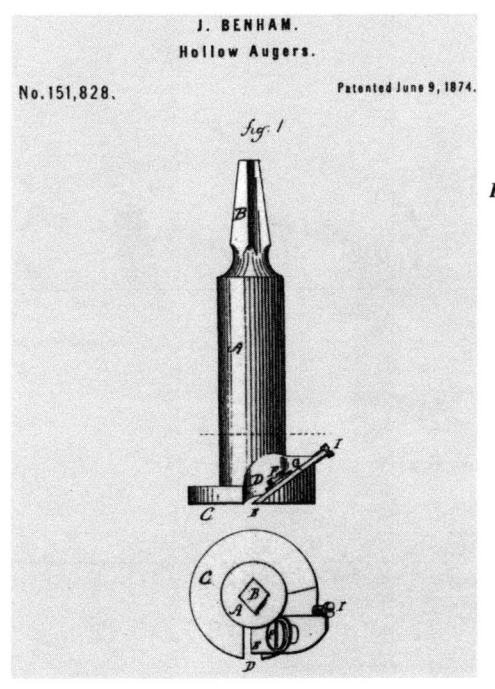

J. BENHAM.
Hollow Augers.

No.151,828.   Patented June 9, 1874.

fig. 1

Fig,2

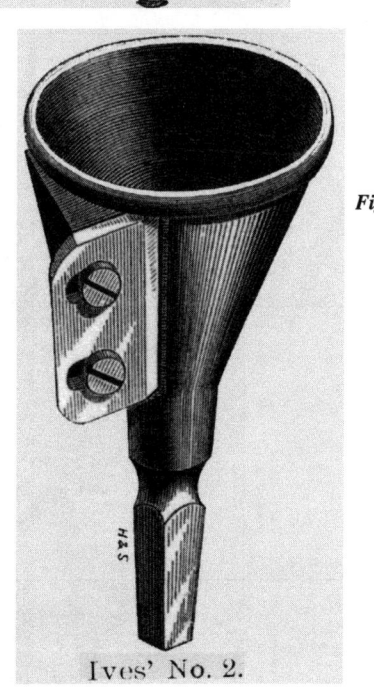

Fig.3

Ives' No. 2.

JACOB'S PATENT WHEEL DRESSING MACHINE CO., New York, NY

Formed in 1864 to make wheel manufacturing machines patented September 15, 1863, by H.S. Jacobs.

Three machines made up a "system of wheel manufacture." In the first (Fig.1) a hub, with spokes in place, was mounted on a mandrel which could be moved in and out; a circular saw cut the spokes to length and a hollow auger E cut the tenon. At the other end of the machine, fellies, already sawed, were squared at the ends and dowel pin and spoke holes were bored.

The fellies were then moved to a second machine (Fig.2) where the inner surface was dressed, "rounding it off perfectly to any desired curve, and forming an oval about the spoke holes."

After assembly, the wheel was moved to a third machine (Fig.3) which dressed the whole surface of the wheel and bored the hole for the box.

Short lived, the firm placed an advertisement in 1866, offering to sell all its machinery and rent out its factory space. *(continued on next page)*

JACOB'S SYSTEM OF WHEEL MANUFACTURE.

Fig.1

Fig.2

Fig.3

JENKINS, DAVID , Sheboygan, WI

Maker, in 1881, of hub machinery, including hub turning, hub mortising, and hub boring machines.

JENKINS & KNIGHT , Kingston, NY

A partnership of Benjamin F. Jenkins and Luke L. Knight formed in 1853 to make a spoke machine (Fig.1, *next page*), jointly patented January 4, 1853.

The machine was of the type in which both the workpiece and the cutters revolved. The workpiece was held between centers on a carriage F which could be fed into the rotating cutters B.

In 1854, the partners advertised "great improvements–the machine is now incontestably far superior to any other spoke machine ever invented." (Fig.2).

Fig.2

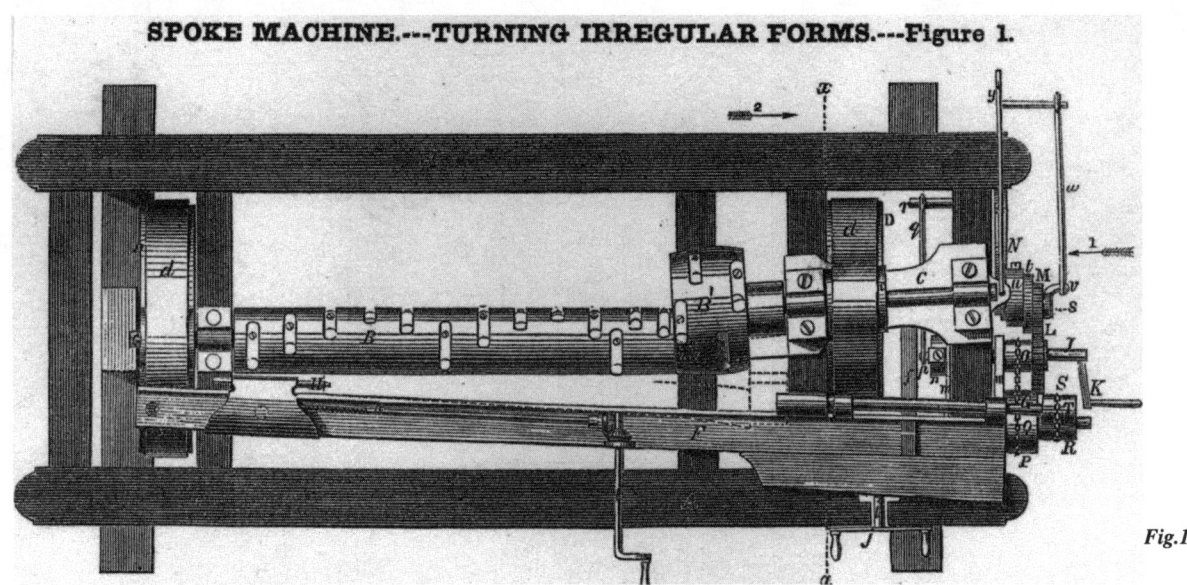

SPOKE MACHINE.---TURNING IRREGULAR FORMS.---Figure 1.

Fig.1

JOHNSON, W.H. , Racine, WI

Maker, beginning in 1885, of a combination shear, punch and forming machine as shown below. Designed for carriage and wagon makers, it would "form king bolts, reach pins, hub bands, hound circles, and stake-irons."

Johnson's Shear, Punch and Forming Machine.

JUSTICE, PHILIP S. , Philadelphia, PA

Formed in 1859 to make a variety of products, including muskets for the Union Army. In 1866, Justice began production of SHAW'S dead stroke power hammer (Fig.1), patented February 27, 1866, by Thomas Shaw. A larger size (Fig.2) was introduced in 1871. The two sizes covered a range of 15 pounds to 2000 pounds stroke force.

The power hammer line was sold to DIENELT & EISENHARDT in 1888; Justice continued business as a commission sales agent.

Fig.1

Fig.2

SHAW'S DEAD-STROKE POWER HAMMER.

THE SHAW & JUSTICE DEAD STROKE POWER HAMMER.

KANE & ROACH , Syracuse, NY

Formed in 1891 by William E. Kane (1866-1945) and his brother-in-law B.F. Roach to make wheelwright machinery. Early products included a hub boring machine patented by Kane November 15, 1892, wheel drills, spoke drivers, band saws, joiners, planers and drill presses.

By 1910, radial drills and metal forming machinery had become the main product lines; production of wheelwright machinery probably ceased at about that time.

KELLEY HARDWARE CO. , Duluth, MN

Maker, in 1917, of the KELLEY, JR. hollow auger shown at right..

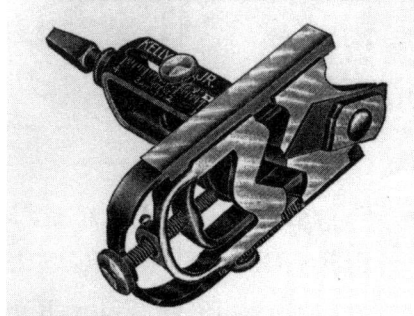

THE KELLY JR. HOLLOW AUGER

The Kelly Jr. Hollow Auger possessing as it does many improvements and advantages over all other hollow augers, is sold at a very reasonable price.

Capacity of Auger—It cuts all size tenons from ¼ inch to 1½ inches in diameter by 4 inches long, which is ¼ inch larger in diameter than is cut by any other ordinary auger.

KEMP & BURPEE MFG. CO. , Syracuse, NY

Founded about 1877 to make manure spreaders invented by J.S. Kemp. By 1885, the firm was also making wheel machinery for its own use and for sale to others. Production included a combination spoke driving and tenoning machine, patented June 9, 1885, by Harry Watkins. Although the combination of spoke driving and tenoning was uncommon, the driving of the spoke just before tenoning, as shown below, would have advantages.

The firm employed 75 hands in 1902 and was active at least as late as 1910.

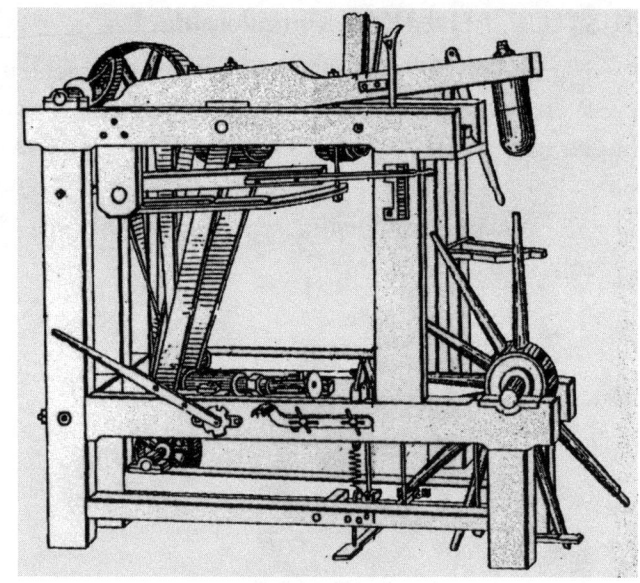

KENDALL, J.B. , Washington, DC

Maker, in 1886, of the NOVELTY axle setter and axle straightener as shown left. By 1889, the tool was a product of the WELLS BROTHERS CO.

KENT, S.W. , Meriden, CT

Maker, in 1888, of the BOWE spoke extractor shown right. Using a heavy screw and T handle for leverage, it would pull any spoke from 3/4" to 3 1/2." By 1893 the device was a product of BUTTS & ORDWAY.

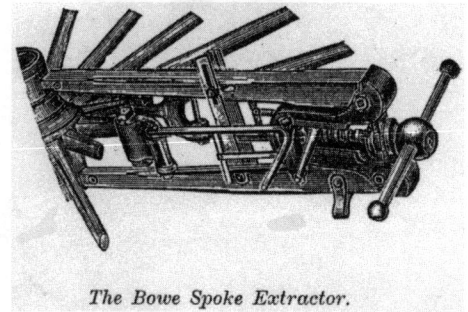

The Bowe Spoke Extractor.

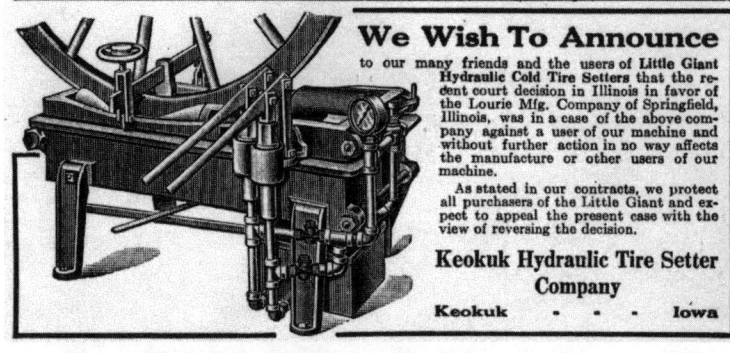

KEOKUK HYDRAULIC TIRE SETTER CO. Keokuk, IA

Maker, in 1914, of the LITTLE GIANT hydraulic cold tire setter. Power was applied by hand pumps as shown at left.

KETTENRING & STRONG, Defiance, OH, later
KETTENRING, STRONG & LAUSTER , Defiance, OH

A partnership of Peter Kettenring and the Strong brothers, formed in 1864 to operate a foundry. By 1868, the firm advertised a line of hub machinery. *(continued next page)*

HUB MACHINERY.—Address
KETTENRING & STRONG, Defiance, Ohio.
16*

In 1869, the firm reorganized as Kettenring, Strong & Lauster when William Lauster (1820-?) became a partner. In 1872 a stock company was formed under the name DEFIANCE MACHINE WORKS.

KIMBALL, GEORGE F. , New Haven, CT

A large maker of carriage wheels, the firm also made a line of wheel making machinery as shown in the 1866 ad below. Offerings included spoke shaving machines, spoke facing and tapering machines, cylinder planers for finishing sides of wheels, felloe rounding machines patented July 17, 1860, by F.W. Mallett, machines for riveting and screwing felloes, boring and doweling machines for felloes, spoke tenoning machines, and spoke polishing machines.

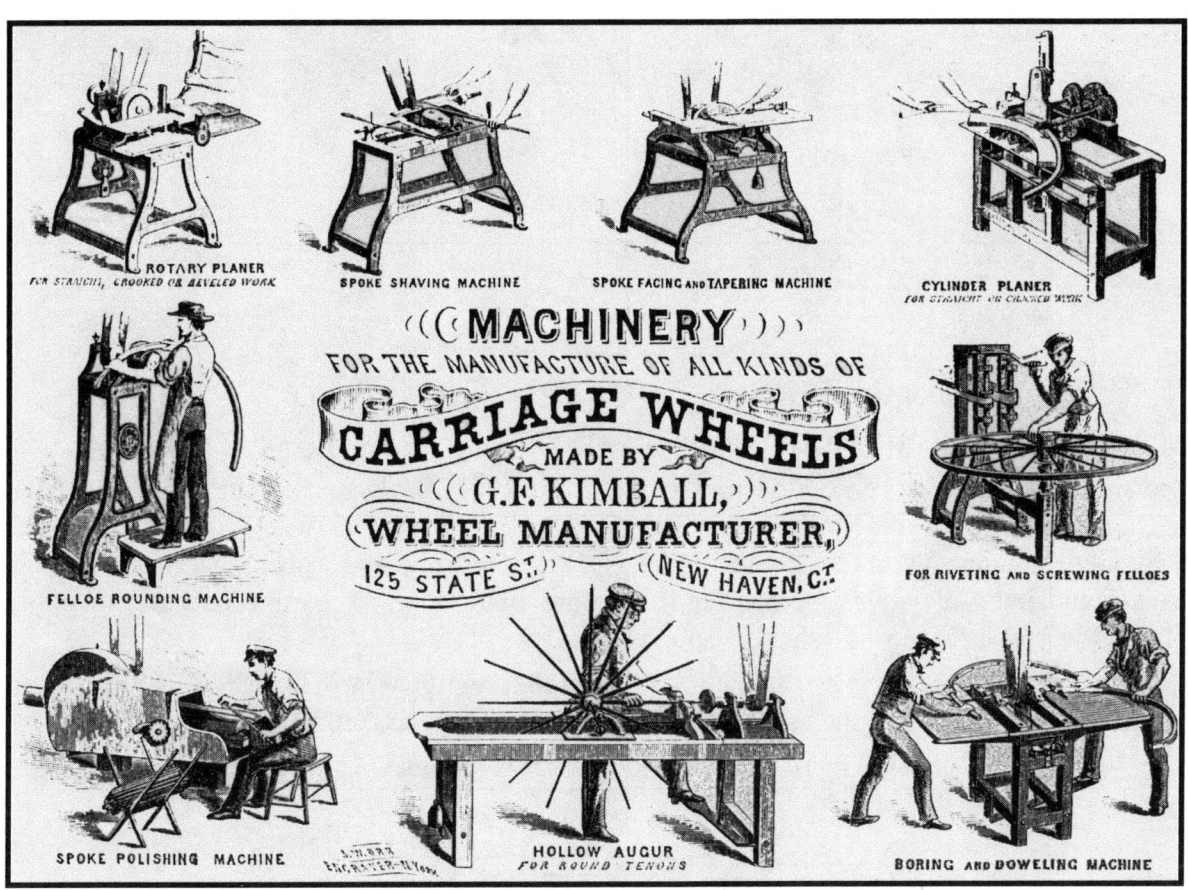

KIMBARK, S.D. , Chicago, IL

Maker, in 1894, of the IDEAL MOLE tire shrinker (Fig.1), one of several MOLE designs made by various makers. Kimbark claimed that "it has been adapted particularly for truck tires, and will shrink a tire with a 2 foot-10 inch circle, or larger while one man can operate it." As shown below, it was offered in four sizes from 2 1/2" to 4". The 4" size weighed 350 pounds.

In 1898, Kimbark introduced Smith's Giant Tire Puller (Fig.2), patented March 23, 1897, by Henry N. Smith. Made in two sizes, it was a simple, and therefore probably very effective, device. *(illustrations on next page)*

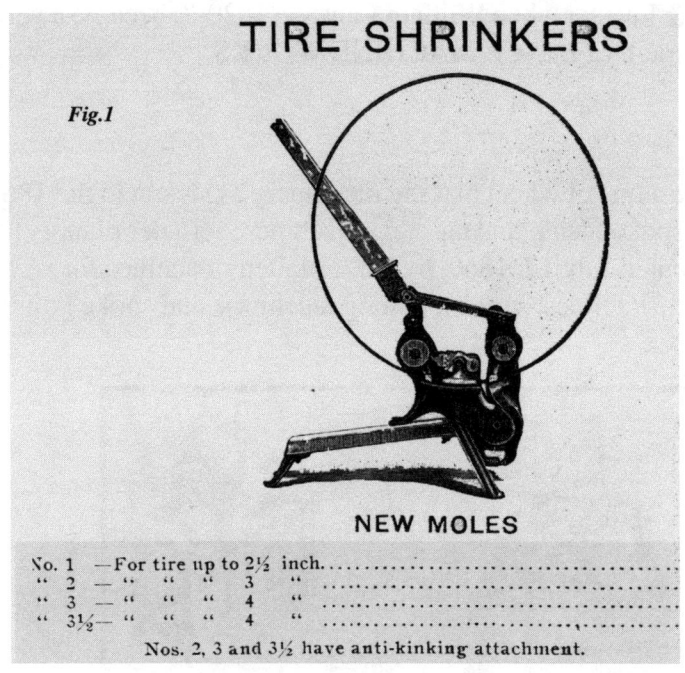

TIRE SHRINKERS

Fig.1

NEW MOLES

No. 1 —For tire up to 2½ inch...
" 2 — " " " 3 " ....
" 3 — " " " 4 " ....
" 3½— " " " 4 " ....

Nos. 2, 3 and 3½ have anti-kinking attachment.

Fig.2

SMITH'S
GIANT TIRE PULLER.

Is a simple, powerful, effective machine for removing tires from wheels without cutting the tire, splitting or defacing the rim.

It is indispensable to the Smith, as it saves time, which is money; saves the rim, which costs money, and satisfies the customer, who pays the money.

Sizes in stock.	Net price each.
No. 1	$6.50
" 2	7.75

KLOTZ & KROMER , Sandusky, OH, later
KLOTZ & KROMER MACHINE CO. , Sandusky, OH

A partnership of August Klotz and Otto Kromer, founded in 1861. The business incorporated in 1870 and was reorganized as the Klotz & Kromer Machine Co. in 1877. Fifty to seventy hands were employed in 1887, producing steam engines, circular saw-mills, axe handle and spoke lathes, hub and wheel machinery, wine and cider presses, steam and hand elevators, pumps, and the Hero binders and self-rake reaper and power corn-shellers. Total 1887 production was valued at $60,000.

The spoke lathe shown below was patented May 22, 1883, and February 23, 1886, by Otto Kromer. The Kromer design was noteworthy by the use a lead screw for traversing the cutting wheel carriage.

The firm went into receivership in 1900 and was eventually reorganized as the Klotz Machine Co.

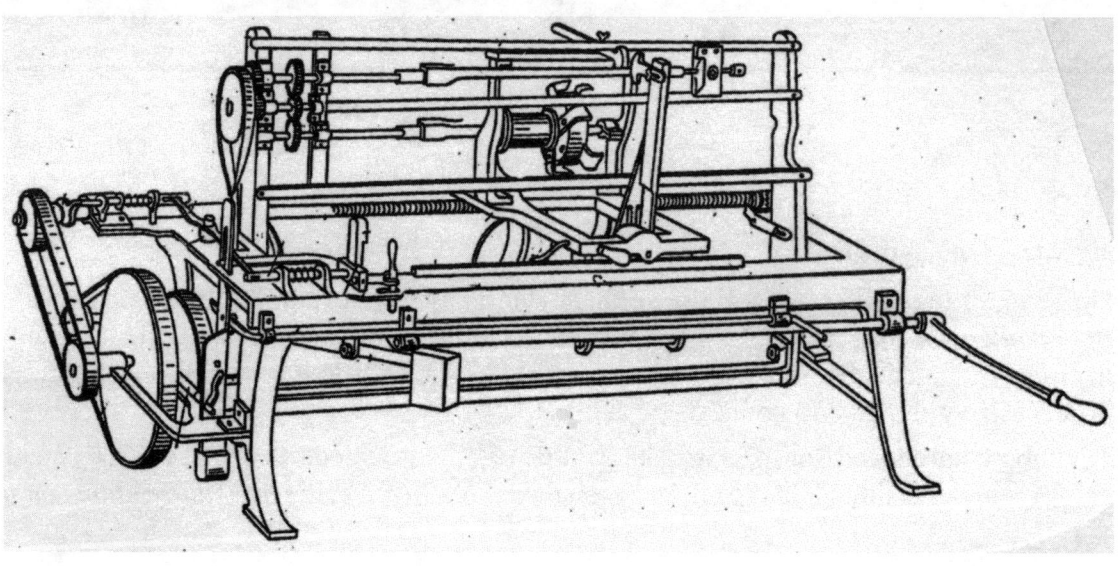

KNAPP & COWLES MFG. CO. , Bridgeport, CT

Reorganized in 1892 with L.S. Catlin, president and George S. Knapp, secretary and treasurer. The firm made a variety of "specialties in hardware and house furnishing goods."

In 1893, it offered the CALIFORNIA tire bender and the CALIFORNIA tire upsetter. The tire bender, although hand operated, was designed for large work up to a 5"x 1" tire. The tire upsetter was also designed for heavy work.

THE CALIFORNIA TIRE BENDER.

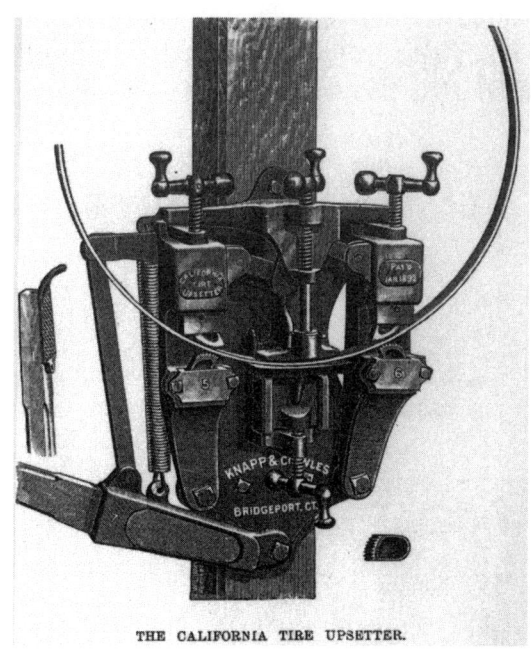

THE CALIFORNIA TIRE UPSETTER.

KNOWLTON MFG. CO. , Rockford, IL

Maker, beginning in 1884, of the BROWN slow raising, quick striking hammer. The machine was designed to move twice as fast on the down (striking) stroke as on the up stroke. This feature was claimed to give 50% more striking force than any other hammer made.

Fig.1

KRITCH & CRANE MFG. CO. , Cleveland, OH

Maker, beginning in 1865, of a hub boring machine or box setter, patented February 23, 1864, by Jacob Kritch. An improved version (Fig.1), patented October 25, 1865, is shown as offered in 1873. Kritch patented additional improvements on March 19, 1878. *(continued on next page)*

Designed to bore straight or tapered holes of any size and angle, it also cut the recesses in the end of the hub for the collar and nut. Although operated by hand power, the maker claimed "any ordinarily smart mechanic can with ease bore from eight to ten sets (32 to 40 wheels) in ten hours."

In 1875, the firm began offering a machine for upsetting and thereby forming collars on iron axles (Fig.2), patented by Kritch on December 7, 1875.

Two styles of machines for turning the arms or spindles of axles were introduced in 1880. Both types used a rapidly rotating form cutter working into a slowly rotating workpiece. The first type, patented December 14, 1880, by Jacob Kritch (Fig.3) was based on milling machine technology; the second type, patented December 28, 1880, by F.D. Bliss (Fig.4) was based on lathe technology.

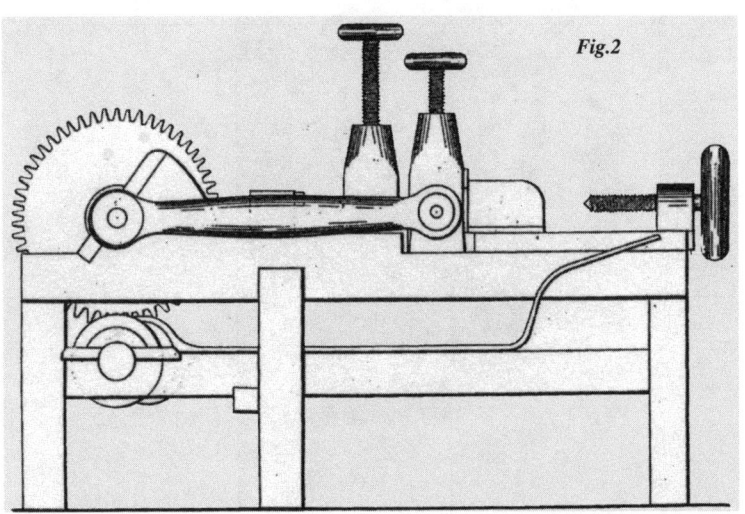

Fig.2

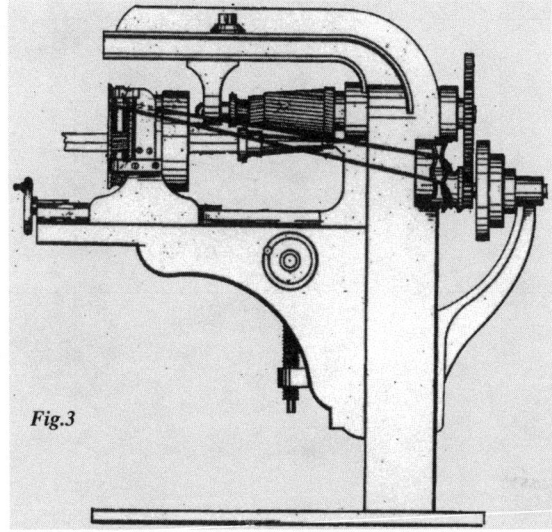

Fig.3

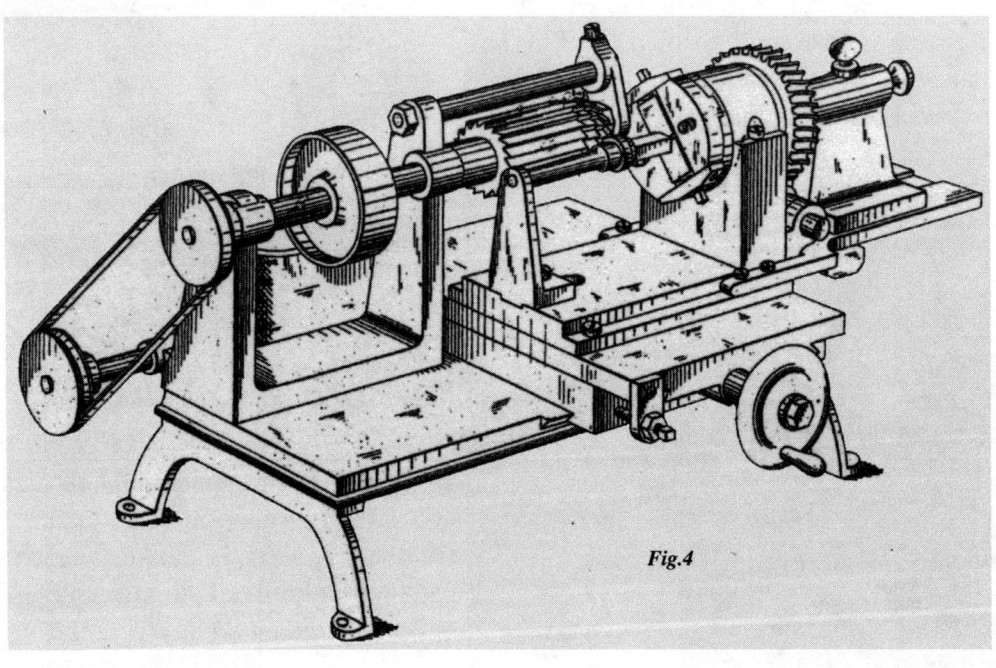

Fig.4

LAIRD & SWEENEY MFG. CO. , St. Johnsbury, VT

Maker, in 1893, of a power hammer patented June 14, 1892. The hammer was counterbalanced and made for quick adjustment.

Fig. 1.—Front Elevation.   Fig. 2.—Rear View.

THE LAIRD & SWEENEY POWER HAMMER

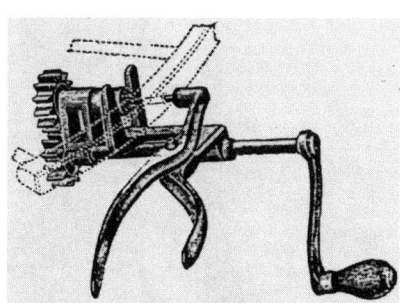

LANDAHL, GUSTAVES , New Carlisle, IL

Inventor and maker of a tire bolt wrench, patented October 26, 1909.

LANE & BODLEY CO. , Cincinnati, OH

A partnership of Philander P. Lane (1821-1900) and Joseph T. Bodley (?-1868) formed in 1852 as a machinery repair business. The firm incorporated in 1876 with a capital of $500,000.

By 1858, the firm advertised as "Manufacturers of wood- working machinery and circular saw mills. Especial attention given to hub, spoke, felloe, and wheel machinery." Among those was the Morris patent wood bender, patented March 11, 1856, and a wheelwrights' machine (Fig.1), patented March 8, 1859, by George W. Miles and P.P. Lane. The machine was designed to shape hubs with a powered axe and a simple rotating mechanism for the hub block. *(continued next page)*

In 1870, it offered a graduated stroke power mortising machine (Fig.2) "adapted to the manufacture of rail cars, furniture, sash and blinds, wagon hubs, etc.." The machine was patented November 14, 1871, by Edward Myers and Samuel R. Smith.

A spoke lathe, of an improved Blanchard type and patented April 4, 1882, by E. Myers, (Fig.3) was offered in 1882.

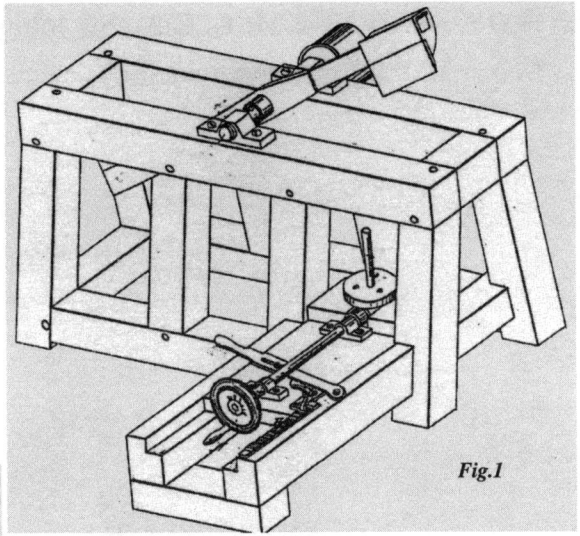

Fig.1

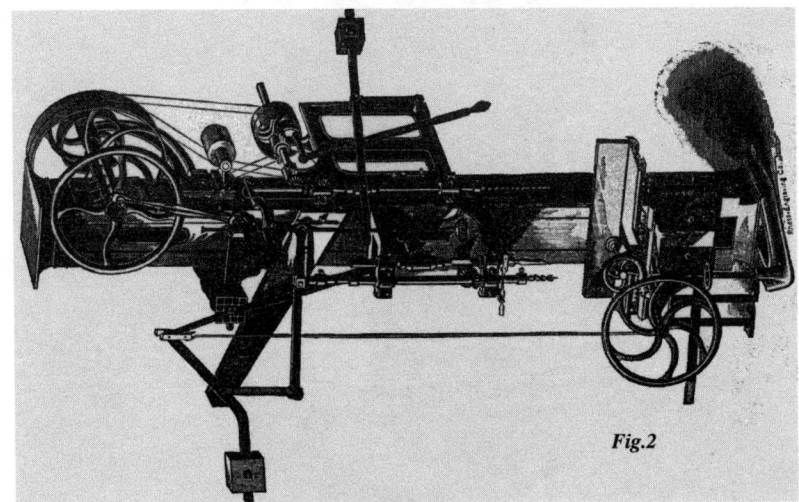

Fig.2

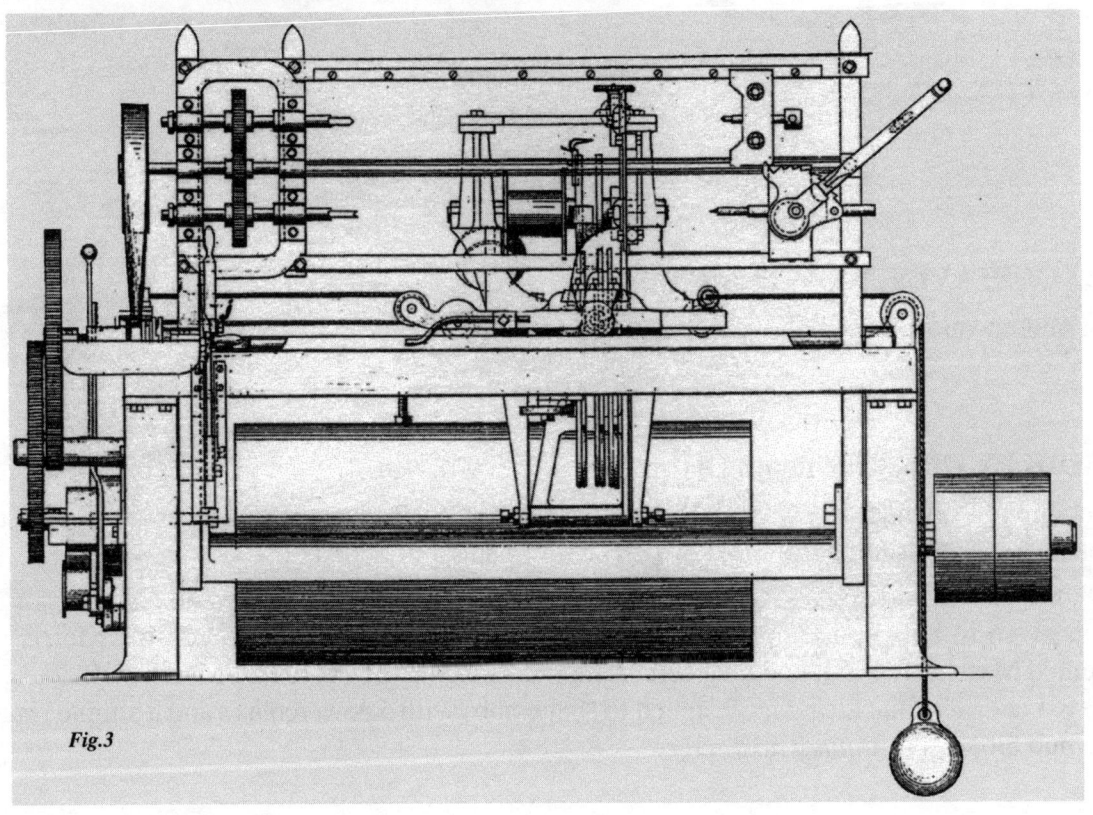

Fig.3

LEFEBER, JAMES , Cambridge City, IN

Inventor and maker, in 1867, of a spoke tenoning machine, patented September 4, and October 2, 1866.

In operation, the hub and spoke assembly was mounted on a vertical arbor which could be rotated and fed forward by a foot treadle; the spokes brought in turn to a hand driven circular saw mounted on arbor E where they were each cut to the same length; and each spoke then tenoned by a hollow auger, Fig. 2 and 3, mounted on a lower arbor and driven by the same hand crank.

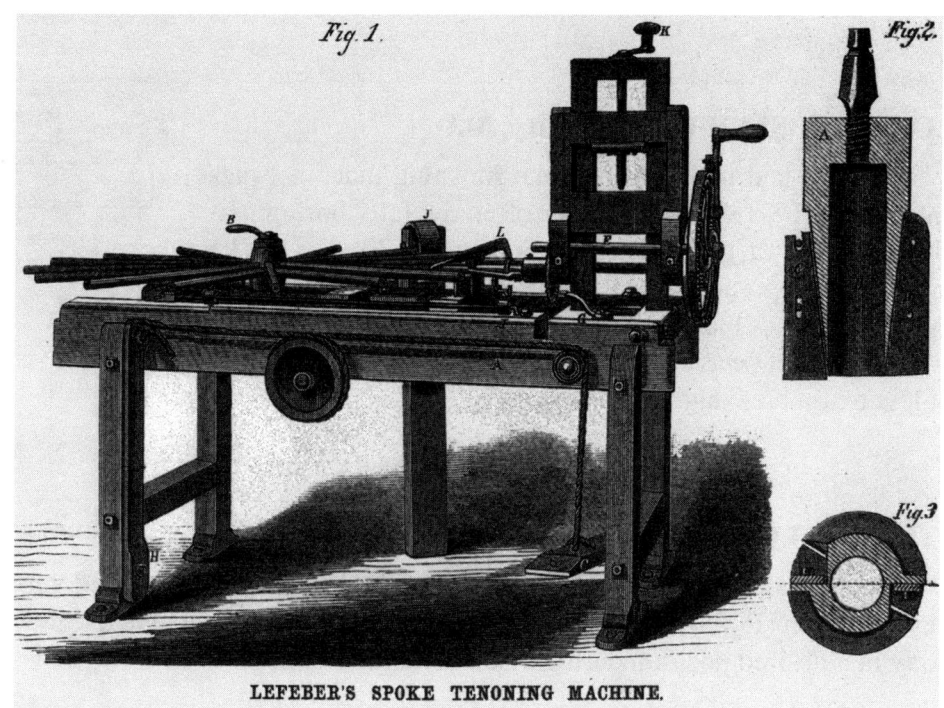

LEFEBER'S SPOKE TENONING MACHINE.

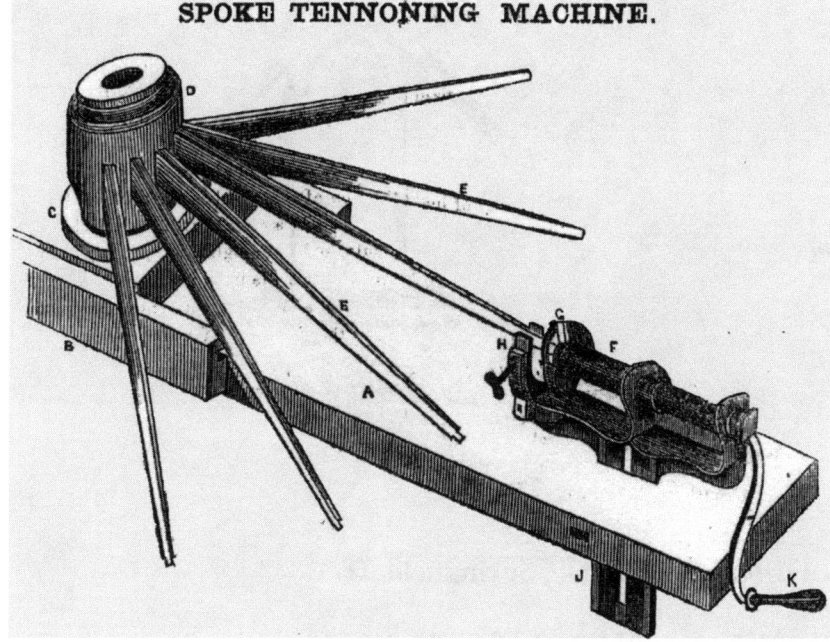

SPOKE TENNONING MACHINE.

LeROY, WELLS & CO. , Sauquoit, NY

Maker, in 1850 of a spoke tenoning machine invented by Edwin A. Palmer. In use, the hub and spoke assembly was mounted as shown at left; each spoke clamped in turn in front of a hand operated hollow auger that was rotated and fed forward to cut the tenon.

LEWIS & CO., WILLIAM B. , Naugatuck, CT

Maker, in 1869, of Ward's patent spoke machines. One of the most popular spoke machines of the period, the WARD spoke lathe, also know as the NAUGATUCK spoke lathe had been designed by Richard Ward of Naugatuck, CT, who received patents February 22, 1853, and June 28, 1853.

The Ward spoke lathe had also been made by PLAMER & CO. beginning about 1859. An improved version was made by PIERCE & CURTIS, based on its patent of August 15, 1871.

LOCKE, JOSEPH R. , Amesbury, MA

Inventor and maker of a spoke finishing machine, patented April 17, 1877. Locke later offered a felly boring machine, shown at right, patented September 20, 1881. The machine incorporated a foot operated vise which compressed the felly stock as the spoke holes were bored. This resulted in an oval hole that was considered a desirable feature, resulting in less tenon breakage as the wheel was used.

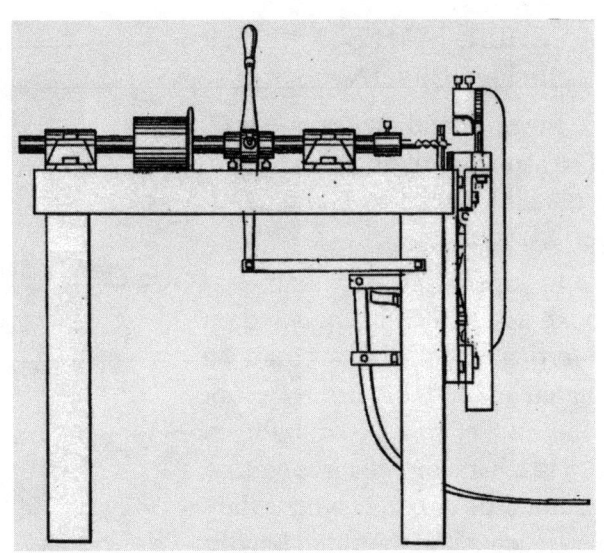

LONG, WILLIAM H. , Miamisburg, OH

Inventor and maker of a Carriage Body Maker's Trestle, patented September 8, 1891. The device, shown below in plan (Fig.1) and elevation (Fig.2), could be both rotated and tilted, and was designed to hold a carriage body in a desired position during assembly and finishing.

Fig.1

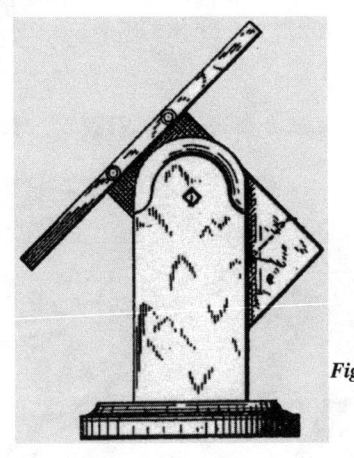

Fig.2

LOURIE MFG. CO. , Springfield, IL

Maker, in 1916, of the SCIENTIFIC hydraulic tire setter, screw arbor presses and hydraulic arbor presses as shown in the ad at left.

LOVE MFG. CO. , Rockford, IL

Formed in 1890 with a capital of $10,000; 35 hands were employed by 1891. Maker, in 1895, of the ROCKFORD tire shrinker. Bringing down the operating lever caused the tire to be gripped by tow clamps; then the portion of the tire between the clamps was forced together. Note the arrow and index which shows the amount of shrinkage done.

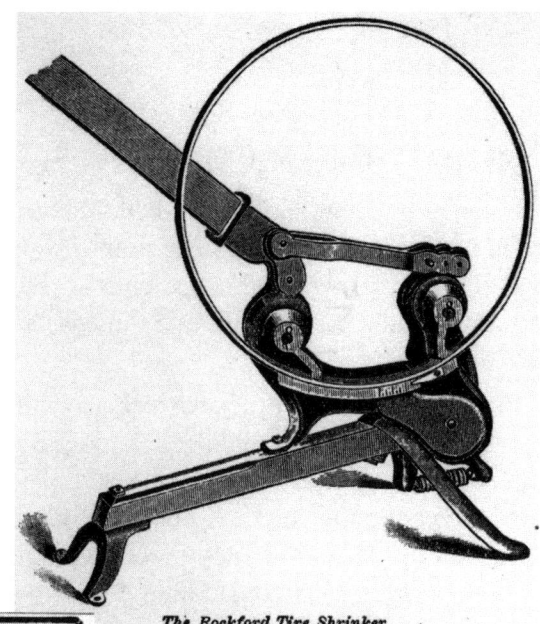

The Rockford Tire Shrinker.

LUTHER MFG. CO. , Olean, NY

Maker, in 1916, of the 1894 combination upset, punch and shear as shown in the ad at left.

MACGOWAN & FINIGAN CORDAGE CO., St. Louis, MO

Maker, in 1916, of the PERFECT power hammer. As shown at right, it was offered in two sizes; 40 pound ram and 80 pound ram.

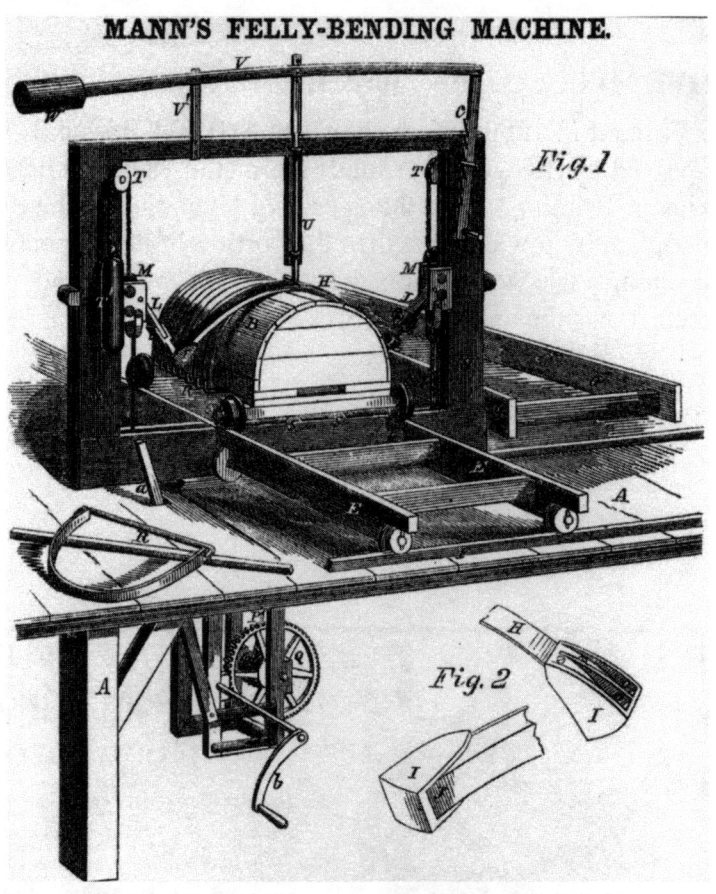

MANN, J.L. , Blandford, MA

Inventor and maker of a felly-bending machine, patented August 31, 1856. As he pointed out, "the bent felly has many advantages, chiefly owing to the grain of wood being continuous and passing in a circle around the wheel."

In use, the fellies were bent over a form B by a windlass pulling down linkages L connected to sockets I holding the felly on each end. The bent fellies were fixed in the bent position by a grip R that stayed in place. The felly pieces were heated, steamed, or both, prior to bending.

MARION MACHINE & TOOL CO. , Marion, IN

Maker, in 1901, of the REYNOLDS tire bolting machine, patented November 8, 1898, by Vestal Reynolds. The machine, shown below, was advertised as a combination bolt-clipper, bolt wrench and tire bolt holder.

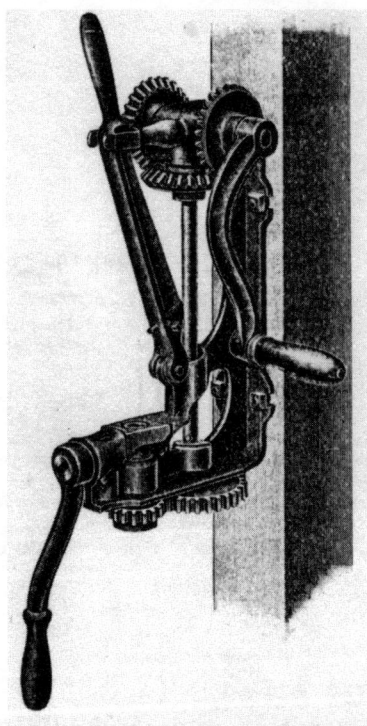

Fig. 1.—The Reynolds Tire Bolting Machine.

Fig. 2. - The Reynolds Machine with Wheel in Position.

MASON PATENT WHEEL CO. , Crown Point, NY

A partnership of Sylvester G. Mason and Charles D. Bogue, the firm was primarily a wheel maker; but also made a spoke-saw and tenoning machine (Fig.1), patented June 3, 1879, by Mason. The unique feature was a combination saw blade and hollow auger (Fig.2) which cut the spoke to length and the tenon to size in one operation. A rim (felloe) boring attachment was furnished with the machine.

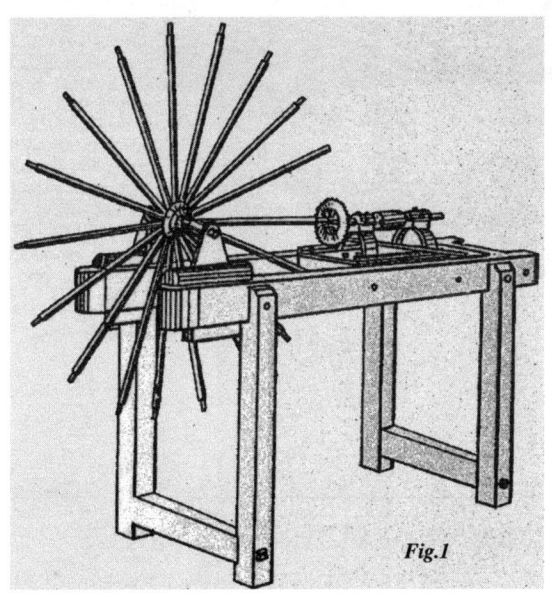

Fig.1

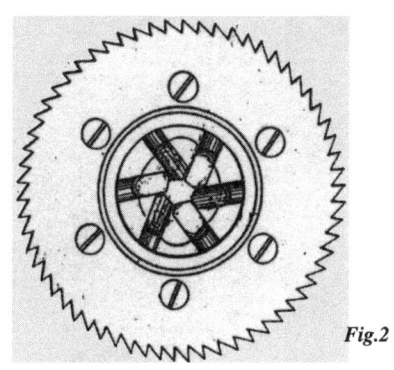

Fig.2

MASSEY, T.C. , Batavia, IL, later

MASSEY VISE CO. , Chicago, IL

Formed in 1884 to make a quick-acting vise invented by Thomas C. Massey. Massey moved to Chicago, IL in 1884, and reorganized as the Massey Vise Co. ca. 1892. The firm appears to have been absorbed by the Morgan Vise Co. prior to 1940.

Products included quick-acting coachmakers' vises (Fig.1) offered in 1884 and a CLINCHER pattern coachmakers' vise introduced in 1908 (Fig.2).

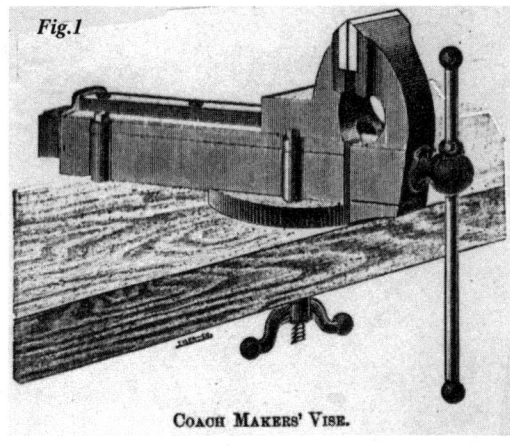

Fig.1

COACH MAKERS' VISE.

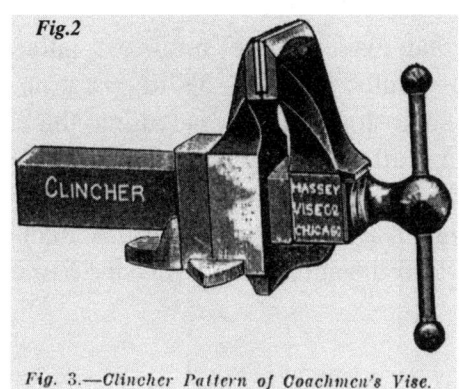

Fig.2

Fig. 3.—Clincher Pattern of Coachmen's Vise.

MATERN, WM. J. , Bloomington, IL

Maker of Matern's ready hub-boxing gauge, patented October 20, 1885. Note that a series of rings of different diameters were inserted into the tapered hole where the proper sizes automatically formed a bushing on which an arm could be rotated. An adjustable pointer at the outer end of the arm would show any out-of-squareness condition between the bore and edge of the wheel.

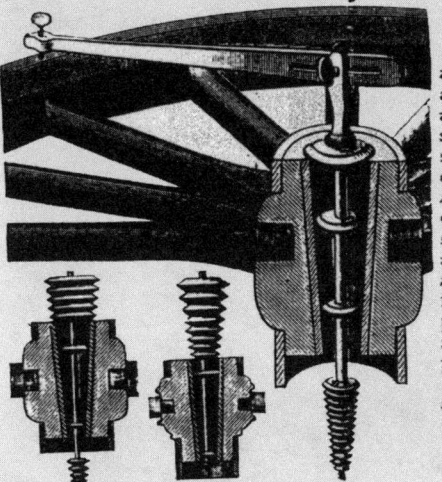

Wm. J. Matern's Ready Hub-Boxing Gauge

Pat. Oct. 20th, 1885.

This gauge of graduated rings is perfectly accurate; works quickly and equally well in large, small or worn boxes. It saves time and trouble, cannot get out of order, and gauges a wheel at once. Two sizes are furnished: one for wooden axles from 2 to 4¾ in., and one for iron axles from ¾ to 2 in. The price is $2.75 for either size, or $5.00 for the pair (two sizes). Descriptive circulars on application. Address

WM. J. MATERN,
306 & 308 W. Front-st.,
Bloomington, Ill.

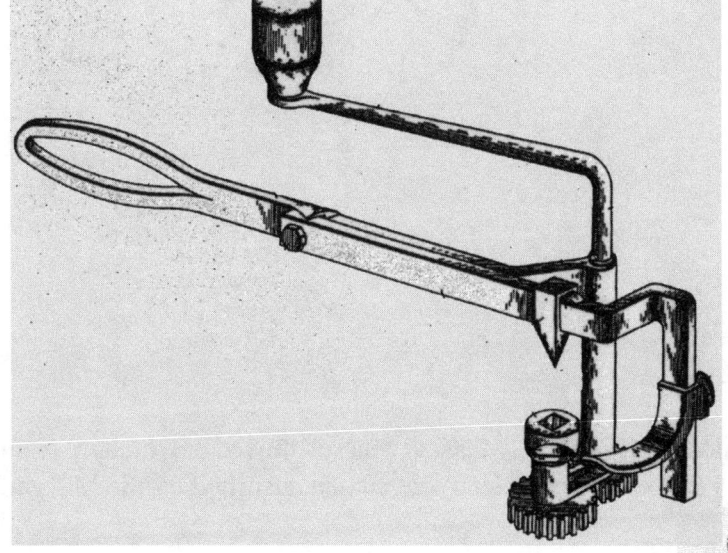

McCOY, WALTER , Conway, KS

Inventor and maker of a combined clamp and wrench for tire bolts, patented September 10, 1895.

McNARY, JOHN , Brooklyn, NY

Inventor and maker of an automatic lathe for turning hubs, patented May 4, 1858. In operation, the workpiece rotated slowly as it was fed into the more rapidly rotating cutter assembly by a handwheel. The machine could be set for any desired hub diameter and was designed to stop feed when that diameter was reached (thus the automatic part of the name).

McNARY'S AUTOMATIC LATHE.

Fig. 1

MERRILL, CHARLES A. , Battle Creek, MI

Inventor and maker of a spoke driving machine (right), patented February 3, 1880. The machine was essentially a trip hammer with a fixture for holding the hub in position as the spoke was driven in.

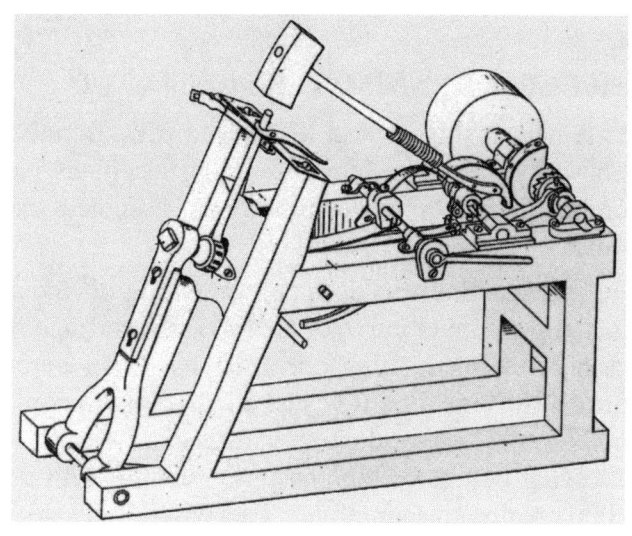

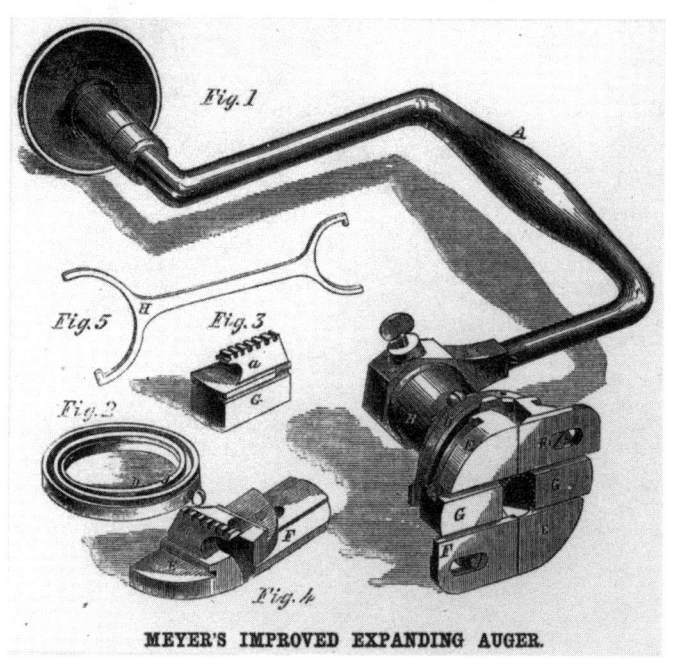

MEYER'S IMPROVED EXPANDING AUGER.

MEYER, C.J.L. , Newark, NJ

Inventor and maker of a spoke tenoning hollow auger (left), patented March 29, 1859. Designed to cut tenons from 1/2" to 1", it was the first to allow quick adjustment, via a rotating ring, so the wheelwright could adjust for size as he was making the spokes.

The tool was sold through Wright's Machinery Depot, Newark, NJ.

MILBURN WAGON WORKS , Toledo, OH

Formed in 1873 by Charles F. Milburn who served as president. In 1893, the firm began making axle lathes, patented May 17, 1892, and March 7, 1893, by Charles F. Milburn and George E. Byrkit, superintendent of the company. The lathe, shown below, was a Blanchard type but was equipped with two cutting heads to allow simultaneous machining on both ends of the axle and on the two cut-outs, one on each side of center.

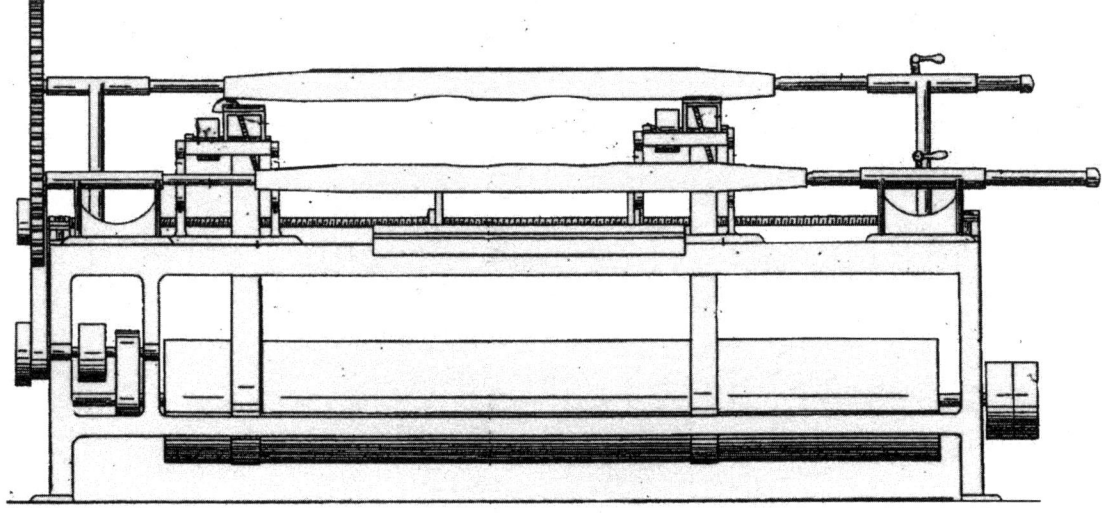

MILLER & DENNISON , Brattleboro, VT

A partnership of Asa Miller and C.H. Dennison, formed about 1859 to make felloe rounding machines patented December 6, 1859, by Dennison who assigned the patent to Miller.

The machine was designed for taking off the corners and finishing the inner curve of the felloes of carriage wheels. The partners claimed; "this operation has been heretofore performed by hand, and it has taken three-quarters of an hour to round the felloes for the four wheels of a carriage; but with the revolving cutters of this machine, running with a velocity of 4,000 revolutions per minute, a set of felloes can be rounded in four minutes."

The felloes were rounded after they were bent and bored for the spokes. There were two sets of cutters, one for the inside edge and the other for the outside.

DENNISON'S IMPROVED TOOL FOR ROUNDING FELLOES.

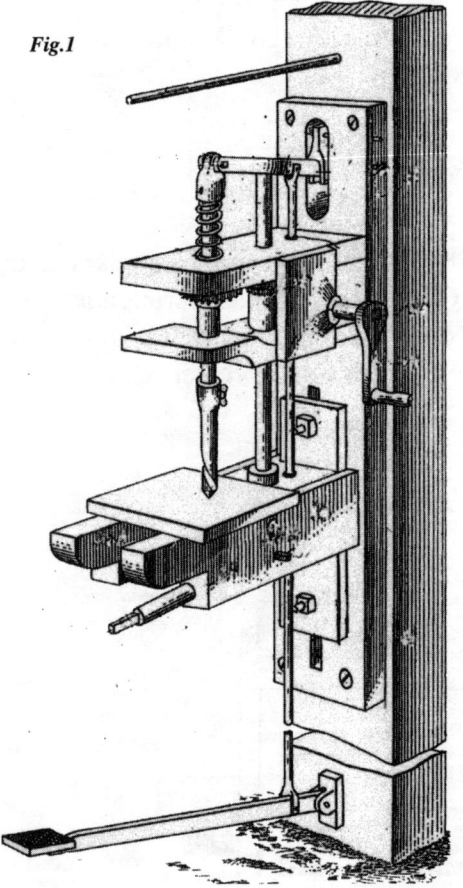

Fig.1

MILLER, GEORGE L. , Socialville, OH

Inventor and maker of a combination tire bolting, boring and drilling machine, patented December 19, 1905. The basic machine (Fig.1) was designed for hand drilling; the addition of a wheel holding device (Fig.2) and the replacement of the drill with a socket wrench converted it to a tire bolting machine.

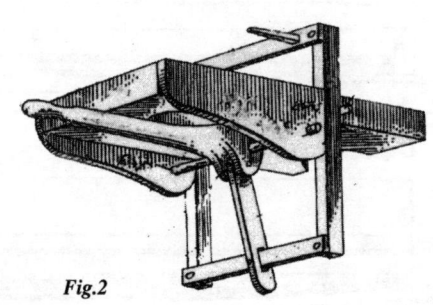

Fig.2

MILLER, HENRY J. , Goshen, NY

Inventor and maker of a spoke tenoning and felly boring machine, patented June 5, 1883. Shown below with the felly boring attachment mounted, it converted to a spoke tenoning machine by removing the felly holding table and mounting the hub and spokes on the center shown at the right end of the machine.

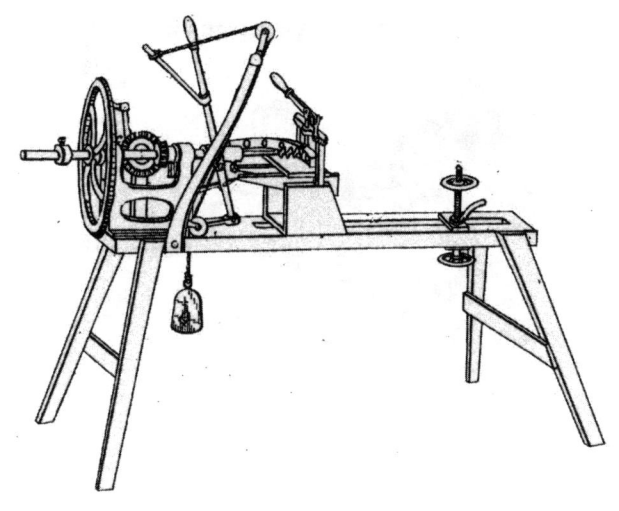

MILLER WRENCH CO. , Ft. Wayne, IN

Maker, in 1909, and as late as 1915, of LANG'S tire bolt wrench (left), patented June 12, 1888, by John S. Lang. The wrench was fitted with a turret containing sockets for 1/8", 3/16" and 1/4" bolts.

MILLERS FALLS CO. , Millers Falls, MA

Formed in 1872 by the merger of the Millers Falls Mfg. Co. and the Backus Vise Co. The George Rogers Co., maker of miter boxes, was also absorbed about the same time. George Rogers joined the Millers Falls Co. and was later vice president and general manager. Henry L. Pratt, president of the Millers Falls Mfg. Co., remained as president of the consolidated companies, serving until his death in December, 1900. Levi J. Gunn was treasurer.

The Langdon Mitre Box Co. became associated with Millers Falls in 1876 and was absorbed in 1906. The Ford Auger Bit Co. was taken over in 1916, and the West Haven Mfg. Co. in 1920. In 1931, the Goodell-Pratt Co. was merged into Miller Falls.

The firm made a great variety of hand tools, primarily for woodworking. Tools for wagon and carriage builders included Goodell's patent adjustable hollow auger (Fig.1) offered in 1883. By 1915, production included spoke trimmers with adjustable depth stops (Fig.2) made in two sizes, and No. 2 (Fig.3) and No. 3 (Fig.4) hollow augers for cutting tenons from 1/4" to 1 1/4". The No. 2 hollow auger was simply the No. 3 hollow auger permanently mounted on a 14" sweep bit brace.

GOODELL'S PATENT
ADJUSTABLE HOLLOW AUGER.

This Auger is believed to be an improvement on anything hitherto in use. It has all the strength, durability and quick adjustability of any other, and it also has to drive it a Steel Bit Brace Sweep of the same size and finish as our No. 10 Brace, to wit: 14 inch sweep. As the Brace Sweep is fitted to the Auger it must always work entirely true, which is not the case when used in an ordinary brace. Besides, it often happens that the Bit Brace on hand is not large enough to drive a spoke Auger.

Price, each, - - $4.00

For sale by most Hardware Dealers, or sent by express by us on receipt of the price.

Millers Falls Co.,
74 CHAMBERS ST.,
NEW YORK.

Fig.1

SPOKE TRIMMERS

Fig.2

Iron casting, exterior black enameled; steel bit shank, nickeled.
Adjustable knife, sharpened ready for use.
ADJUSTABLE STOP GAUGE clamped with a thumb screw.

ADJUSTABLE HOLLOW AUGER
No. 2

Fig.3

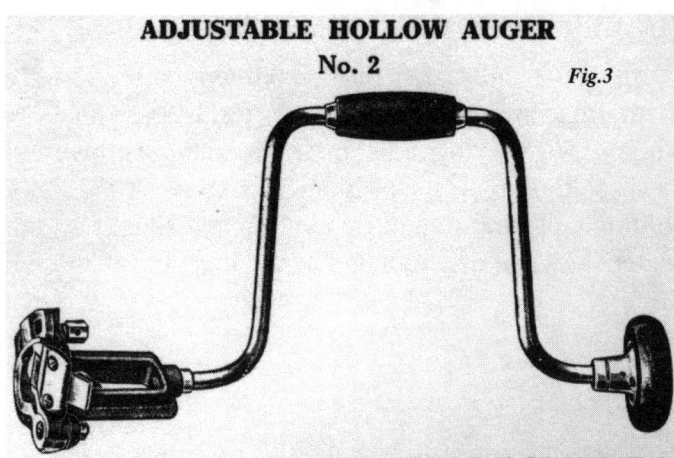

A 14-inch sweep bit brace of our No. 10 pattern, with **BALL BEARING HEAD**, especially fitted to the auger, causing the latter always to work true.

ADJUSTABLE HOLLOW AUGER
No. 3

Fig.4

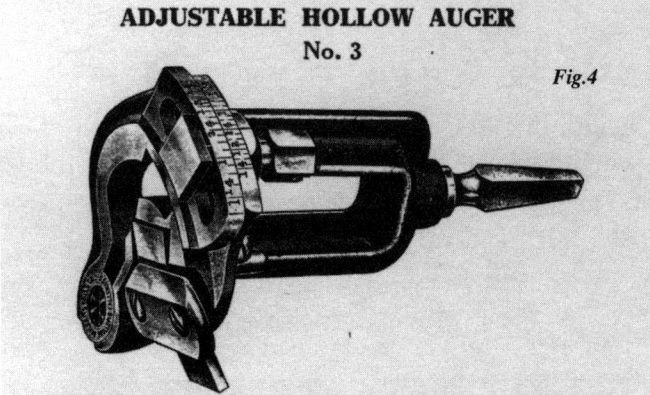

The same as Hollow Auger No. 2, shown next preceding, except that, instead of a bit brace sweep, a bit stock shank is furnished to fit into the chuck of a bit brace.

MORELAND AND NIXON'S MORTISING MACHINE.

MORELAND & NIXON , Adrian, MI

Maker of a hub mortising machine (right), patented February 22, 1853. In use, the hub was mounted on a carriage that was moved back and forth by a hand lever driving a pinion and rack. The hub was located by an index plate that positioned it for each mortise cut. Cutting was done by two chisels and a rotating auger bit.

MORGAN, THOMAS S. , New Columbia, IL

Inventor and maker of a spoke setting machine (right), patented March 25, 1876.

In operation, the hub was fastened to an arbor with clamp C, the spokes placed but not driven into the hub, and the adjustable frame moved up or down until the center line of the hub was on a level with the guide ring D. The hub was then moved above the leveling straight edge, and the move-able frame lowered by cranks B until the desired dish or set of the spokes was obtained. "It now only remains to rest the spokes upon the guide ring, and to drive them into the hub."

MORGAN'S SPOKE-SETTING MACHINE.

MORRIS, WM. B. , Boise City, ID

Maker, in 1877, of CARLTON'S axle gauge, patented June 27, 1876, and September 26, 1876, by William C. Carlton of Boise City, ID. The gauge (Fig.1) was used take the center and dish of a wheel, set the axle spindle for the dish, and set the gather. Morris also offered a bolt cutter patented June 27, 1876, by Carlton.

In slightly modified form (Fig.2) the gauge was offered as late as 1902.

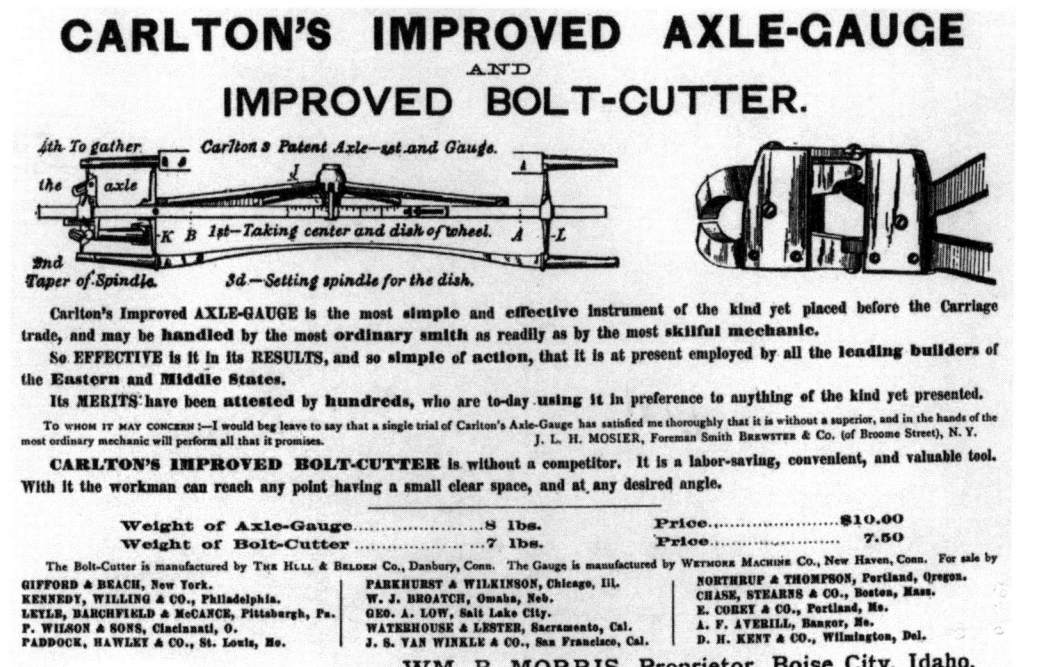

Fig.1

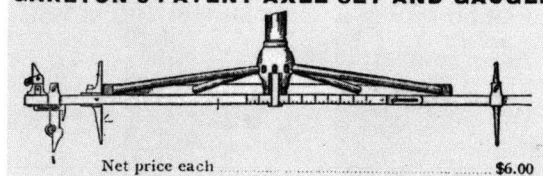

Fig.2

MOWRY AXLE & MACHINE CO. , Greeneville, CT

Maker of Reed & Bowen's patent combined upsetter, shear and punch and J.B. West's American tire setter. See WEST TIRE SETTER CO.

MOYER, H.A. , Syracuse, NY

Operator of the Moyer Wagon Works, Moyer also offered, beginning in 1882, the MOYER hub borer, patented July 11, 1882. The machine was offered in 1891 at least as late as 1906.

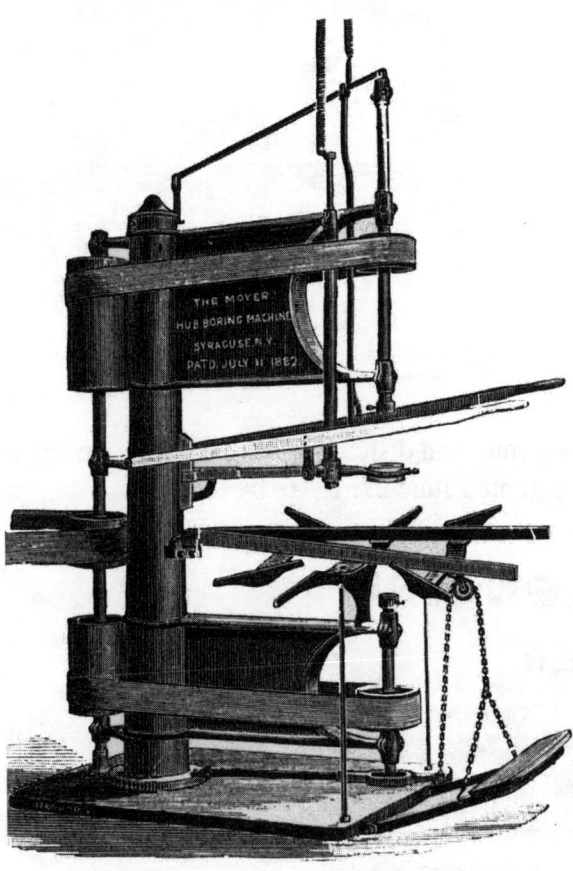

THE KING OF ALL.

The Moyer Patent Hub Borer is a great success. Best record in America. Awarded Silver Medal, Cincinnati Exposition, 1882. Used by over 100 of the largest Carriage Manufacturers in the U. S.

Centers and bores a set of four wheels in less than half a minute at a cost, including the setting of boxes, of only TWO cents. If you manufacture 1000 jobs a year it will pay you forty per cent. on investment.

Machine Guaranteed to do all I claim for it.

MANUFACTURED BY

H. A. MOYER,

SYRACUSE, N. Y.

NATIONAL HARDWARE CO. , Cincinnati, OH

Maker, in 1892, of a multiple spindle drilling machine, patented February 24, 1891, by Joseph Faske. The machine was designed to drill and countersink up to ten holes at a time in one half the circumference of a wheel. Although set up time would have been very lengthy, machining time would have been reduced about 80% over a conventional drill press.

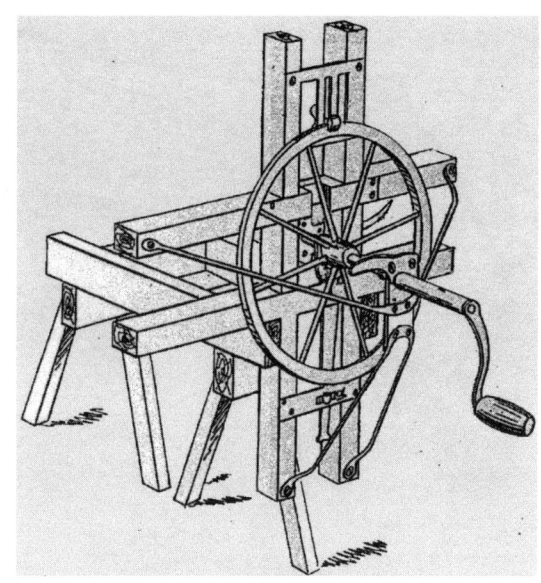

NEWELL, JOHN A. , Kalamazoo, MI

John A. Newell (1834-1908) operated as a carriage maker, but also invented and made wheel machinery. Products included a box-setting machine, shown at right, patented December 17, 1872, and improved with the addition of a self-centering hub chuck, patented December 16, 1873. Newell received a medal for the machine at the 1876 Centennial Exposition.

NOVELTY IRON WORKS , Dubuque, IA

Maker, in 1907, of the BOSS power hammer "for wagon and buggy factories." The firm also made key seating machines, hand punches and blacksmith bending tools.

OBER LATHE CO. , Chagrin Falls, OH, later
OBER MFG. CO. , Chagrin Falls, OH

Founded in 1873 to make lathes for turning irregular forms, patented June 27, 1865, and spoke tenoning machines, patented July 16, 1867, both by G.H. Ober. An improved version of the lathe was patented February 17, 1885. Ober also received patents for other improved versions on July 29, 1890, and June 1, 1897.

The firm's ca. 1895 catalog offered the No. 1 spoke lathe, patented February 17, 1885, (Fig.1) for work 8" to 43" in length; No. 2 lathe, patented July 29, 1890, (Fig.2) made in three sizes, 33", 36" and 44" length; and No. 11 lathe, also patented February 17, 1885, (Fig.3) for work 8" to 36" in length.

In 1904, the firm reorganized as the Ober Mfg. Co., maker of sad irons, lathes, sanders, shapers, chucks, and countershafts. Its 1919 ad offered "machinery for turning wiffletrees, neck yokes, and handles of various kinds."

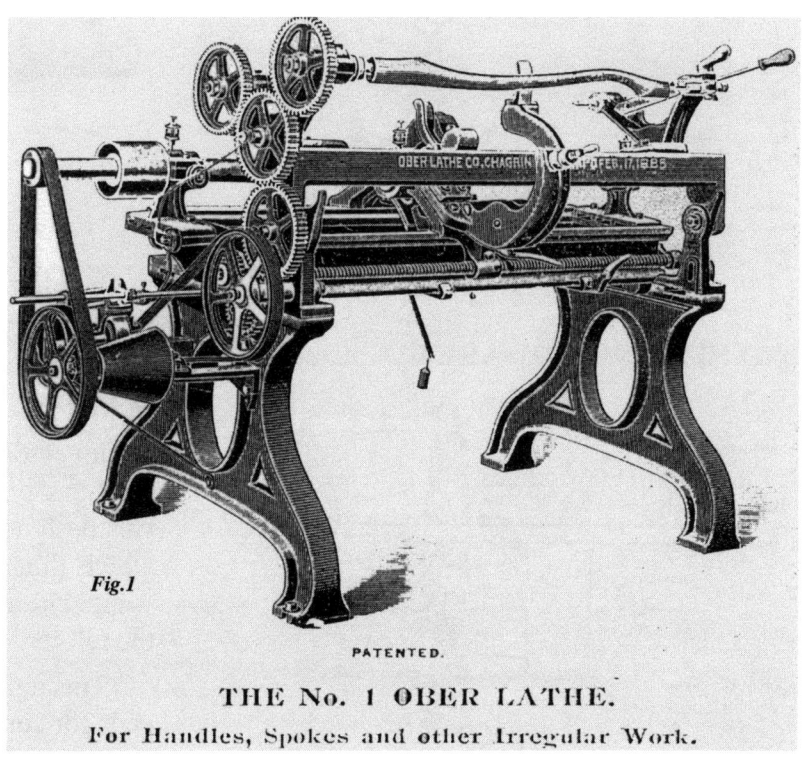

Fig.1

PATENTED.

THE No. 1 OBER LATHE.
For Handles, Spokes and other Irregular Work.

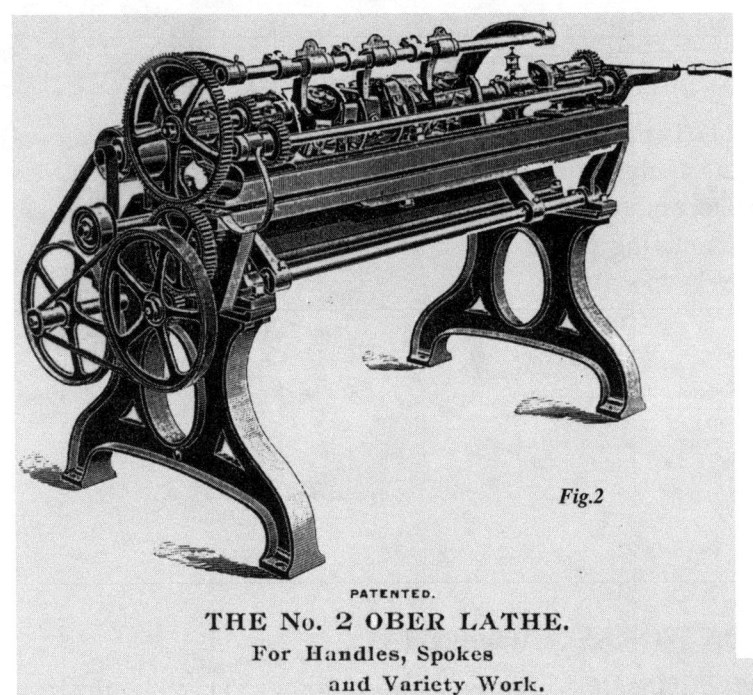

PATENTED.

THE No. 2 OBER LATHE.
For Handles, Spokes
and Variety Work.

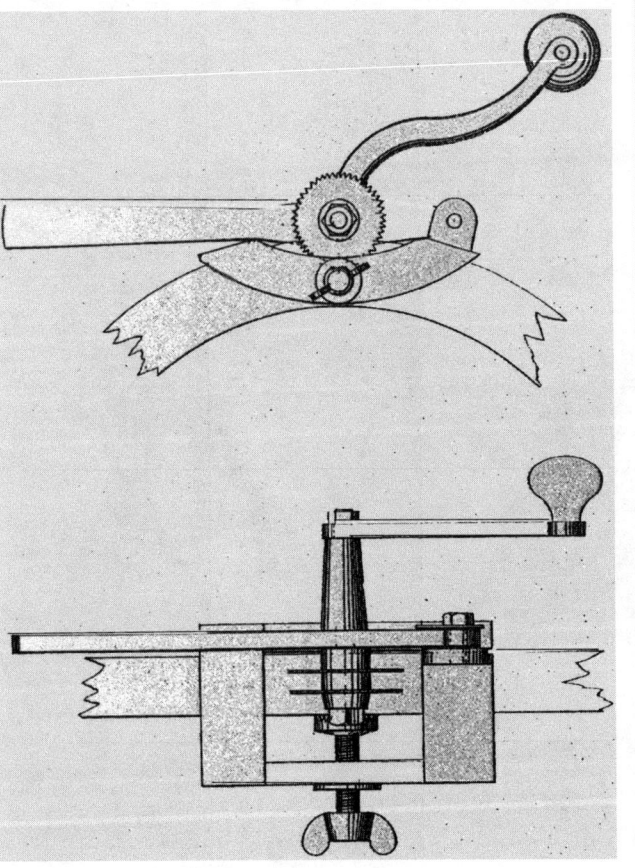

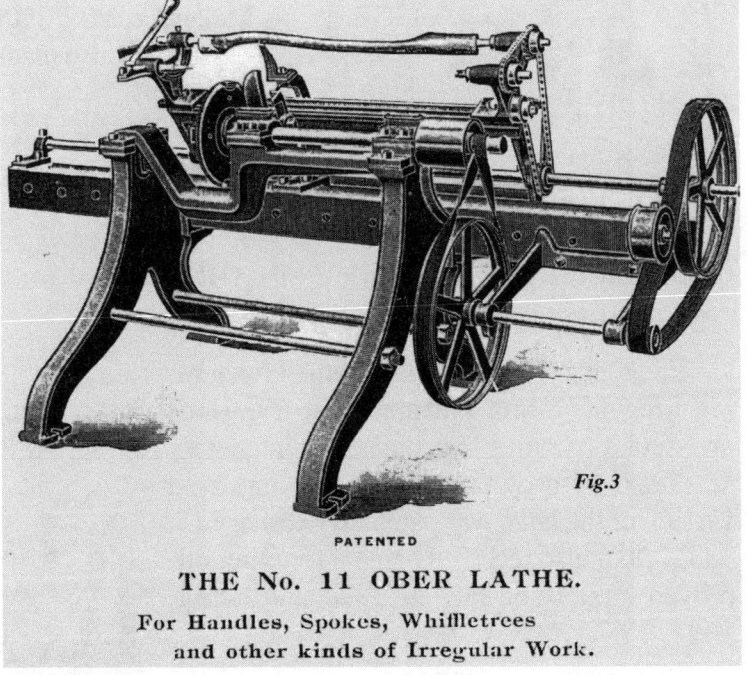

PATENTED

THE No. 11 OBER LATHE.
For Handles, Spokes, Whiffletrees
and other kinds of Irregular Work.

O'BRIEN, JOSEPH P. , Kewanee, IL

Inventor and maker of a hand operated felloe doweling machine, patented July 30, 1872. The device, shown at left, was designed to cut slots or kerfs at the felloe joints, into which thin metal pieces were inserted. The metal pieces were held in place by the tires after they were shrunk over the felloes.

This replaced the old system of boring holes in the felloe ends for conventional wooden dowels.

OLMSTEAD & DINSMORE , Chicago, IL

Maker of a tire upsetter, patented January 12, 1864, by Joseph Olmstead. By 1882, the upsetter was a product of the ILLINOIS IRON & BOLT CO., which made it into the 20th century.

OTIS & COTTLE , Syracuse, NY

Maker of the Otis Mortising, Boring and Hub-Mortising Machine, patented February 20, 1846, by B.H. Otis and improved in 1853. As shown below, the boring spindle was power operated while the chisel was forced down by foot power and raised by a heavy spring.

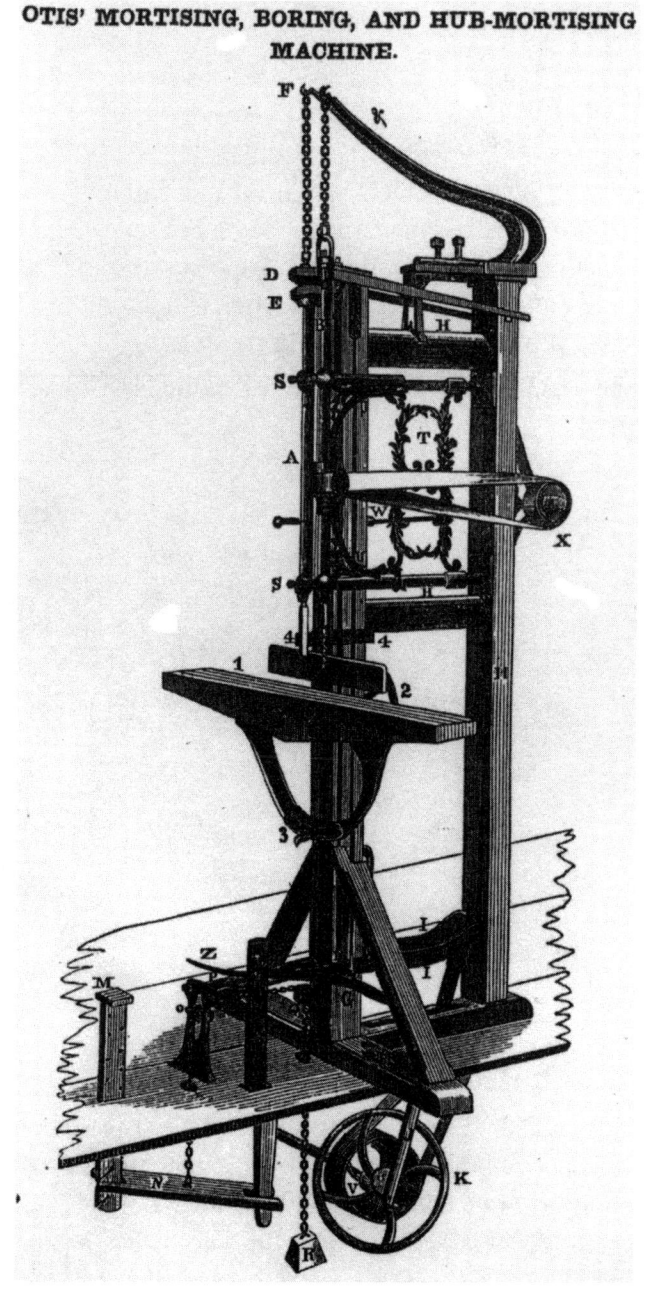

OTIS' MORTISING, BORING, AND HUB-MORTISING MACHINE.

PACKARD, O.L. , Milwaukee, WI, later
PACKARD MACHINERY CO., O.L. , Milwaukee, WI

Formed ca. 1870 as a machinery dealership selling machine tools, woodworking machinery, and steam engines. The firm began offering its only known proprietary product, PENNY'S spring cushioned helve hammer, in 1884. Production appears to have continued into the twentieth century. In 1891, the firm incorporated as the O.L. Packard Machinery Co.

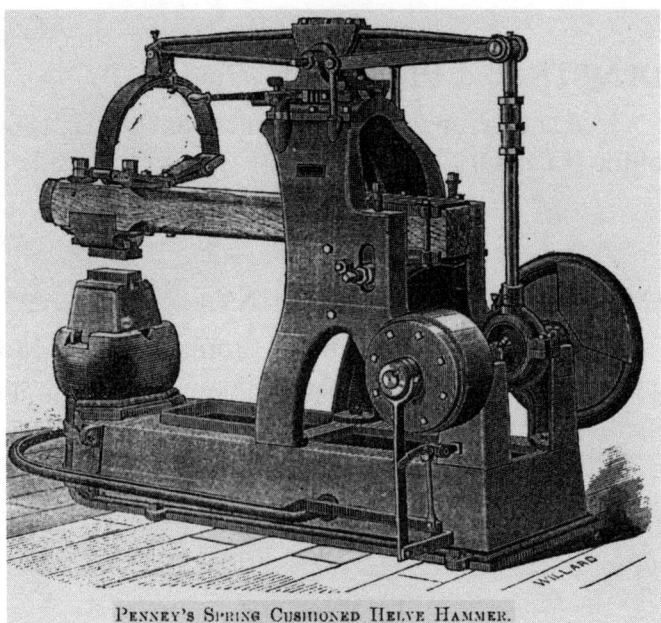

PENNEY'S SPRING CUSHIONED HELVE HAMMER.

PALMER & CO. , New York, NY

Maker, in 1859, of the WARD spoke turning lathe, patented by Richard Ward of Naugatuck, CT, on February 22, 1853, and June 28, 1853. The machine consisted of two sections. The first (Fig.1) cut the oval shape of the spoke by rotating and feeding the blank in and out in front of a rotating set of cutters A. The second section (Fig.2) cut the hub-tenon on the end of the spoke by indexing the spoke and feeding it into the large rotating cutter I.

By 1869, the WARD spoke lathe, also called the NAUGATUCK spoke lathe, was produced by WILLIAM B LEWIS & CO.

WARD'S MACHINE FOR TURNING IRREGULAR FORMS.

PARRY MFG. CO., Indianapolis, IN

A large buggy maker (Fig.1), the firm also made some wheel machinery for its own use and for sale to others. Products included a hub boring machine (Fig.2) patented February 12, 1889, by David M. Parry and a hand powered axle bending machine (Fig.3), patented June 11, 1901, by Thomas H. Parry and William J. Byers. The firm was active at least as late as 1911. *(illustrations on next page)*

146

The
Largest
and
Best Equipped
Factory
on Earth
for
Producing
Superior
Vehicles.

Fig.1

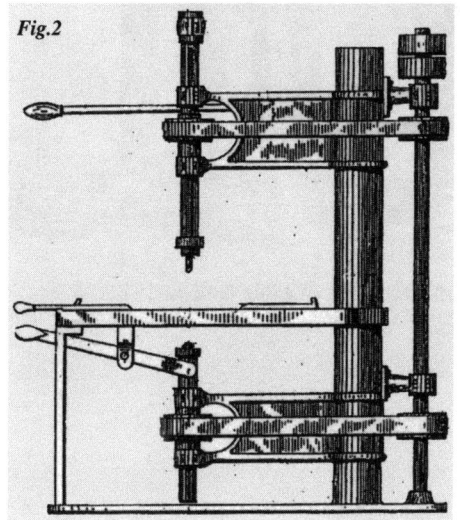

Fig.2

Fig.3

PEACE & CLARK, Salem, MO

Maker of of a hand operated spoke tenoning machine, patented February 1, 1876, by John G. Peace. It was later offered with a felly boring attachment patented May 11, 1880, also by Peace. As shown below, it could cut tenons from 1/4" to 1 1/4" and sold for $15.00. The device was listed in dealers catalogs as late as 1902.

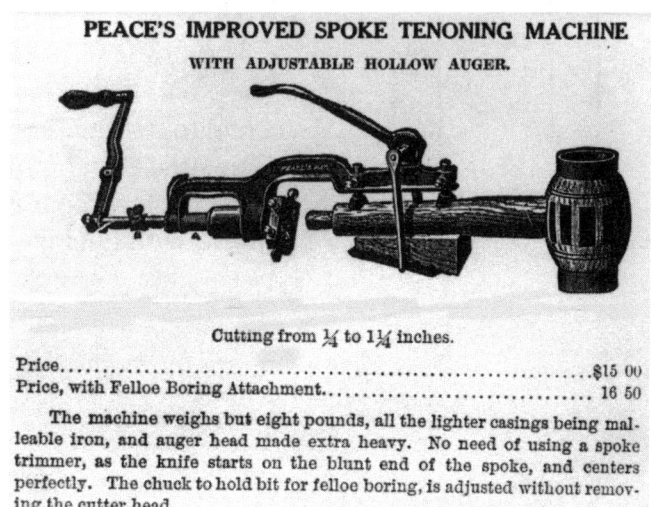

PEACE'S IMPROVED SPOKE TENONING MACHINE
WITH ADJUSTABLE HOLLOW AUGER.

Cutting from 1/4 to 1 1/4 inches.

Price...$15 00
Price, with Felloe Boring Attachment............................. 16 50

The machine weighs but eight pounds, all the lighter casings being malleable iron, and auger head made extra heavy. No need of using a spoke trimmer, as the knife starts on the blunt end of the spoke, and centers perfectly. The chuck to hold bit for felloe boring, is adjusted without removing the cutter head.

PEARSALL, G.T., Apalachin, NY

Maker of Pearsall's wagon-box setter, patented September 30, 1862, by T.G. Pearsall and S.A. Garrison. In use, the wheel was clamped by the rim to the machine so that "the workman cannot fail, and the hole must be square with the fellies." The hole was then bored by a cutter rotated and fed by a hand crank and screw and arranged to cut either a straight or tapered bore.

Pearsall claimed that the workman "cannot fail to bore the hub as square and true with the rim, as if it was secured to the face plate of a lathe." He also pointed out that "fitting a set of wheels with a gouge and chisel to receive the boxes, if well done, is a tedious operation. Workmen generally cut out every part too large except for the rim of the hub, in order to make a quicker job." (This has the ring of truth and should tempt us to rethink our ideas about old time craftsmanship.)

PEARSALL'S WAGON-BOX SETTER.

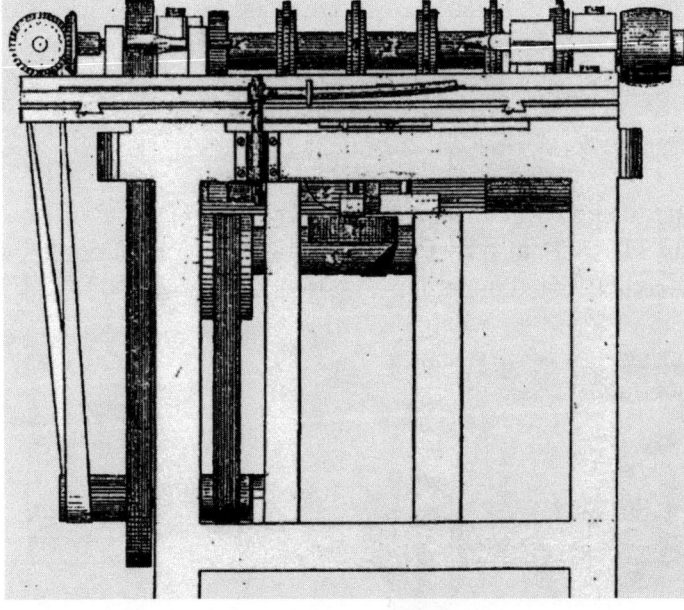

PIERCE & CURTIS, New Haven, CT

Maker, in 1871, of an improved WARD spoke lathe, patented August 15, 1871. The machine was originally patented February 22, 1853, and June 28, 1853, by Richard Ward of Naugatuck, CT, and was made by PALMER & CO. and later, WILLIAM B LEWIS & CO.

The original WARD design required two machines, one to cut the tapered spoke section and a second to cut the rectangular tenon. The Pierce & Curtis design combined the tenoning section, mounted on a separate slide and with a separate pattern, with the taper turning section.

PRYIBIL, P., New York, NY

Formed by Paul Pryibil (1834-1897) in 1878, as a reorganization of bandsaw maker First & Pryibil. In 1880, Pryibil offered "superior wood working machinery, principally for the cabinet, piano, and piano action makers."

The only wagon and carriage makers' machinery thus far observed is a Combined Sawing, Boring and Chamfering Machine for Wagon and Carriage Makers shown at right. It was equipped with a 12" circular saw, chamfering cutter and boring bit all carried on separate arbors, running at proper speeds and not interfering with each other. Offered in 1893, the machine weighed about 700 pounds.

COMBINED SAWING, BORING AND CHAMFERING MACHINE.

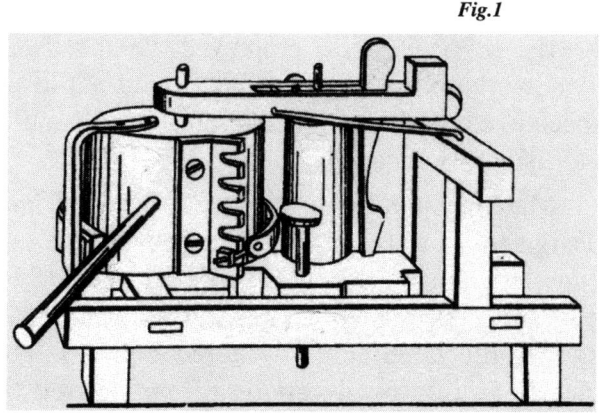

LIGHTNING TIRE UPSETTER.

STODDART'S PATENT.

PRICES.

2 inch Upsetter........each		$20 00
4 " " .... "		25 00
4 " Tire and Axle Upsetter Combined..........		28 00

REIMOLD, Christian J., Saginaw, MI

First maker of the LIGHTNING tire upsetter, patented February 9, 1875, by Nolton Stoddard. In 1882, it was offered in 2" and 4" sizes and as a 4" combination tire and axle upsetter.

The STODDARD LIGHTNING tire upsetter was eventually made by several different companies, including ILLINOIS IRON & BOLT and CHAMPION BLOWER & FORGE, and as late as World War I.

REYNOLDS, EDWARD K., Salem, NJ, later Philadelphia, PA

Inventor and maker of the first felloe bending machine, patented July 17, 1835, (Fig.1). The machine was less than successful due to the breakage of about 30% of the stock as it was bent. This was caused by severe elongation of the fibers in the outer part of the curve.

The breakage problem was solved by Thomas Blanchard's patent of December 18, 1849, which prevented elongation by compressing the material lengthwise as it was bent. Edwards appears to have licensed the Blanchard patent and began production of the Reynolds-Blanchard machine (Fig.2 - *next page*) in 1849.

The business was moved to Philadelphia in 1852, shortly after the Salem factory was destroyed by fire.

Fig.1

149

Fig.2

REYNOLDS, JAMES A., Wabash, IN

Inventor and maker of the Reynolds axle gauge, patented April 29, 1902. Reynolds claimed it was "the simplest and best axle gauge on the market and must be seen to be appreciated."

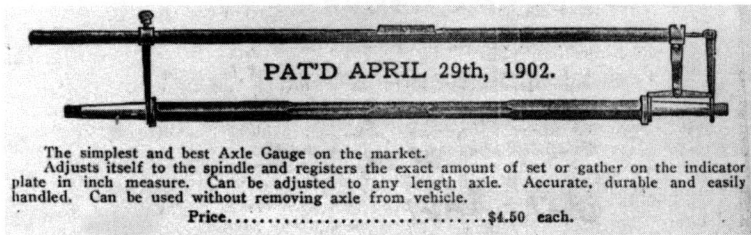

PAT'D APRIL 29th, 1902.

The simplest and best Axle Gauge on the market.
Adjusts itself to the spindle and registers the exact amount of set or gather on the indicator plate in inch measure. Can be adjusted to any length axle. Accurate, durable and easily handled. Can be used without removing axle from vehicle.
Price..............................$4.50 each.

ROFF, ERASTUS W., Newark, NJ

Established in 1865 to make a variety of wheel and woodworking machinery. In 1880, he advertised a spoke tenoning machine, but by 1885 was no longer operating.

ROGERS CO., C.B., Norwich, CT

Originally founded in 1848 as the Norwich, CT branch of J.A. FAY & CO., with C.B. Rogers as resident partner. The firm was organized as a stock company when the Fay firm began to break up in 1861 and Rogers bought the Norwich factory.

By 1876, the firm employed 200 hands making a variety of woodworking machinery, which filled a 140 page catalog. Rogers specialized in large planing machines, moulding machines, and mortising machines.

Machines made for carriage and wagon makers included a Fay design foot mortise machine with hub attachment (Fig.1 - *right*), patented January 17, 1842, offered from 1856 or earlier; a large hub mortising machine (Fig.2) offered in 1876; and a spoke and axe handle lathe (Fig.3) offered in 1880. The latter machine is clearly an improved version of one offered by J.A. FAY & CO. about 1855.

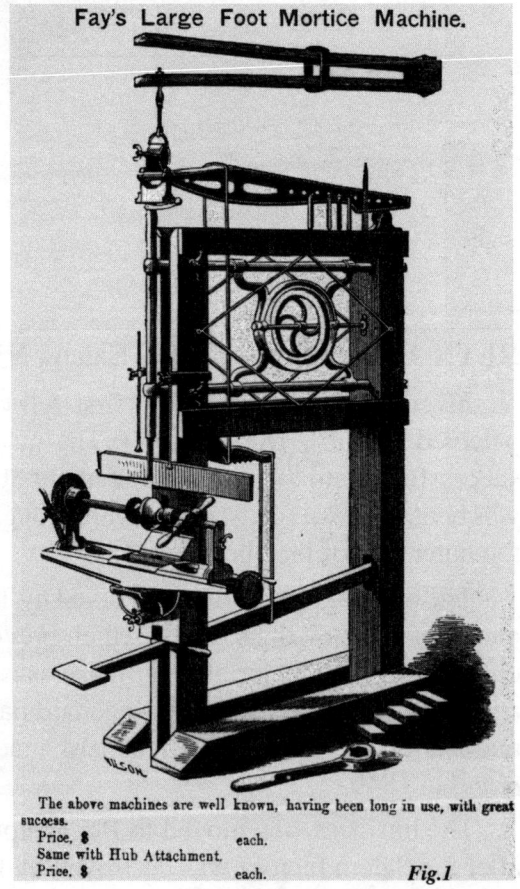

Fay's Large Foot Mortice Machine.

The above machines are well known, having been long in use, with great success.
Price, $ each.
Same with Hub Attachment.
Price, $ each.   Fig.1

(Illustrations continued on next page)

Fig.2

Fig.3

ROHRER & CO., HENRY, Stockton, CA

Maker, in 1886, of Rohrer's improved wheel and method of setting tires. Rohrer's machine allowed the tire to be put on cold "so that steel may be used as well as iron." In use, the wheel, less tire, was placed on the machine where a band was tightened, causing the spokes to buckle horizontally. The fellies were clamped at the now decreased diameter, the band removed, the tire put in place, and the clamps released to complete the tire setting operation.

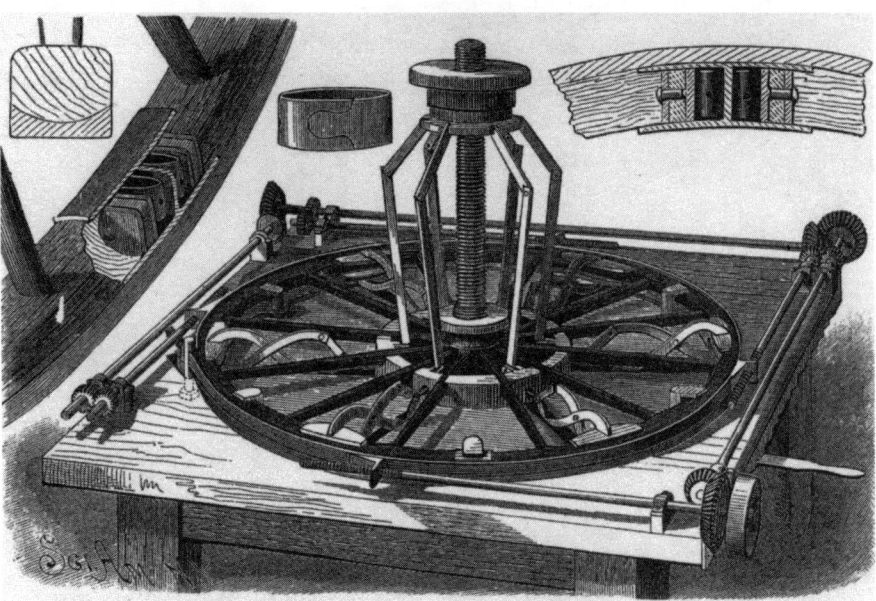

ROHRER'S IMPROVED WHEEL AND METHOD OF SETTING TIRES.

ROYS & FRENCH, Detroit, MI

A partnership of Reuben D. Roys and Newell French. Maker, in 1853, of Roys & French's hub mortising machine, *left*, jointly patented January 23, 1845, "which will lay off, bore, and mortise a hub of ordinary size in 15 minutes, turning it out completely finished, the mortises having any required disc."

SARVEN, JAMES D., Columbia, TN

Inventor and maker of a wood bending machine, patented January 20, 1857. Made for bending fellies for wheels, bows for carriage tops, shafts at heel, poles, seat pieces, sleigh runners, goose necks and body pieces, it was aimed at carriage and wagon makers.

In operation, the piece was clamped to the front of a semi-circular mold by turning the handwheel K. The frame was then rotated as required up to 180 degrees, bending the piece, which had been steamed or heated, over the mold. A different mold was required for each radius to be bent.

SCHREIDT & MILLER CO., Mansfield, OH

Formed about 1880 to make iron fittings for carriage and wagon makers. The firm also made a line of machinery for production of carriage irons which included: upsetting machines for rough forming the ends of top irons (Fig.1); filing machines for finishing the ends of top irons (Fig.2) which utilized form files (Fig.3) made to size and shape for each purpose; metal sawing machines (Fig.4) which cut mortises and tenons into opposite ends of the irons; and special drilling machines (Fig.5) for drilling holes in the ends. All were patented in November, 1887, by Frank Schreidt. *(Illustrations continued next page)*

SARVEN'S PATENT WOOD BENDING MACHINE.

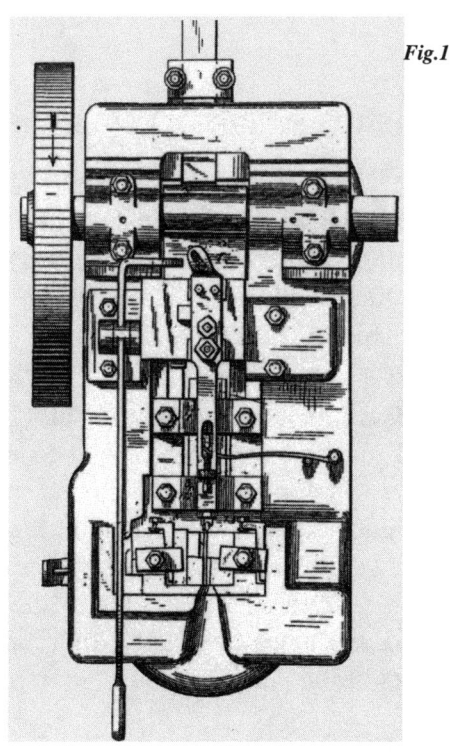

Fig.1

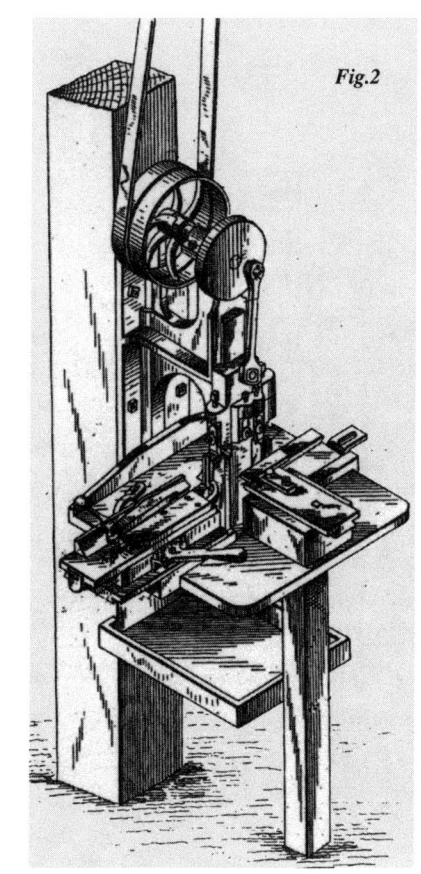

Fig.2

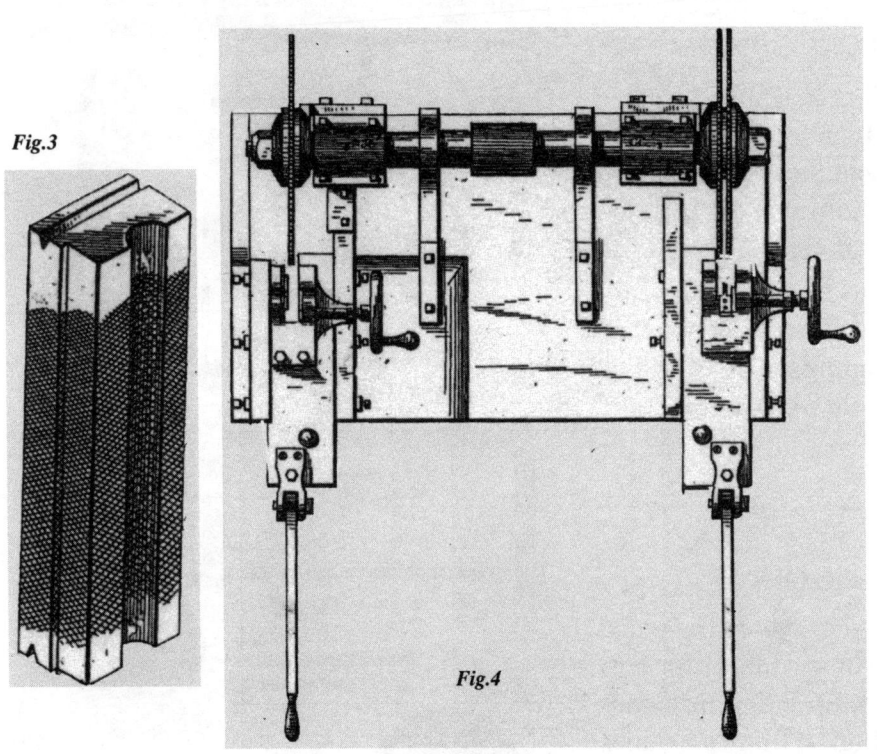

Fig.3

Fig.4

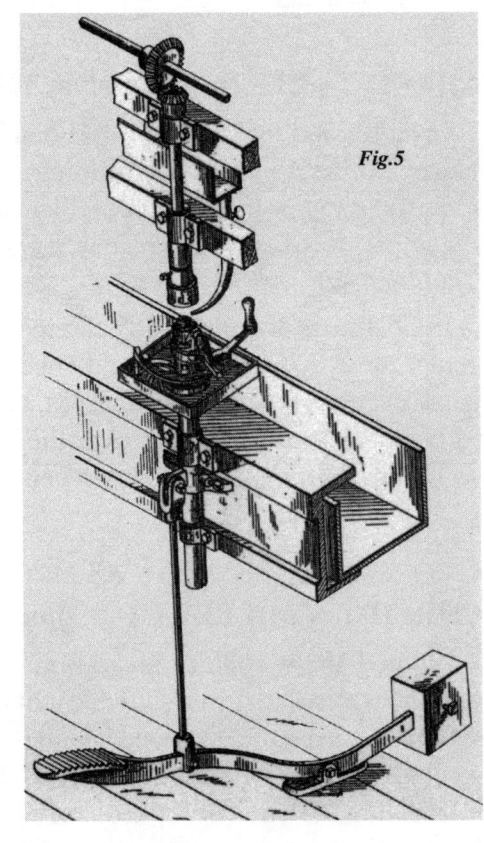

Fig.5

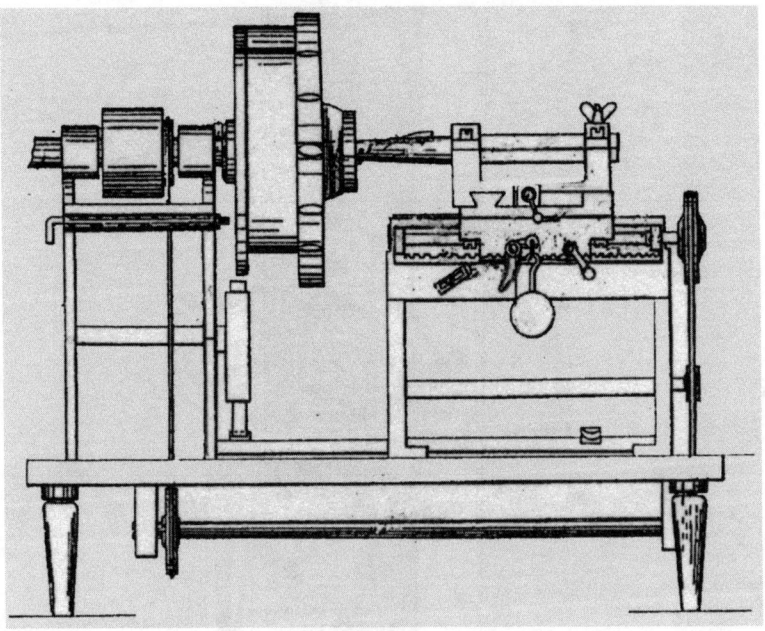

SCHUTTLER, PETER, Chicago, IL, later SCHUTTLER & HOTZ, Chicago, IL

Wagon maker established in 1843 by Peter Schuttler. The firm reorganized in 1869 as Schuttler and Hotz, when Schuttler took Christopher Hotz as a partner. The factory was burned in the great fire of 1871, but was soon rebuilt.

The firm, as was common at the time, developed machinery for its own use and for sale to others. Such machinery included the hub boring machine shown at left, patented May 2, 1865, by Peter Schuttler. Equipped with a compound slide that was swiveled to set the desired taper to be bored, the machine was far more advanced than others of the period.

SCRANTON & CO., New Haven, CT

Formed in 1894 to take over production of power hammers previously made by the BELDEN MACHINE CO.

SCRIBNER, J.M., Middleburgh, NY

Maker, in 1868, of Rickart's patent hub lathes, patented September 7, 1858, and June 28, 1859, by A. Rickart.

RICKART'S Patent Hub Lathe is a success. Is in constant use by Am. Hub Co. Rights and Lathes for sale. Apply for circular, giving full particulars of its merits, to J. M. SCRIBNER, Middleburgh, N. Y. 1*

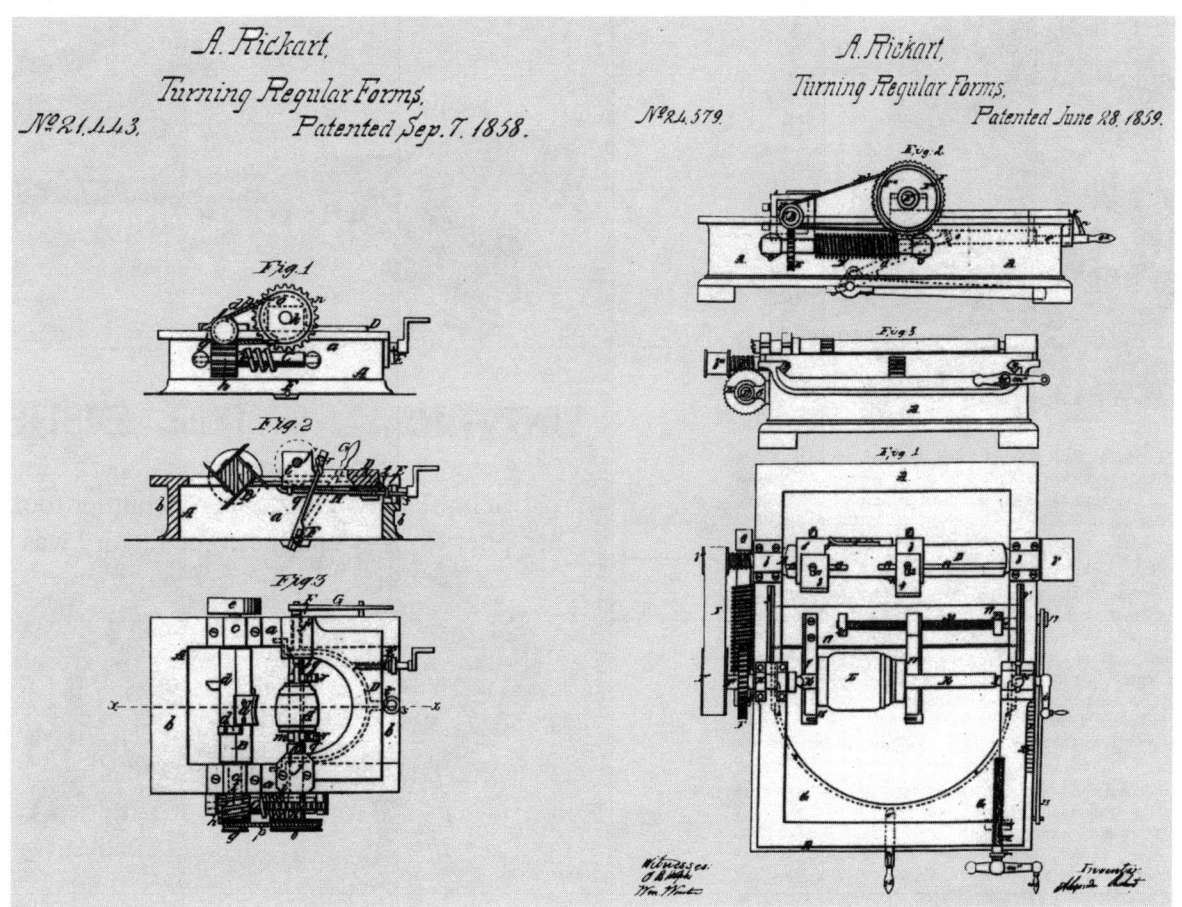

SELLEW, ADAMS & CO., Gowanda, NY

A large maker of farm machinery, the firm also offered, in their 1871 catalog, the very simple tire bender shown below.

SHADBOLT & BOYD IRON CO., Milwaukee, WI

Established in 1863 as a hardware jobber. By 1917, the firm specialized in wagon and carriage hardware, carriage makers' and blacksmiths' tools, and carriage trimmings and mountings.

Its July, 1917 catalog offered a great variety of the above, including several which may have been proprietary. These were the EUREKA hub borer (Fig.1) made in three sizes, the UNIVERSAL axle setting machine (Fig.2), and UNIVERSAL wheel disher (Fig.3).

Fig.1

No. 1 Eureka is built for light and medium work. It takes in a wheel 5 feet 2 inches high and will bore a hub 9 inches long; boring for the nut, a fit for the box, chamber the spokes, cut the collar on the back, and presses in the light boxes without removing the wheel from the machine. It has one boring bar, presser bar, knives, wrenches, etc.

No. 2 Eureka is the principal one of these machines, and there are ten of them sold to one of the other sizes. It is the best adapted to general work for a hand machine of any that we build. It has two boring bars, one for light and one for heavy work; it will bore from a ¾ inch axle box p to a hub 17 inches long, and a hole 8 inches in diameter, taking on a wheel 5 feet 6 inches high; the jaws will catch from a 1¾ inch up to 11½ front band, so it takes in the general run of work.

No. 3 Eureka is built for extra heavy work, but will do light work as well as No. 1 or No. 2. It has two bars and will bore from a ¾ inch axle box up to hub 22 inches long, taking on a wheel over 6 feet high; will take in a 13½ front band and bore a hole 10 inches in diameter. The bars and frame are heavier than a No. 2. Every machine is tested before shipping and guaranteed perfect in every respect.

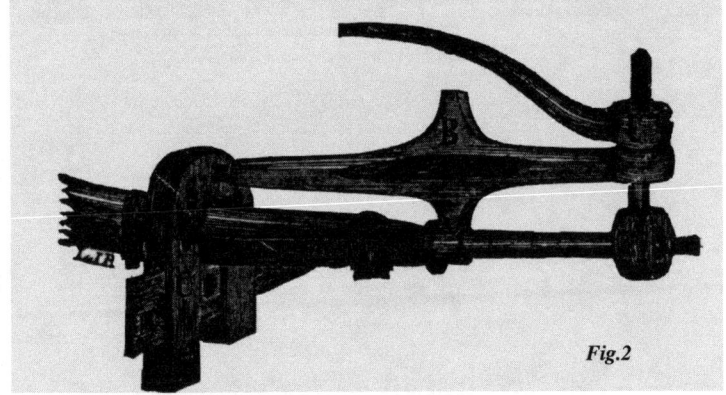

UNIVERSAL AXLE SETTING MACHINE

Fig.2

UNIVERSAL WHEEL DISHER

Fig.3

SHERBURNE & CO., Boston, MA

Maker, in 1887, of Reed's patent gas tire heating machine for heating carriage tires as shown below.

SILVER & DEMING, Salem, OH, later
SILVER & DEMING MFG. CO., Salem, OH, later
SILVER MFG. CO., Salem, OH

A partnership of Albert R. Silver (1823-1900) and John Deming (1817-1894) formed in 1868 as a reorganization of DOLE, SILVER & DEMING. The firm incorporated as the Silver & Deming Mfg. Co. in 1874 with Silver as president and Deming vice president and treasurer. In 1890 the company split into the Deming Co., which continued the pump and hydraulic machinery business added about 1882, and the Silver Mfg. Co. which continued the drill and wheel machinery lines.

Early production included all the carriage and wagon makers' machinery and tools previously made by DOLE, SILVER & DEMING. New products began with an improved hub boxing machine (Fig.1), patented by Silver August 11, 1868; Silver's patent double chuck taper hub-boxing machine (Fig.2), patented July 12, 1870;

HUB BOXING MACHINES

SILVER'S Fig. 710

No. 1—For medium and heavy work, up to
    11 x 13 inch hubs......................$25.00

"   2—For extra heavy work, up to 16 x 24
    inch hubs.......................... 35.00

Extra mandrel and bits for light work, for
    No. 1.................................. 3.00

Bits per set (4) for No. 1..................... .75

"   "   "   (4) "   "   2..................... 1.00

NOTE—This machine will not bore tapering.

Fig.1

SILVER'S PATENT DOUBLE CHUCK TAPER HUB-BOXING MACHINE.

Fig. 4 shows the Chuck for the large end of the hub, with the device for varying the taper of the hole. Fig. 5 shows the reverse, or Chuck for the smaller end, giving also a view of the "Silver's Open Nut" as applied to this machine and by the aid of which perfect freedom is obtained for the Mandrel to oscillate, as well as to cut a level shoulder if desired. The "Adjustable Rule" enables the operator to set the Bits for cutting either straight or taper hole, as may be desired. Directions in full accompany each Machine.

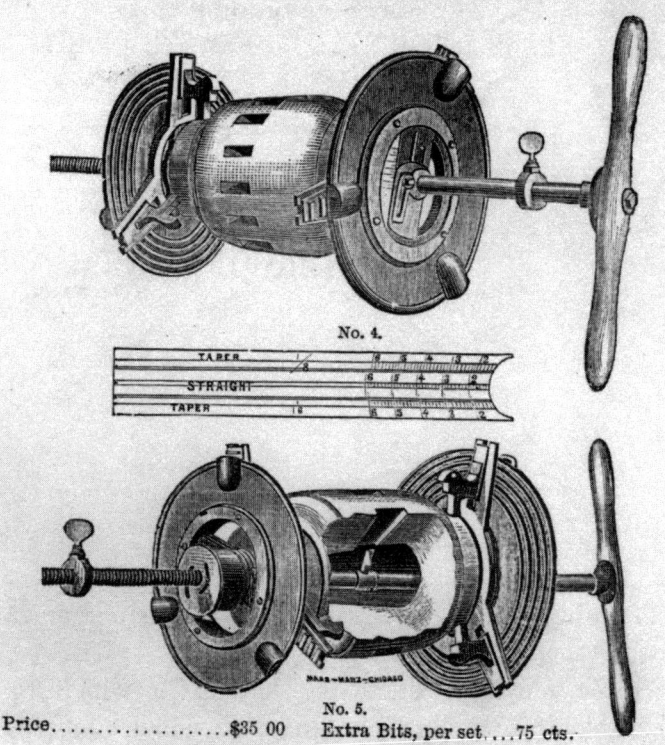

No. 4.

No. 5.

Price....................$35 00　　Extra Bits, per set....75 cts.

Fig.2

DOLE & DEMING'S PATENT SPOKE TENONING MACHINE.

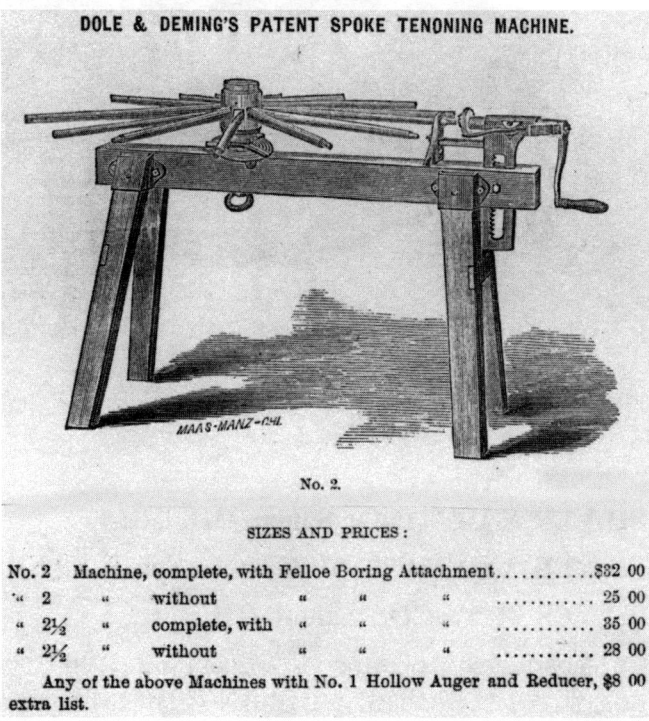

No. 2.

SIZES AND PRICES :

No. 2	Machine, complete, with Felloe Boring Attachment					$32 00
" 2	"	without	"	"	"	25 00
" 2½	"	complete, with	"	"	"	35 00
" 2½	"	without	"	"	"	28 00

Any of the above Machines with No. 1 Hollow Auger and Reducer, $8 00 extra list.

Fig.3

Fig.4

and an improved version of the spoke tenoning machine (Fig.3) with a hub centering device patented by Deming on May 17, 1870.

By 1877, the company was offering a variety of products (Fig.4), including feed cutters, horse powers, meat choppers and stuffers, and blacksmiths' drills, in addition to the hub boxing and spoke tenoning machines.

In 1891, the Silver Mfg. Co. offered an improved spoke tenoning and felly boring machine (Fig.5), now fitted for power operation, and the newly introduced Silver's taper hub-boring machine mounted on a cast iron stand. Martin's combined rim wrench and bolt clipper, patented July 28, 1891, and February 23, 1892, (Fig.6) was introduced in 1892.

The STAR hollow auger, first patented by L.A. Dole in 1860, and improved by John Deming in his patent of December 3, 1872, was offered in four sizes (Fig.7) in 1894.

By 1917, Silver had introduced a new design taper hub boring machine (Fig.8), patented May 18, 1909, by Stoten A. Taylor.

The Silver Mfg. Co.'s 1911 catalog, ten pages of which are reproduced below, offered many of the older products, and added a power operated taper hub-boring machine.

(Illustrations continued next page)

Fig.5

DOLE & DEMINGS PATENT SPOKE TENONING MACHINE,
with the celebrated "Star" Hollow Auger, for hand and power.

Fig. 718

No. 3. Complete, with Felloe Boring Attachment and Nos. 1 and 2 Star Augers, cuts tenons ⅞ to 1¼ inches . . $45 00
No. 3½. Complete, with Felloe Boring attachment and Nos. 1 and 3 Star Augers, cuts tenons ⅞ to 1½ inches . . $50.00
Cuts a perfectly true square-shouldered tenon, has an established reputation of over thirty years, and is the best machine of the kind in use.

SILVERS' NEW TAPER HUB-BORING MACHINE.

with "Self-Centreing" Hub Chuck, and Quick-acting Open Feed Nut. For hand use.

Fig. 709

Centers the hub instantly and accurately, trues the wheel at the rim, bores straight or any desired taper, and cuts all necessary recesses, including that at the spokes, consequently the box is set without wedging.
No. 2. For light and medium work, up to 7¼ x 10 in. hubs, weight, 100 lbs. $35.00
No. 3. With two mandrels for light and heavy work, up to 9½ x 13 in. hubs, weight, 170 lbs. $45.00
Either size furnished without iron stand to go on work-bench, at $5.00, less list, if so ordered.
Also "Dole's" and "Silver's" Old Standard Hub Boring Machines, Figs. 710 and 711, and Silver's Upright Post Drills, with steel spindles, and upright column, and latest improved swing table.
No. 1½. Single-geared, drills ¾ in. and to centre of 12 in. circle, 55 lbs. $6.00
No. 2. Double back geared, drills 1 in. and to center of 14½ in. circle, 100 lbs. $10.00
No. 3. Drills 1¼ in. and to centre of 16 in. circle, 140 lbs. $14.00

THE SILVER MFG. CO., Salem, Ohio, U.S.A.
HENION & HUBBELL, Chicago, N. W. Agents.

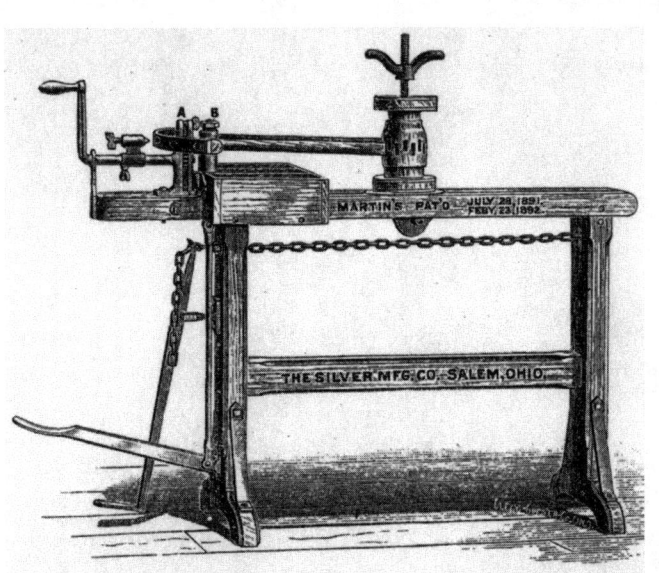

Martin's Combined Rim Wrench and Bolt Clipper.

Fig.6

Sizes and Prices.

No. 4—For light and medium work up to hubs 5½ inches in diameter at Point by 10 inches long, weight crated 130 pounds..........................$35.00

No. 5—For medium and heavy work up to hubs 7½ inches in diameter at point by 13 inches long, weight crated 150 pounds.........................$45.00

Fig.8

Fig.7

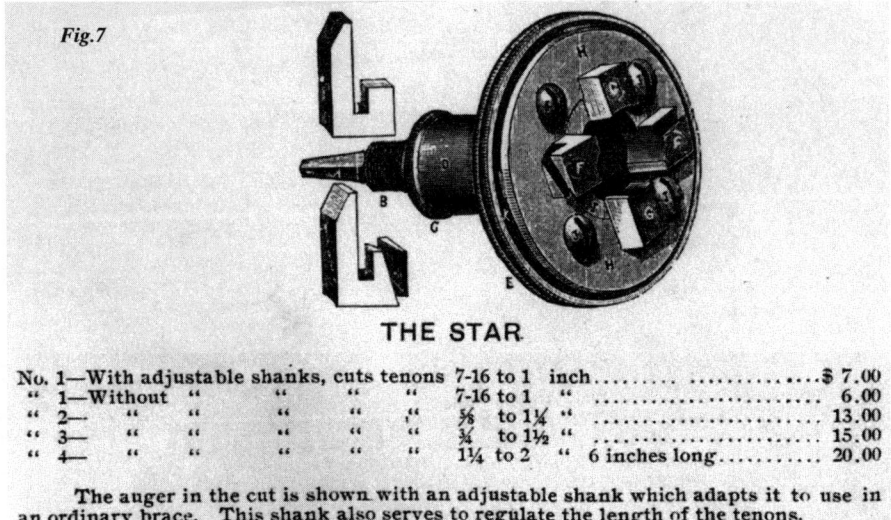

THE STAR

No. 1—With adjustable shanks, cuts tenons				7-16 to 1 inch					$ 7.00
" 1—Without "	"	"	"	"	"	7-16 to 1	"		6.00
" 2— "	"	"	"	"	"	⅝ to 1¼	"		13.00
" 3— "	"	"	"	"	"	¾ to 1½	"		15.00
" 4— "	"	"	"	"	"	1¼ to 2	"	6 inches long	20.00

The anger in the cut is shown with an adjustable shank which adapts it to use in an ordinary brace. This shank also serves to regulate the length of the tenons.

R   FACTURING COMPANY, SALT , U. S. A.

Silver's New Taper Hub-Boring

With Self-Centering Hub Chuck and Quick-Acting Open Feed Nut

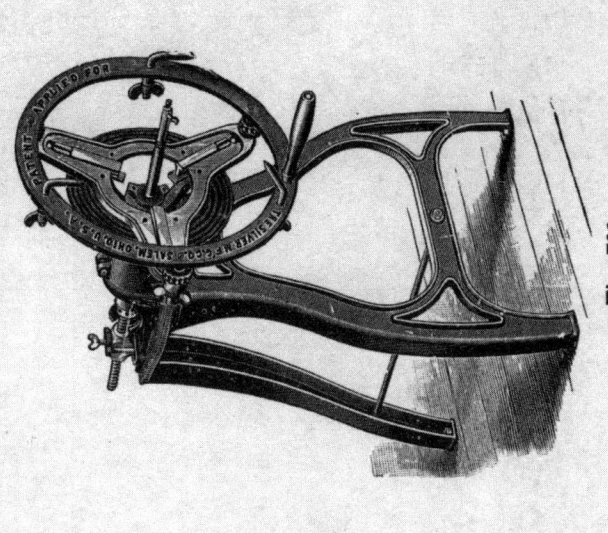

Fig. 709

Centers the Hub Instantly and Accurately

SIZES AND PRICES

No. 2 For light and medium work, up to 7¼x10 inch hubs, mounted on legs as shown, weight 150 lbs......$35.00   Ofvid
No. 2 For light and medium work, up to 7¼x10 inch hubs, without legs, to mount on bench, weight 80 lbs. . 30.00   Ofvuz
No. 3 With two mandrels, for light and heavy work, up to 9½x13 inch hubs, mounted on legs as shown, weight 230 lbs...... 45.00   Ofwer
No. 3 With two mandrels, for light and heavy work, up to 9½x13 inch hubs, without legs, to mount on bench, weight 180 lbs. ...... 40.00   Ofwop
Extra bits, per set (four) for small mandrel...... 4.00   Ogbac
Extra bits, per set (four) for large mandrel...... 1.00   Ogbez
No. 3 will be found as well adapted to light buggy wheels as the largest work for which it is recommended.

Boxed for Export

No. 2   Net 115 pounds, gross 190 pounds, 86 kilos, 8 cubic feet.
No. 3   Net 210 pounds, gross 295 pounds, 133 kilos, 9½ cubic feet.

6

THE SILVER MANUFACTURING COMPANY, SALEM, OHIO, U. S.

Silver's Power Taper Hub-Boring Machine

ADAPTED ALSO FOR HAND USE.

With Self-Centering Hub Chuck and Quick-Acting Open Feed Nut

Fig. 708

See description on opposite page

Centers the Hub Instantly and Accurately

SIZES AND PRICES

With two mandrels for light and heavy work, up to hubs 7½ inches in diameter at point by 13 inches long, weight 385 pounds, floor space 32x34 inches................$75.00   Ofxod
Extra bits, per set, (five) for small mandrel.............. 1.25   Ogbig
Extra bits, per set, (five) for large mandrel.............. 1.25   Ojros

Boxed for Export

Net 355 pounds, gross 450 pounds, 204 kilos, 11½ cubic feet

8

Dole's Old Standard Hub-Boxing Machine

With Silver's
Patent Open
Adjustable
Feed Nut

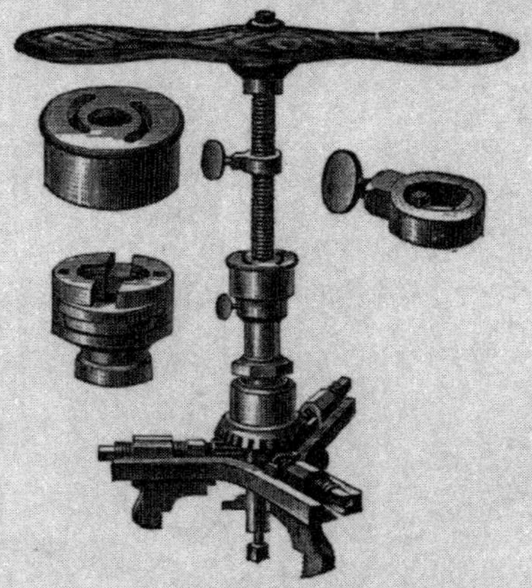

This cut represents Dole's Old Standard Hub-Boxing Machine, with Silver's Patent Open Adjustable Feed Nut. It is still made with the solid feed nut, but with the addition of the Silver's Open Feed Nut it is regarded as more desirable as it admits of the mandrel being drawn from the hub with one motion, instead of screwing it back.

Fig. 711

Machine No. 1 is suitable for buggy and carriage work. It will bore holes from 1¾ to 5 inches in diameter, 4½ inches deep, and by reversing the wheel, 9 inches deep. The hub jaws will grasp from 2 to 7 inches in diameter.

Machine No. 2 is suitable for buggy, carriage and wagon work. It will bore holes from 1¾ to 5 inches in diameter, 4½ inches deep, and by reversing the wheel, 9 inches deep. The hub jaws will grasp from 2 to 12 inches in diameter.

Machine No. 3 is suitable for all the heaviest class of wagon work. It will bore holes from 2 to 5¾ inches in diameter, 7½ inches deep, and by reversing the wheel, 15 inches deep. The hub jaws will grasp from 2½ to 15 inches in diameter.

When ordered we furnish the Nos. 1 and 2 with an extra mandrel made light at the end, with an extra set of small bits, which makes them suitable for the lightest class of work.

This is the original "Dole" Hub-Boxing Machine, invented by L. A. Dole in 1854. Our present large business was established on the manufacture and subsequent sale and success of this machine. This machine will not bore a taper hole.

SIZES AND PRICES

No. 1 Suitable for buggy and carriage work, weight net, $20.00 Ogath
24 lbs.
No. 2 Suitable for buggy, carriage and wagon work, weight
net, 28 lbs. 23.00 Ogauc
No. 3 Suitable for heavy wagon work, weight net, 40 lbs. 27.00 Ogava
Special mandrel and bits for light work, No. 1 or No. 2 3.00 Ogawo
Bits, per set, No. 1 .60 Ogaxe
Bits, per set, No. 2 .75 Ogayo
Bits, per set, No. 3 .85 Ogazi

Boxed for Export

Fig. 711 Nos. 1 or 2, gross 40 pounds, 18 kilos, 2 cubic feet
Fig. 711 No. 3, gross 70 pounds, 32 kilos, 2¾ cubic feet

11

Silver's Old Standard Hub-Boxing Machine

This machine is of more recent construction than the Dole Hub-Boxing Machine, and combines all the good qualities of that popular machine, besides having some features not possessed by it. The open feed nut, which admits of withdrawing the mandrel from the hub after boring the required depth, by simply turning the cap to the left, is an important consideration. The peculiar form of the chuck admits of a better view of the work, while the movement of the jaws being effected by the aid of screw pinions working directly through the jaws, gives the machine great power for clamping the hub. The jaws are arranged with two shoulders for clamping large and small hubs, and are provided with sharp steel plates for gripping patent wheels with iron bands.

Machine No. 1 will bore holes 1⅜ to 5 inches diameter, 6½ inches deep, and will grasp hubs 2 to 9¾ inches diameter measuring at the end.

Machine No. 1½ will bore holes 1¾ to 5 inches diameter, 8 inches deep, and will grasp hubs 3 to 12½ inches diameter, measuring at the end.

Machine No. 2 is intended only for very large, heavy wheels, and is sold principally in foreign countries. It will bore 2⅜ to 6 inches diameter, 12½ inches deep, and will grasp hubs 9 to 14½ inches diameter, measuring at the end.

When ordered we furnish No. 1 with an extra small mandrel and bit, making it suitable for light work. This machine will not bore tapering.

By making slight changes and adjustments in the bits and mandrels, the user can vary the range of work somewhat from sizes given herein.

Fig. 710

SIZES AND PRICES

No. 1 For medium and heavy work, up to 11x13-inch hubs,
weight, 23 lbs. $25.00 Ofylk
No. 1½ For medium and heavy work, up to 13x16-inch hubs,
weight, 40 lbs. 30.00 Ofyrt
No. 2 For extra heavy work, up to 16x24-inch hubs, weight,
70 lbs. 35.00 Ofzin
Extra mandrel and bits for light work, for No. 1 3.00 Ofzub
Bits per set (four), for No. 1 and No. 1½ .75 Ogaoj
Bits per set (four), for No. 2 1.00 Ogasm

Boxed for Export

No. 1 Net 23 pounds, gross 50 pounds, 23 kilos, 1⅞ cubic feet
No. 1½ Net 40 pounds, gross 85 pounds, 39 kilos, 3⅛ cubic feet
No. 2 Net 70 pounds, gross 100 pounds, 45 kilos, 4 cubic feet

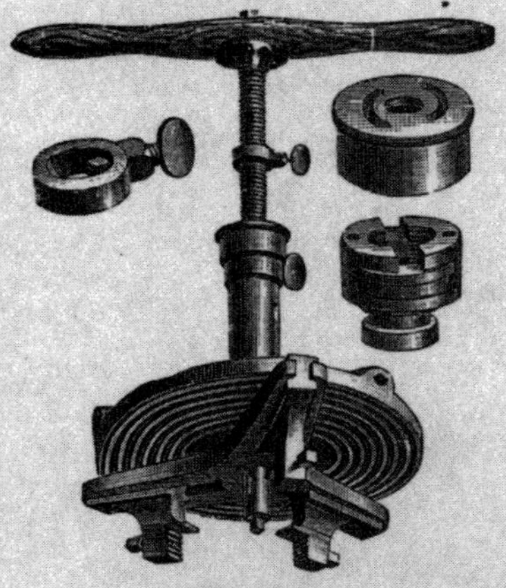

10

Silver's Patent Double Chuck Taper Hub-Boxing Machine

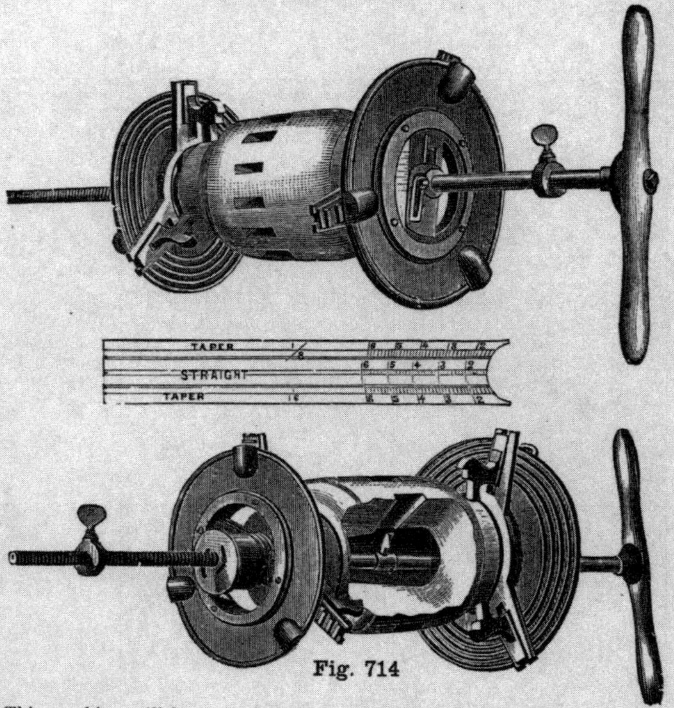

Fig. 714

This machine will bore straight or any desired taper, and is designed for use on large, heavy wheels that are cumbersome to handle, and too large for our improved machine, Fig. 709. Its work is accurate and the box is set perfectly without wedging.

It will bore 2 to 5½ inches diameter, 15½ inches deep.

The large chuck will grasp hubs 6 to 12 inches diameter, and the small one 3 to 9 inches. The engraving shows two views of the same machine. The upper one illustrates the chuck for the large end of the hub, with the device for varying the taper of the hole, and the lower one the reverse or chuck for the smaller end; cut also shows a view of Silver's Open Feed Nut, as applied to this machine, which provides for the free oscillation of the mandrel.

The adjustable rule enables the operator to set the bits for cutting a straight or taper hole any size desired.

SIZE AND PRICE

Complete, weight boxed 75 pounds	$35.00	**Ogbuj**
Bits, per set (four)	.75	**Ogbyd**

Boxed for Export

Net 55 pounds, gross 90 pounds, 41 kilos., 3 cubic feet

THE SILVER MANUFACTURING COMPANY, SALEM, OHIO, U. S. A.

The Celebrated "Star" Hollow Auger

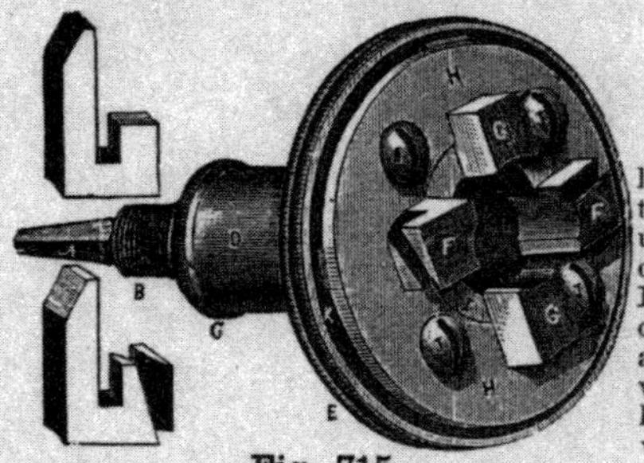

Fig. 715

Fig. 715 represents our new Star Hollow Augur. It is an improvement on the Dole Hollow Augur, which was manufactured by us for many years previous to the invention of the Star Augur. It combines all the valuable qualities of the Dole Augur, as well as some novel and desirable features of its own, and we confidently recommend it as the best hollow augur made. The bits are provided with two cutting edges, arranged at right angles with each other, one cutting the shoulder while the other pares off the surface of the tenon, leaving it a model for mechanical neatness. The adjustable shank shown in above illustration is furnished only with No. 1 Augur, and makes the augur suitable for use in the ordinary brace. This shank also serves to regulate the length of tenon. The form of the bits and blanks is also shown in the engraving.

We have supplied a number of manufacturers of universal wheel machinery with these augurs to go on their machines, consequently they are in use in most of the large wagon factories throughout the country. This is one of the strongest indorsements that could be given of the merits of this tool.

SIZES AND PRICES

No. 1	Augur, with adjustable shank, cutting tenons $\frac{7}{16}$ to 1 inch diameter	$ 7.00	**Ogcad**
No. 1	Augur, with round shank for power use, cutting tenons, $\frac{7}{16}$ to 1 inch diameter	7.00	**Ogcec**
No. 1	Augur, without shank, cutting tenons $\frac{7}{16}$ to 1 inch diameter	6.00	**Ogcov**
No. 2	Augur, cutting tenons ⅝ to 1¼ inches diameter, 4 inches long, used on Fig. 717, No. 2, and Fig. 718 No. 3	13.00	**Ogcus**
No. 2	Augur, cutting tenons ⅝ to 1¼ inches diameter, 6 inches long, used on Fig. 718, No. 3, when arranged to cut tenons 6 inches long	14.00	**Ogcyx**
No. 2	Augur, cutting tenons ⅝ to 1¼ inches diameter, 6 inches long with large shank to suit Fig. 718, No. 4 and No. 4½	15.00	**Ogdak**
No. 3	Augur, cutting tenons ¾ to 1½ inches diameter, 4 inches long, used on Fig. 717, No. 2½, and Fig. 718, No. 3½	15.00	**Ogdes**
No. 3	Augur, cutting tenons ¾ to 1½ inches diameter, 6 inches long, used on Fig. 718, No. 3½, when arranged to cut tenons 6 inches long	16.00	**Ogdot**
No. 4	Augur, cutting tenons 1¼ to 2 inches diameter, 6 inches long	20.00	**Ogdra**

Bits and Blanks for the "Star" Augur

Bits for No. 1 Augur, per pair	$ 1.00	**Ogduy**
Bits for 2, 3 or 4 Augur, per pair	1.50	**Ogian**
Blanks for No. 1 Augur, per pair	.60	**Ogiey**
Blanks for No. 2, 3 or 4 Augur, per pair	.80	**Ogihy**

Bits and Blanks for the "Dole" Augur

Bits for No. 1 Augur, per pair	$ 1.00	**Ogiis**
Bits for No. 2 Augur, each (only one to an augur)	1.00	**Ojcag**
Blanks for No. 1 Augur, per pair	.60	**Ojced**
Blanks for No. 2 Augur, per pair	1.00	**Ojcim**
Files for sharpening the bits	.25	**Ojcob**
Oil stones for finishing same	.15	**Ojcuk**

No. 1 Augur can be adjusted to cut ⅜-inch tenons when especially ordered.

THE SILVER MANUFACTURING COMPANY, SALEM, OHIO, U. S. A.

Dole & Deming's Patent Spoke Tenon Machine

Fig. 717—Nos. 2 and 2½

The accompanying illustration represents our large Hand Tenon Machines, Nos. 2 and 2½. These machines are similar in construction to No. 1, Fig. 716, but intended for larger and heavier work. They are furnished with felloe boring attachment as shown. Round hole bit chuck for Cook's patent machine bits always sent, unless square hole chuck is ordered.

No. 2 is fitted with No. 2 Star Hollow Augur, and will cut tenons any size from ⅝ to 1¼ inches.

No. 2½ is fitted with No. 3 Augur, and will cut tenons any size from ¾ to 1½ inches.

When ordered we supply these machines with No. 1 Star Augur and reducer. The reducer renders the augurs interchangeable on the machines, and gives No. 2 a range of work from ½ to 1¼, and No. 2½, ⅞ to 1½ inches.

Boring Bits to use in connection with felloe boring attachment are not included in price of machines, but will be found listed on another page.

Floor space fo Fig 717, 28x56 inches.

SIZES AND PRICES

No. 2	With felloe boring attachment, cuts tenons ⅝ to 1¼ inches, weight 145 pounds..............................	$32.00	Ojder
No. 2	Without felloe boring attachment, cuts tenons ⅝ to 1¼ inches, weight 125 pounds..............................	25.00	Ojdio
No. 2½	With felloe boring attachment, cuts tenons ¾ to 1½ inches, weight 145 pounds.............................	35.00	Ojdol
No. 2½	Without felloe boring attachment, cuts tenons ¾ to 1½ inches, weight 125 pounds..............................	28.00	Ojdug
Either size, with No. 1 Augur and reducer, extra..............		8.00	Ojdyc

Boxed for Export

Net 145 pounds, gross 200 pounds, 91 kilos, 5½ Cubic feet

15

THE SILVER MANUFACTURING COMPANY, SALEM,, OHIO, U. S. A.

Dole & Deming's Patent Spoke Tenon Machine

Fig. 716—No. 1

This cut represents our No. 1 Spoke Tenon Machine, which is adapted to hand use. It is fitted with our No. 1 Star Hollow Augur, and will cut tenons any size from ½ to 1 inch. The hub is held in a self-centering chuck, which can be revolved to present the spokes to the hollow augur. The spokes are held firmly on the rest, and in line with the augur. Thus all tenons are cut with the shoulders uniform in width and in the same plane. With a slight transformation it can be changed into a boring machine, for boring the felloes for the spokes, giving that accuracy in the work that can be alone attained by machinery.

Our new illustration shows the felloe boring attachment on the machine as shipped. Bit chucks with ½-inch round hole always furnished with the felloe boring attachment unless otherwise ordered. When specially ordered we can furnish chuck with square hole, so the ordinary brace bits can be used in the machine. This size is now furnished complete with legs, as shown, without additional cost.

Boring bits to use in connection with felloe boring attachment are not included in price of machine, but will be found listed on another page.

Floor space for Fig 716, 20x45 inches.

SIZES AND PRICES

No. 1	With felloe boring attachment, weight 90 pounds...	$23.00	Ojcyn
No. 1	Without felloe boring attachment, weight 80 pounds..	18.00	Ojdaz

Boxed for Export

Net 90 pounds, gross 125 pounds, 57 kilos, 4 cubic feet

14

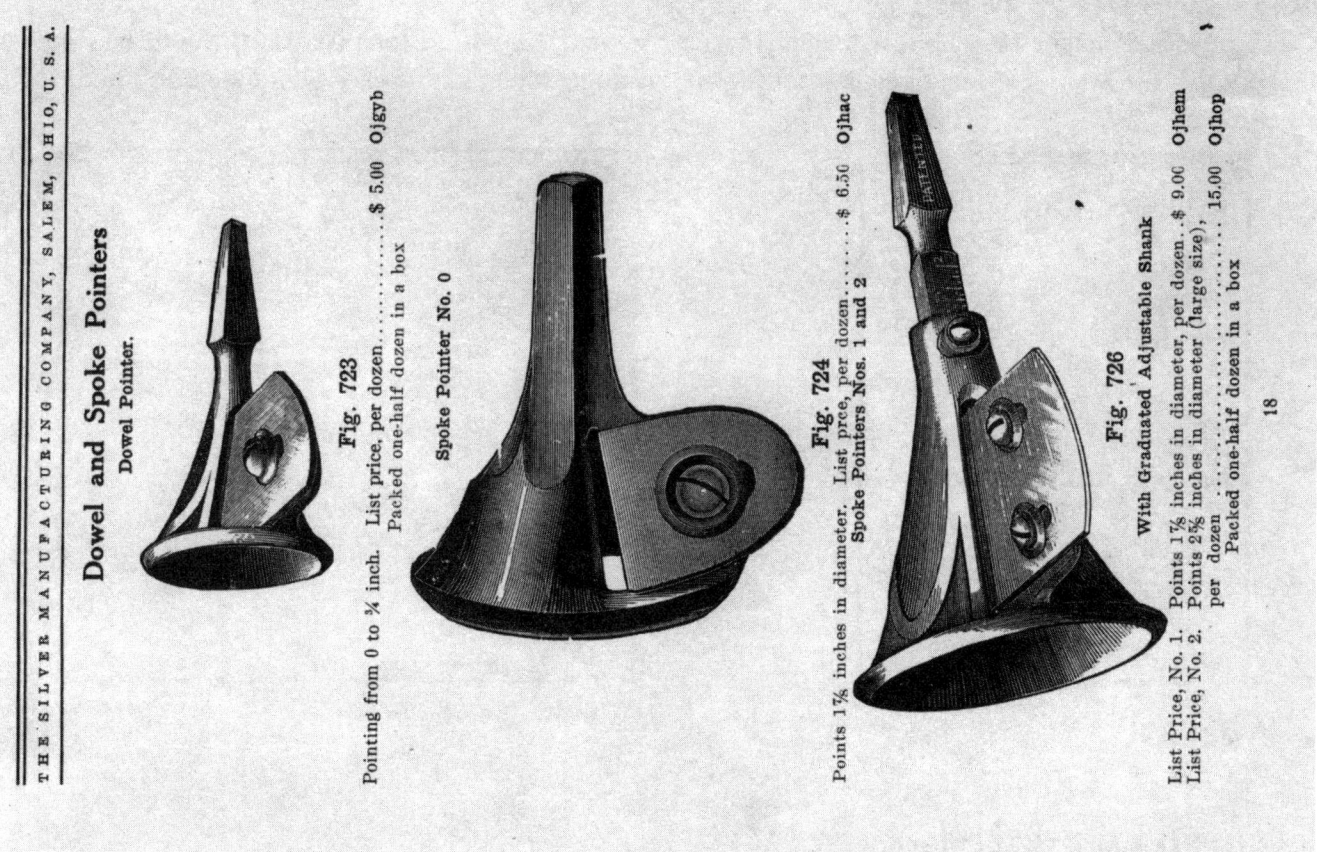

Dole & Deming's Patent Spoke Tenon Machine

For Hand or Power, Fitted with Star Hollow Auger

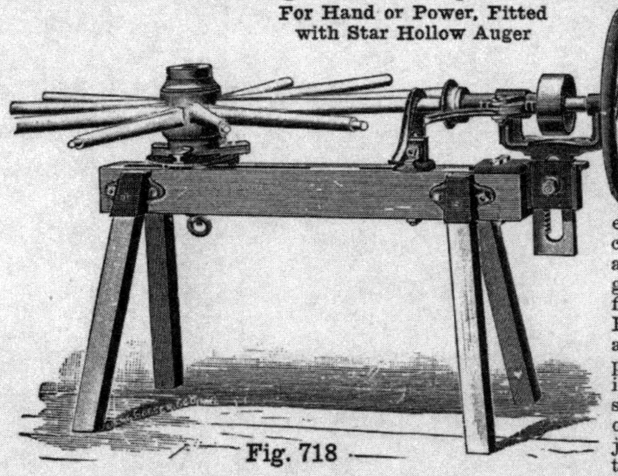

Fig. 718

This machine has been long and favorably known to the carriage tool trade and its sale increases each year. The accuracy of its work adapts it to high grade wheels. It is fitted with the Star Hollow Auger and is arranged for hand or power, which adapts it for use in every shop, whether a large or small number of jobs are manufactured.

A fly wheel and handle has lately been substituted for hand use instead of crank, which is regarded a marked improvement. When power is applied the wheel should be removed.

Another improvement is a machined cast iron way for head or main casting to move in, instead of the old-fashioned wooden way.

Felloe boring attachments with round hole bit chuck furnished with all machines unless otherwise ordered. See Fig. 717 for felloe boring attachment.

For price of boring bits see another page, these are extra.

Speed for power about 1,200 revolutions per minute.

Floor space for Fig. 718, 23x58 inches.

SIZES AND PRICES

No. 3	With felloe boring attachment and No. 1 and No. 2 Augurs, cutting tenons $\frac{7}{16}$ to 1¼ inches diameter, 4 inches long, weight 175 pounds	$45.00	Ojfab
No. 3½	With felloe boring attachment and No 1 and No. 3 Augurs, cutting tenons $\frac{7}{16}$ to 1½ inches diameter, 4 inches long, weight 175 pounds	50.00	Ojfel
No. 4	With felloe boring attachment and No. 2 and No. 4 Augers, cutting tenons ⅝ to 2 inches diameter, 6 inches long, weight 230 pounds	60.00	Ojfid
No. 4½	With felloe boring attachment and No. 1, No. 2 and No. 4 Augurs, cutting tenons $\frac{7}{16}$ to 2 inches diameter, 4 inches long from $\frac{7}{16}$ to ⅝ inches diameter and 6 inches long from ⅝ to 2 inches diameter, weight 230 pounds	68.00	Ojfof
	Nos. 3 and 3½ furnished without No. 1 Auger and reducer at reduction of	8.00	Ojfux
	Any of the above sizes furnished without felloe boring attachment at reduction of	7.00	Ojfym
	Nos. 3 and 3½ arranged to cut tenons 6 inches long, additional	5.00	Ojgal
	Suitable countershaft, with tight and loose pulleys, for these machines	10.00	Ojgen

Boxed for Export

No. 3 or 3½. Net 175 pounds, gross 250 pounds, 113 kilos., 6⅛ cubic feet
No. 4 or 4½. Net 230 pounds, gross 345 pounds, 156 kilos., 9½ cubic feet

Dowel and Spoke Pointers

Dowel Pointer.

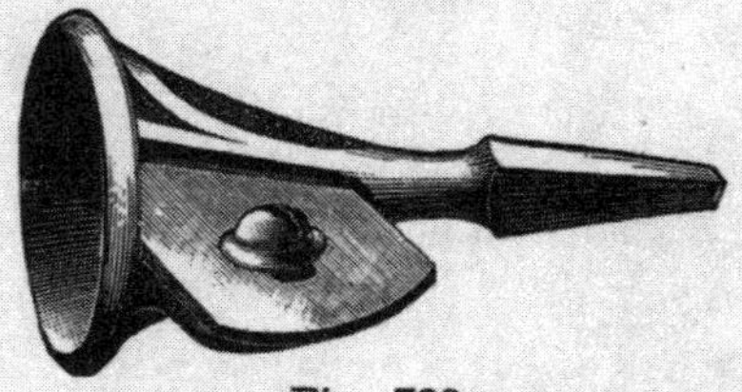

Fig. 723

Pointing from 0 to ¾ inch. List price, per dozen.............$ 5.00 Ojgyb
Packed one-half dozen in a box

Spoke Pointer No. 0

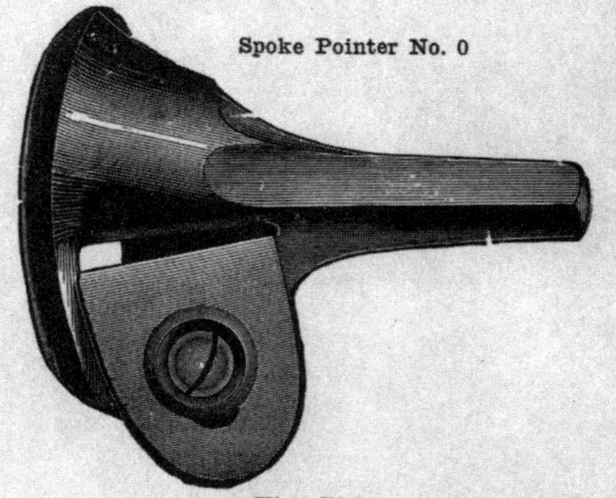

Fig. 724

Points 1⅞ inches in diameter. List prce, per dozen........$ 6.50 Ojhac

Spoke Pointers Nos. 1 and 2

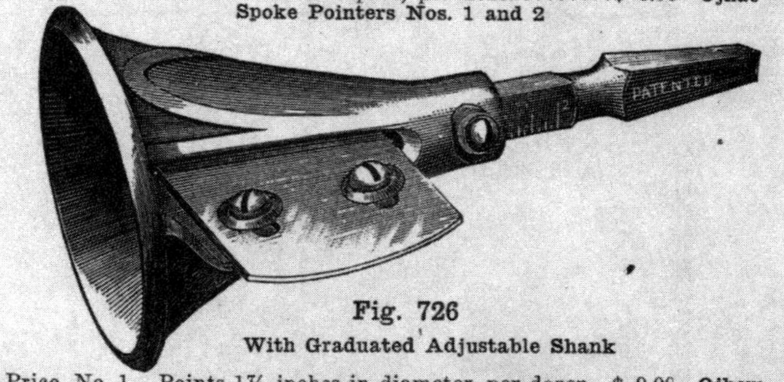

Fig. 726

With Graduated Adjustable Shank

List Price, No. 1. Points 1⅞ inches in diameter, per dozen..$ 9.00 Ojhem
List Price, No. 2. Points 2⅝ inches in diameter (large size), per dozen .... 15.00 Ojhop
Packed one-half dozen in a box

SMITH, J. HESTON, Pineville, PA, later Lambertville, NJ

Inventor and maker of a hollow auger (Fig.1), patented July 17, 1866. By 1880 Smith had moved to Lambertville, NJ, where he continued to offer the hollow auger along with a variety of other tools and machines (Fig.2).

Fig.1

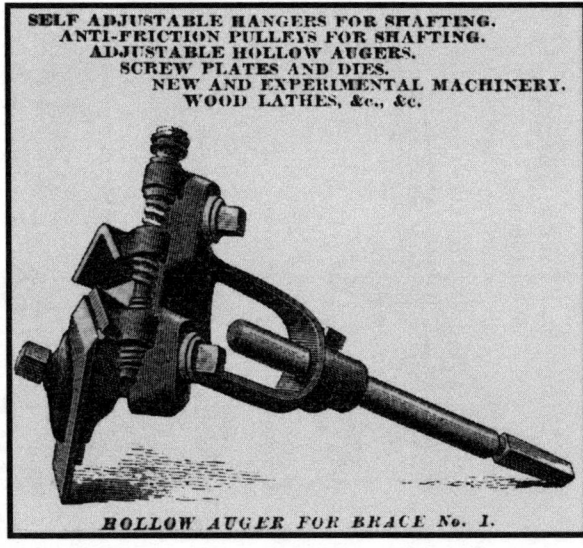

Fig.2

STANDARD AXLE CO., Wheeling, WV

A large maker of axles for the coach, carriage and buggy industry, the firm was producing 25,000 to 30,000 sets of axles yearly in the 1890s.

Production at that rate required highly productive machinery, and the firm appears to have designed and built some of its own. These machines included an axle box machine (Fig.1) for hollow milling both outside diameters of axle boxes, patented December 11, 1894; a machine for reaming the inside of axle boxes (Fig.2), patented July 6, 1897, capable of machining three axle boxes at a time; and an axle lathe (Fig.3), patented December 13, 1898, capable of machining three axles at a time. All three patents were issued to Ralph R. Spears.

It is noteworthy that the latter two machines are the earliest noted which were designed for simultaneously machining multiple workpieces for carriage and wagon makers. *(Illustrations continued on next page)*

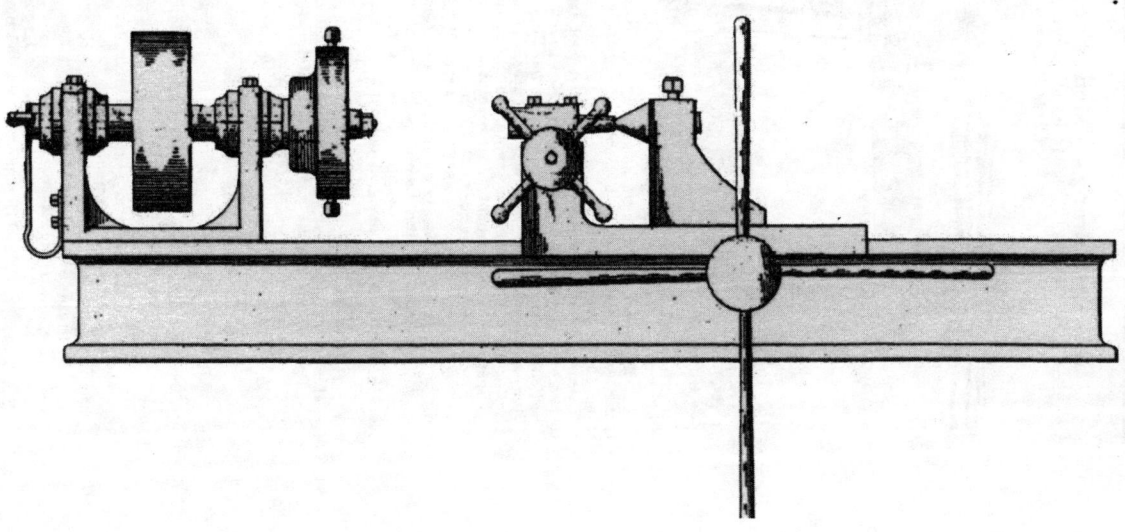

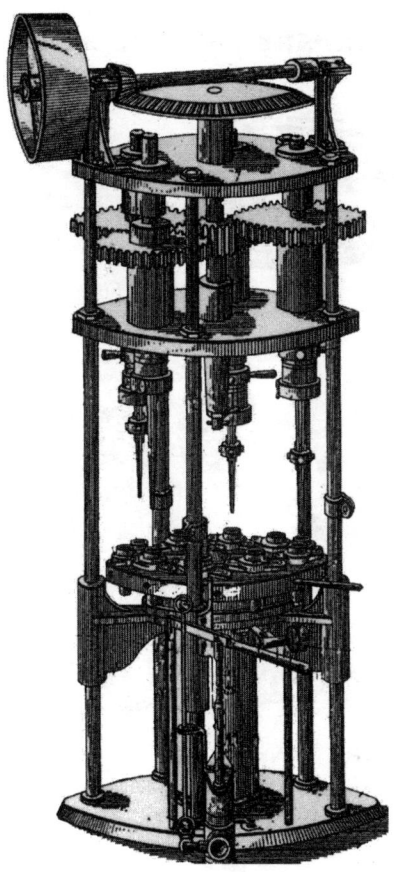

Fig.2

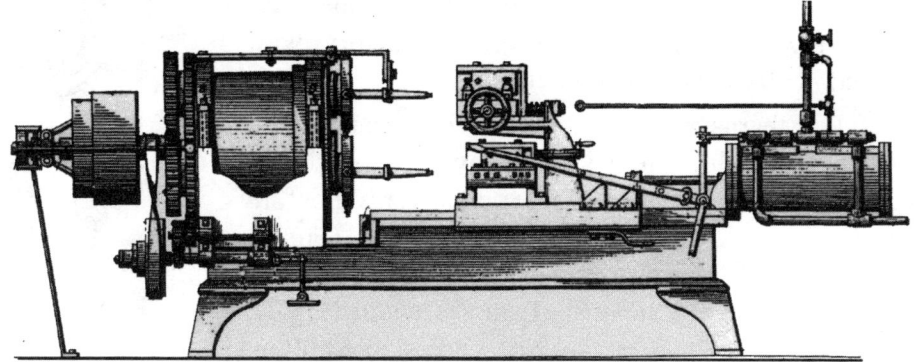

Fig.3

STANDISH, A., Columbus, OH

Maker, in 1881, of a foot-powered hammer (right) "specially adapted to weld small pieces that it is difficult to weld by hand, such as all descriptions of carriage irons."

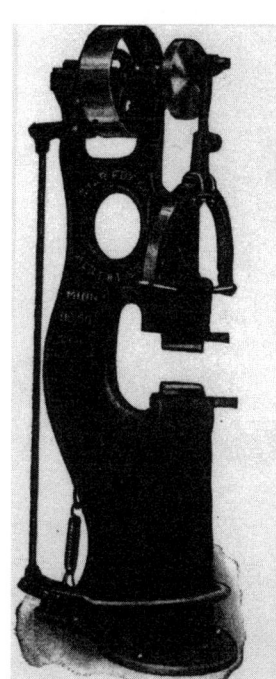

THE STANDISH FOOT POWER HAMMER.

STAR FOUNDRY CO., Albert Lea, MN

Maker, in 1917, of the STAR No. 50 power hammer as shown in the ad at left.

STEARNS & CO., E.C., Syracuse, NY

A partnership of Edward C. Stearns, son of George N. Stearns, and Mrs. Avis (Stearns) Mead, formed in 1877 to make a variety of small tools. In 1889, the firm was incorporated with Stearns as president and E.P. Hasbrouck as treasurer. Robert E. Dudley, Jr. was president when the factory was burned in 1945 and never rebuilt.

E.C. Stearns made a line of carriage and wagon makers' tools including spoke shaves patented December 13, 1870; expansion fore augers for use before a hollow auger, patented September 5, 1876, (Fig.1); Stearns' No. 1 hollow augers, patented November 23, 1880, (Fig.2); No. 2 Stearns' expansive augers (Fig.3), patented March 5, 1878; and No. 3 adjustable hollow augers patented May 7, 1878, (Fig.4); all patented by George N. Stearns. No. 5 (Fig.5) and No. 6 (Fig.6) hollow augers, both made to cut only one size, were offered by 1883.

The firm also made adjustable spoke pointers with graduated shanks, patented October 7, 1879, (Fig.7) by E.C. Stearns, offered in two sizes; and BONNEY'S improved hollow auger (Fig.8), patented August 2, 1870, by Charles S. Bonney and improved by G.N. Stearn's November 23, 1880, patent.

WOOD'S adjustable hollow aguer (Fig.9), patented by A.A. Wood August 10, 1875, and G.N. Stearns May 7, 1878, was offered as late as 1904.

In an 1883 advertisement (Fig.10) the firm offered No. 0 hollow augers patented March 16, 1880, by E.C. Stearns; band setters patented February 10, 1880, by G.N. Stearns; screw clamps; and taper augers patented June 12, 1877, by G.N. Stearns.

Later production included improved spoke pointers (Fig.11); Stearns new adjustable hollow augers No. 33 (Fig.12) and No. 44 (Fig.13), both patented June 5, 1900; Sargent's No. 50 adjustable (Fig.14); and the No. 55 universal hollow auger (Fig.15).

STEARN'S PATENT EXPANSION FORE AUGER.

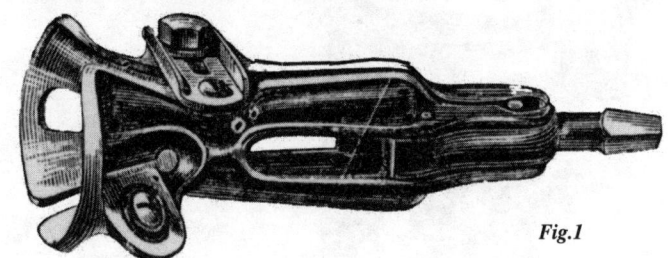

Fig.1

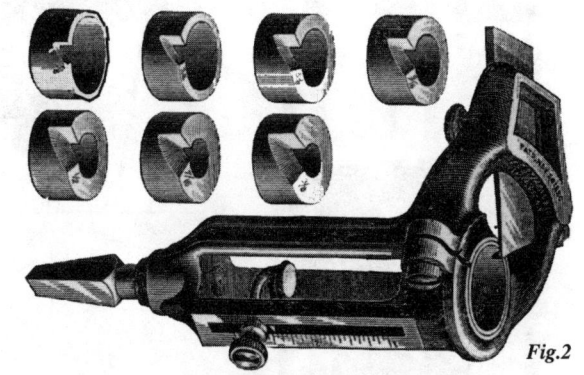

STEARNS' No. 1

Fig.2

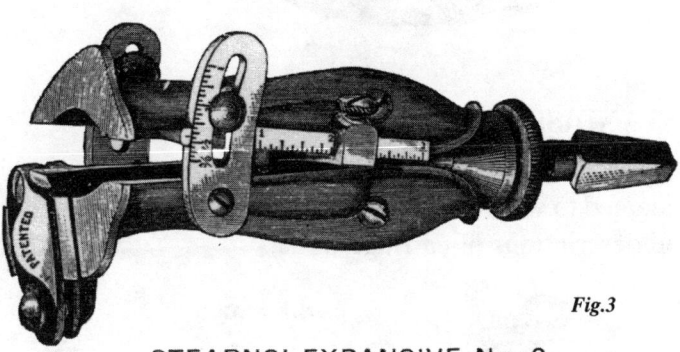

STEARNS' EXPANSIVE No. 2

Fig.3

STEARNS' ADJUSTABLE, No. 3

Fig.4

Fig.5

No. 5, with Adjustable Shank.

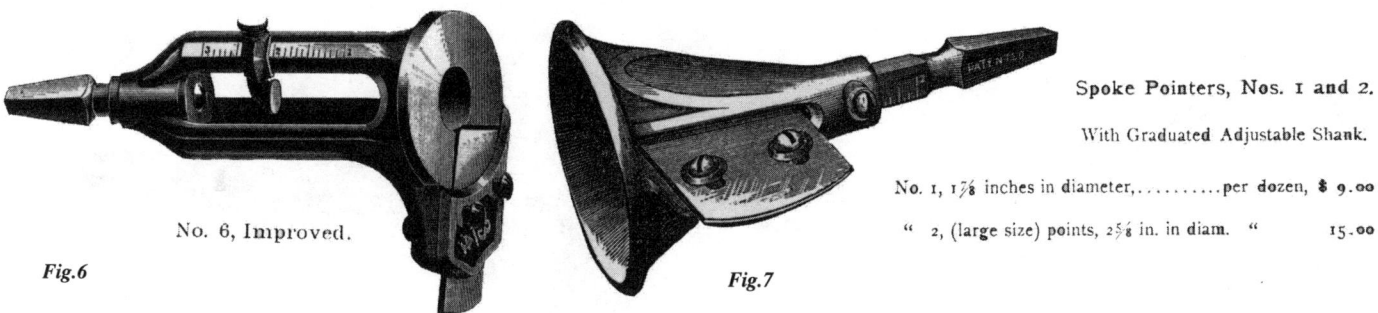

No. 6, Improved.

Fig.6

Fig.7

Spoke Pointers, Nos. 1 and 2.

With Graduated Adjustable Shank.

No. 1, 1⅞ inches in diameter,.........per dozen, **$ 9.00**

" 2, (large size) points, 2⅝ in. in diam. " 15.00

Fig.8

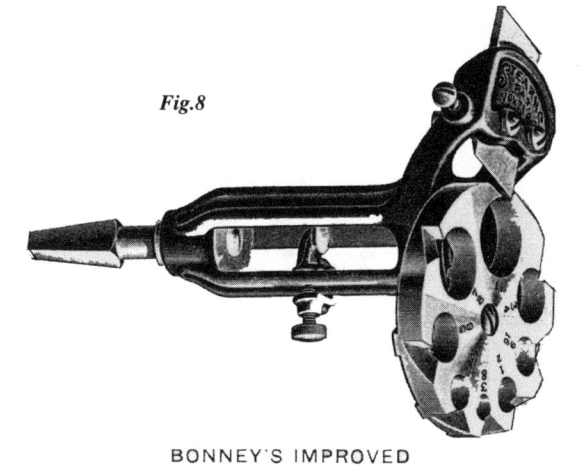

BONNEY'S IMPROVED

⅜ to 1 inch...each, $4.00

Wood's Adjustable

Cuts from ¼ to 1½ in.

Each...................$4.00
Extra cutters.... Each, .28

Fig.9

E. C. STEARNS & CO.,
MANUFACTURERS OF NEW TOOLS FOR CARRIAGE BUILDERS,
SYRACUSE, N. Y., U. S. A.

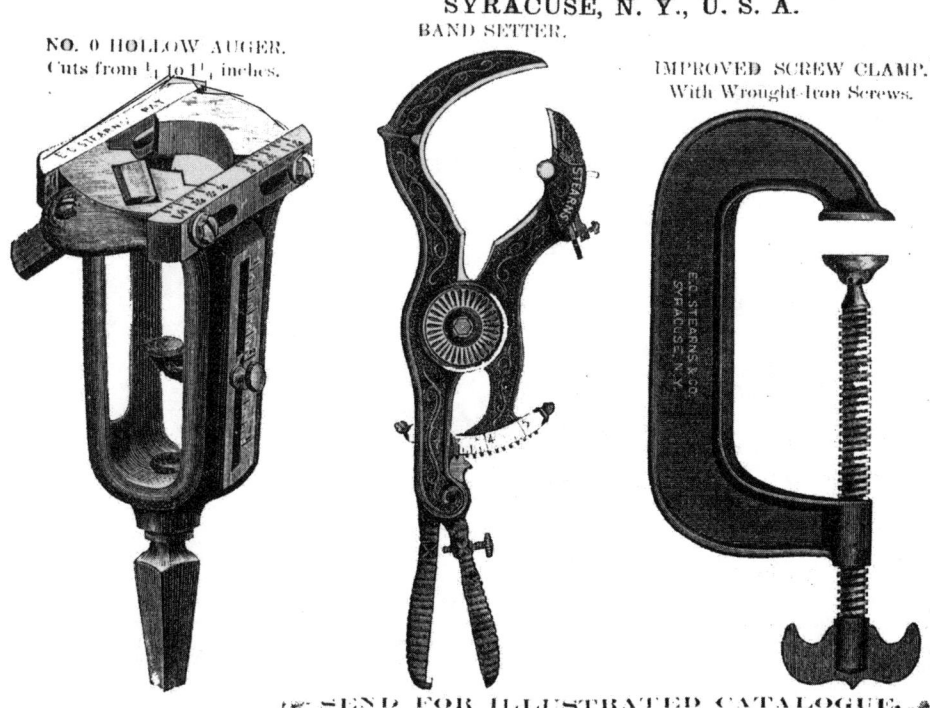

NO. 0 HOLLOW AUGER.
Cuts from ¼ to 1¼ inches.

BAND SETTER.

IMPROVED SCREW CLAMP.
With Wrought-Iron Screws.

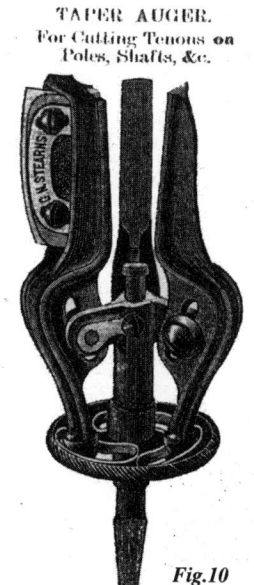

TAPER AUGER.
For Cutting Tenons on
Poles, Shafts, &c.

Fig.10

☛ SEND FOR ILLUSTRATED CATALOGUE. ☚

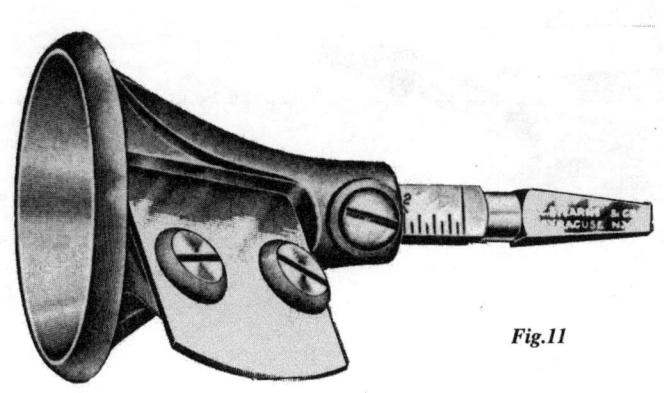

Fig.11

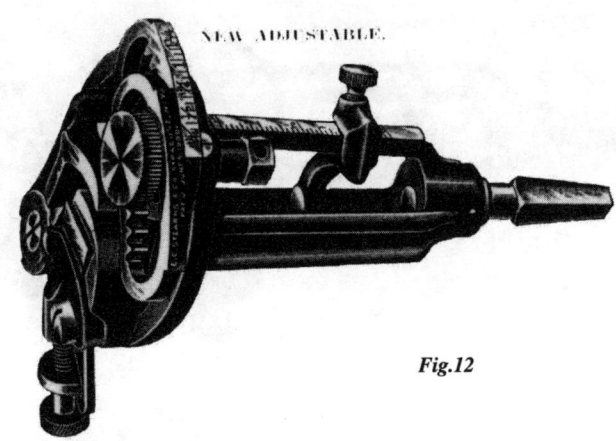

Fig.12

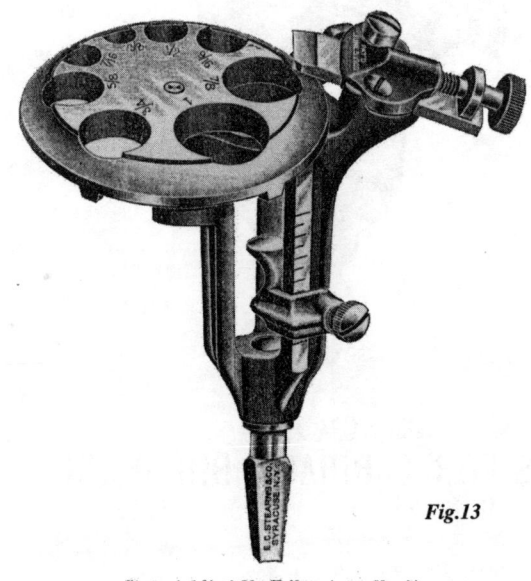

Fig.13

Stearns' Adjustable Hollow Auger No. 44.

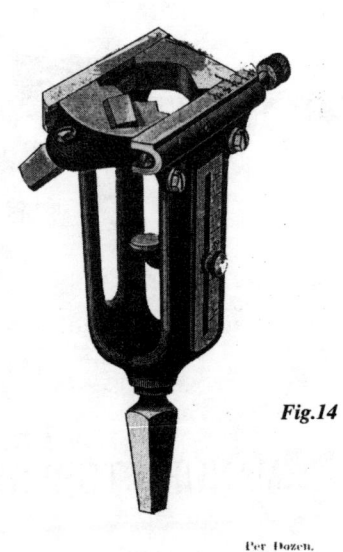

Fig.14

Per Dozen.

No. 50—Sargent's Adjustable,
Cuts ¼ to 1½ in., $60.00

UNIVERSAL HOLLOW AUGER

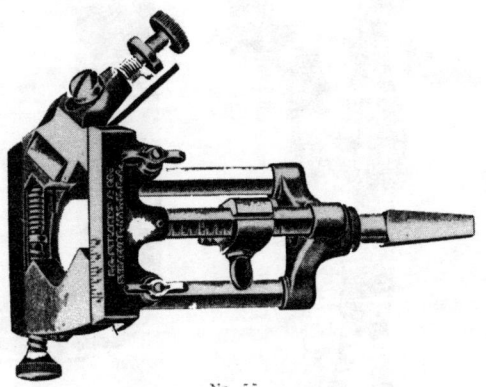

Fig.15

No. 55.

This new auger has our patented adjustment which allows
the knife to be moved forward and backward entirely without the use of tools by simply turning the knurled head adjusting screw.

STEARNS, G.N., Syracuse, NY, later
STEARNS & CO., G.N., Syracuse, NY

Founded by George N. Stearns in 1853 to make a hand powered hub boring and mortising machine (Fig.1). As shown below (Fig.2), the hub index mechanism could be removed in order to use the machine for mortising flat work. An improved version (Fig.3), was patented March 11, 1856.

The firm of G.N. Stearns & Co. was first listed in city directories in 1873, as a maker of machinists' tools, augers, and hollow augers; no mention was made of mortising machines. The listing continued until 1877 when the business appears to have been taken over by his son E.C. Stearns.

Products included extension hollow augers (Fig.4), patented September 8, 1863, by Stearns; BONNEY'S hollow augers, patented August 2, 1870, by Charles S. Bonney (Fig.5); double edge spokeshaves, patented December 13, 1870, by Stearns; and taper augers, patented June 12, 1877, by Stearns (Fig.6).

See E.C. STEARNS & CO. entry for more G.N. Stearns designs.

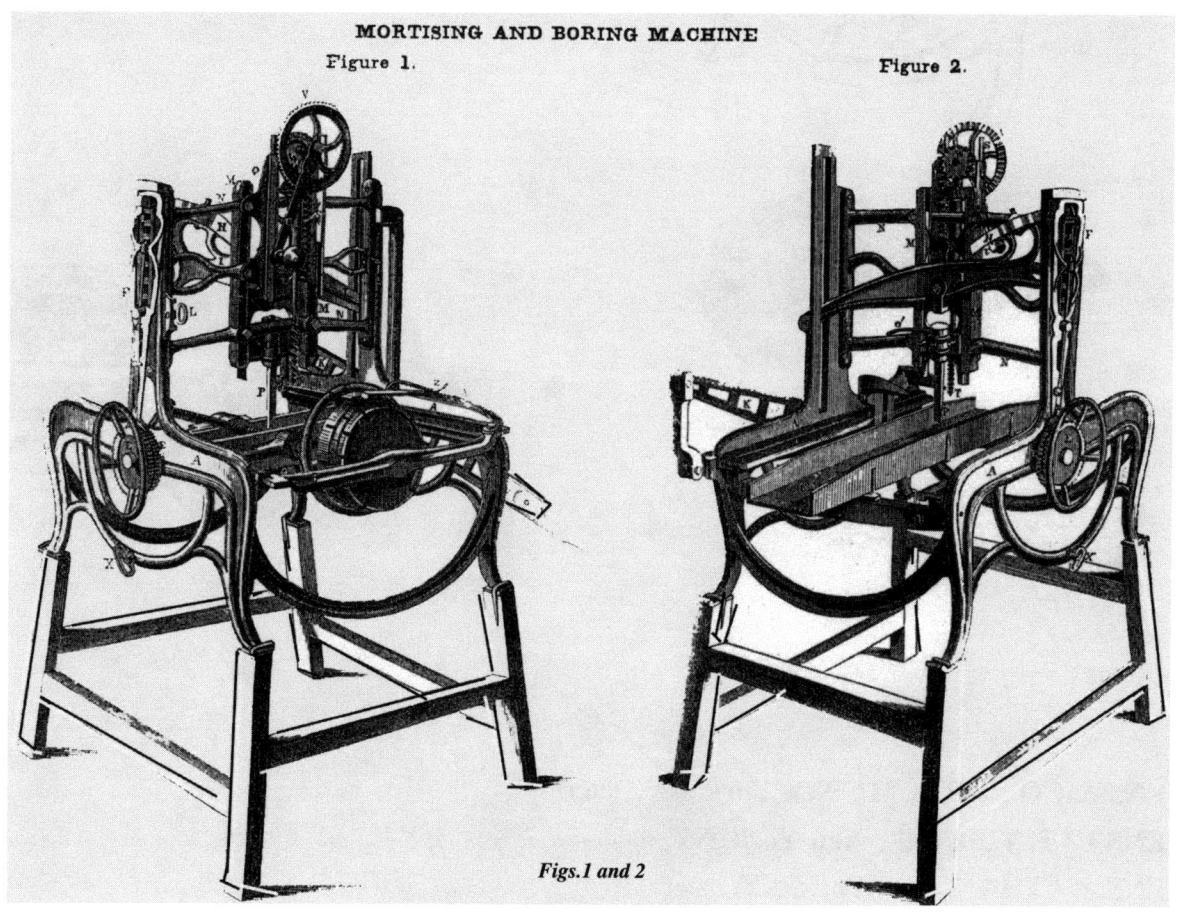

MORTISING AND BORING MACHINE

Figure 1.　　　　Figure 2.

Figs.1 and 2

171

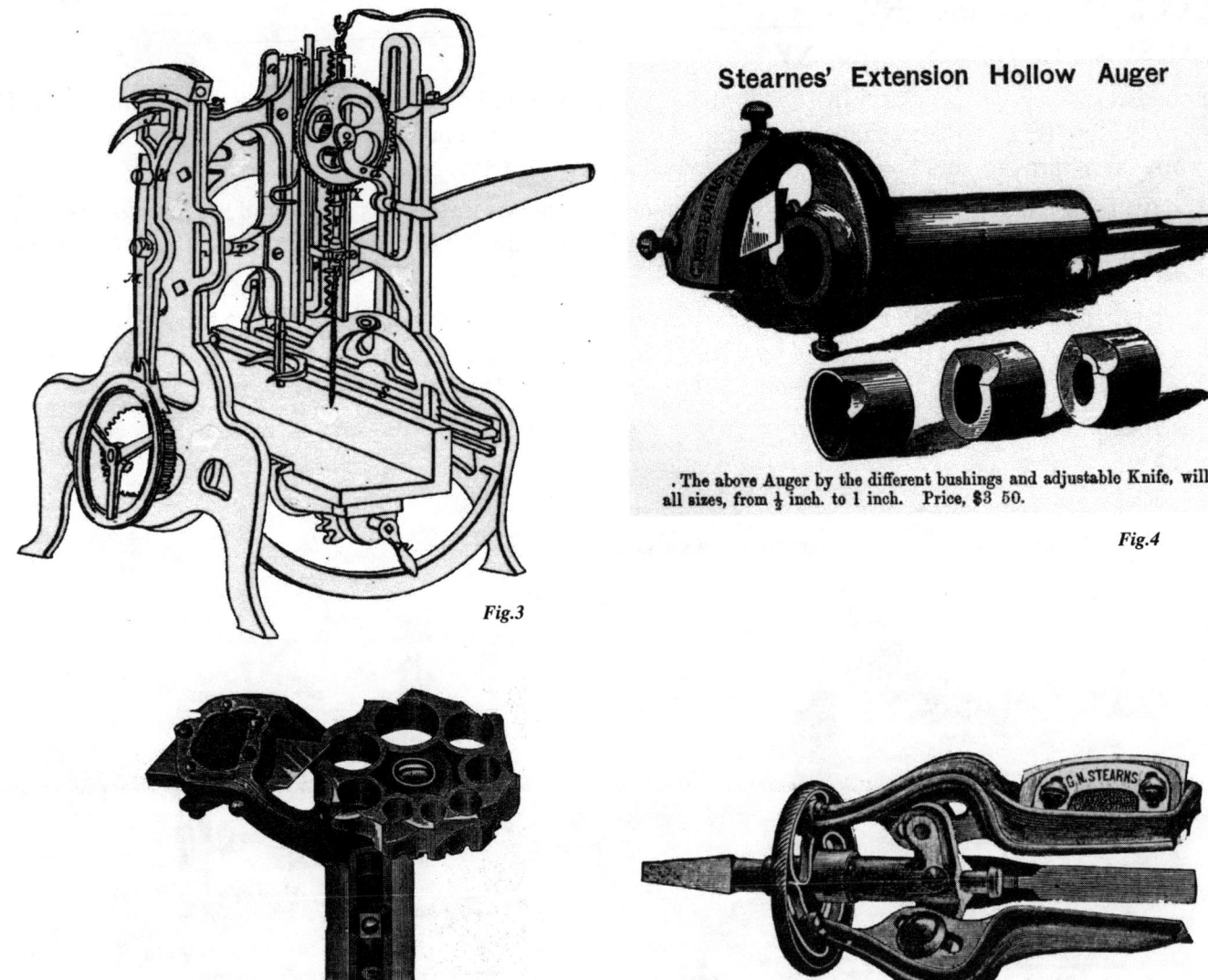

Fig.3

Stearnes' Extension Hollow Auger

. The above Auger by the different bushings and adjustable Knife, will cut all sizes, from ½ inch. to 1 inch.   Price, $3 50.

Fig.4

Fig.5

Fig.6

STEPHENS & CO., A.P. & M., New York, NY, later
STEPHENS PAT. VISE CO., New York, NY, later
STEPHENS, NATHAN, New York, NY, later
STEPHENS, MELVIN, New York, NY

A partnership of Anson P. Stephens and Melvin Stephens formed about 1869 to make quick-acting vises patented April 5, 1864, October 26, 1869, and July 19, 1870, by Anson P. Stevens. By 1878, the firm had become the Stephens Pat. Vise Co., which became Nathan Stephens by 1884, Melvin Stephens by 1886, and sold out to Tower & Lyon in 1888.

The firms specialized in smaller vises for jewelers but also made a line of larger vises. The larger sizes included the coach or wagon makers' vise offered in 1883 and shown on next page.

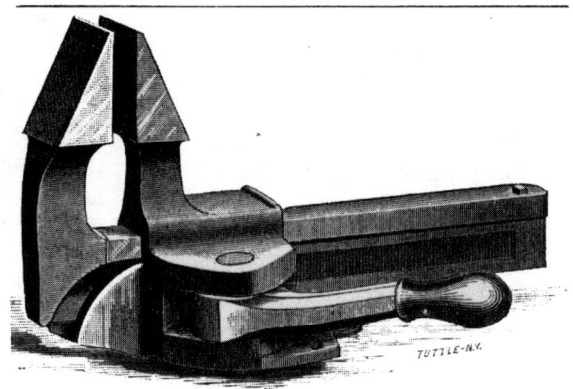

STEPTOE, JOHN, Cincinnati, OH, later

STEPTOE & McFARLAN, Cincinnati, OH, later

STEPTOE & CO., JOHN, Cincinnati, OH

Founded in 1843 by John Steptoe (1804-1888) to make wood working machinery and, later, machine tools. In 1860 Steptoe formed a partnership with Thomas McFarlan which continued business until failing in 1872. Steptoe then reorganized as John Steptoe & Co., which he operated until his death in 1888.

Machinery for wagon and carriage makers included a foot power mortiser made from 1843 to 1868 or later (Fig.1) and a hub lathe, patented June 7, 1881, by James Mills (Fig.2).

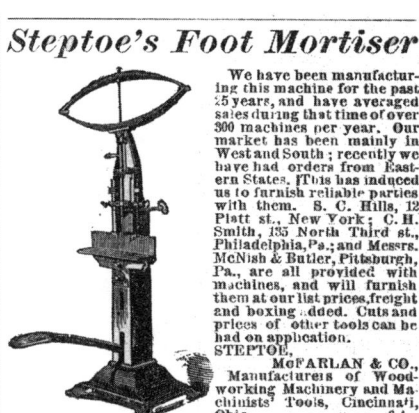

Steptoe's Foot Mortiser

We have been manufacturing this machine for the past 25 years, and have averaged sales during that time of over 300 machines per year. Our market has been mainly in West and South; recently we have had orders from Eastern States. This has induced us to furnish reliable parties with them. S. C. Hills, 12 Platt st., New York; C.H. Smith, 135 North Third st., Philadelphia, Pa.; and Messrs. McNish & Butler, Pittsburgh, Pa., are all provided with machines, and will furnish them at our list prices, freight and boxing added. Cuts and prices of other tools can be had on application. STEPTOE, McFARLAN & CO., Manufacturers of Woodworking Machinery and Machinists' Tools, Cincinnati, Ohio. 64

Fig.1

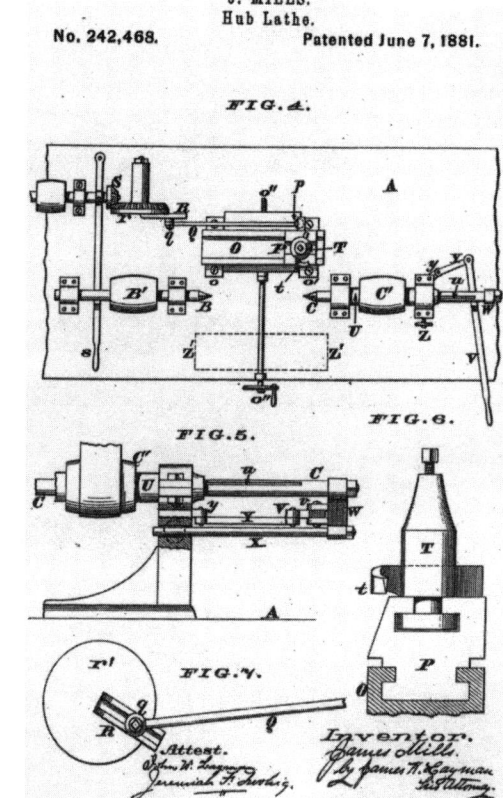

Fig.2

STONE & HERBERT, Amesbury, MA

A partnership of Charles E. Stone and Alfred Herbert formed in 1868 to make a tool for fitting hub-bands (right), jointly patented July 14, 1868. Adjustable to a large range of diameters, the tool was fitted with a marking and scribing cutter C and a chisel D. "In operation the wheel is swung and revolved while the workman holds the tool on the hub."

20   CHAS. A. STRELINGER & CO.

CARRIAGE MAKERS' TOOLS.

No. 1. **No. 2.**

No. 1. Carriage Makers' Smooth Plane, Double Iron, to 1⅝ inch.	Each, $1 10
No. 2. " " " " Circle Face, Double Iron, to 1⅝ inch,	" 1 25

No. 3. **No. 5.**

No. 3. Carriage Makers' Rabbet Plane, 1 inch,	Each, $1 00
No. 4. " " " " Circle Face, 1 inch,	" 1 10
No. 5. " " T " "	" 1 20
No. 6. " " T " " Circle Face,	" 1 35

No. 7.

No. 7. Carriage Makers' Beading Tool,	Each, $1 75

No. 9.

No. 8. Carriage Makers' Router, Single Cutter,	Each, $1 00
No. 9. " " " Double Cutter,	" 1 20

No. 10.

No. 10. Carriage Makers' Router, Double Cutter, with Guard,	Each, $1 40
No. 11. " " Panel Router,	" 5 00
No. 12. " " Boxing Tool,	" 1 60

All Tools sold by us are *fully warranted* in every particular, and we will gladly replace any found defective.

STRELINGER & CO., CHAS. A., Detroit, MI

A large dealer in machinery and tools of all types. A selection of carriage makers' tools, including planes, beading tools, routers, drawing knives, and chisels were offered in its 1886 catalog as shown at left and on next page.

SOCKET FIRMER CHISELS AND GOUGES.

COACH MAKER AND FRAMING CHISELS.

We wish again to call attention to the *Beveled Edge Chisels.* They are fast gaining favor for their lightness, strength, and convenience of handling.

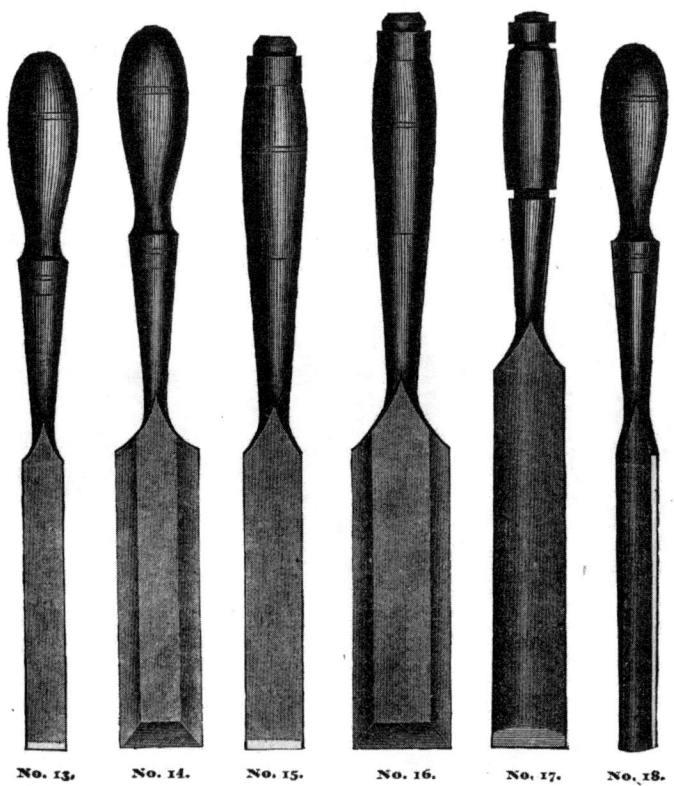

No. 13.   No. 14.   No. 15.   No. 16.   No. 17.   No. 18.

PATENT ADJUSTABLE HANDLE DRAWING KNIVES.

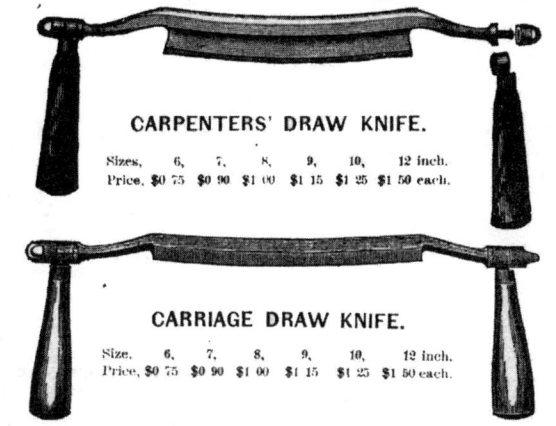

CARPENTERS' DRAW KNIFE.

Sizes.	6,	7,	8,	9,	10,	12 inch.
Price.	$0 75	$0 90	$1 00	$1 15	$1 25	$1 50 each.

CARRIAGE DRAW KNIFE.

Size.	6,	7,	8,	9,	10,	12 inch.
Price,	$0 75	$0 90	$1 00	$1 15	$1 25	$1 50 each.

COACH DRAW KNIFE. (Same as Carpenters', but heavier).

Size,	6,	7,	8,	9,	10,	12 inch.
Price,	$0 80	$0 95	$1 05	$1 20	$1 30	$1 55 each.

SWAN CO., JAMES, Seymour, CT

Founded by James Swan (1831-1908) in 1877 when he bought the DOUGLASS MFG. CO. where he had been superintendent. Swan reorganized as the James Swan Co. where he served as president until 1904 and treasurer from 1904 until his death in 1908. He was succeeded as president by Benjamin A. Hawley, a vice president of Russell & Erwin Mfg. Co., which had financed Swan's purchase of the Douglass Mfg. Co. Swan's son, William B. Swan, was serving as president when he died in 1932.

Products offered to wagon and carriage makers included spoke trimmers (Fig.1); AMES improved hollow augers (Fig.2) originally made by Oliver Ames & Son, predecessor to the Douglass Mfg. Co.; and improved universal hollow augers (Fig.3), patented August 30, 1870, by Austin F. Cushman, also previously made by the Douglass Mfg. Co.

An improved version of the universal hollow auger, fitted with an adjustable depth stop, patented May 29, 1894, by James Swan (Fig.4) was offered as late as 1915.

IMPROVED SPOKE TRIMMER

Fig.1

THIS Tool is required to trim the ends of carriage spokes, chair rounds, &c., before using the Hollow Auger.

AMES' IMPROVED HOLLOW AUGER

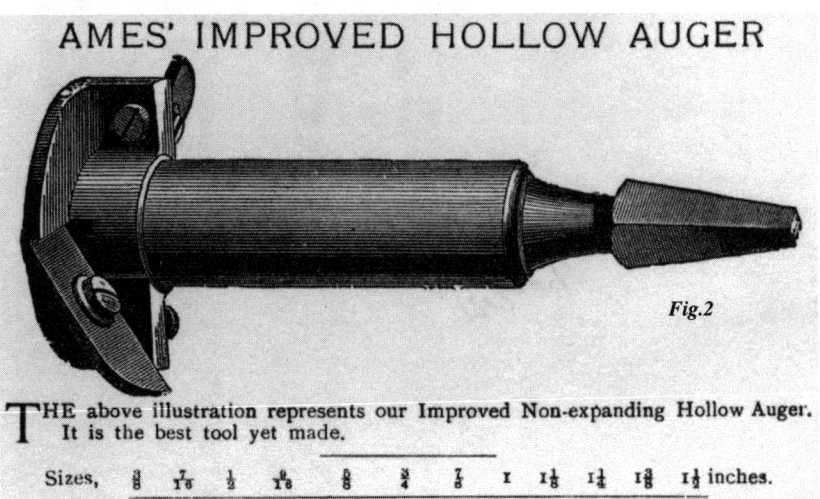

Fig.2

THE above illustration represents our Improved Non-expanding Hollow Auger. It is the best tool yet made.

Sizes, $\frac{3}{8}$ $\frac{7}{16}$ $\frac{1}{2}$ $\frac{9}{16}$ $\frac{5}{8}$ $\frac{3}{4}$ $\frac{7}{8}$ 1 $1\frac{1}{8}$ $1\frac{1}{4}$ $1\frac{3}{8}$ $1\frac{1}{2}$ inches.

IMPROVED UNIVERSAL HOLLOW AUGER

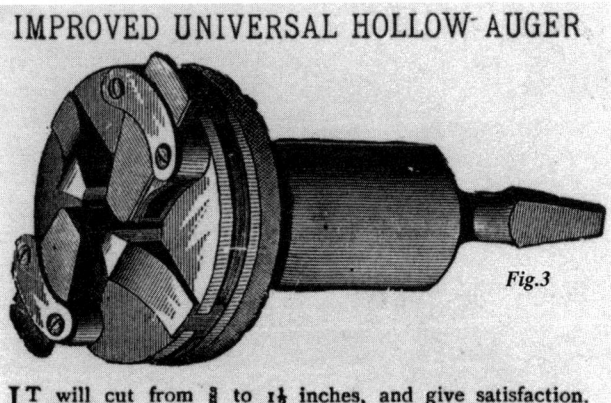

Fig.3

IT will cut from $\frac{3}{8}$ to $1\frac{1}{2}$ inches, and give satisfaction. Any part can be replaced if broken, as it is all made to a gauge.

Fig.4

Swan Universal Improved No. 6001

Has a depth gauge to regulate length of tenon. The face is graduated so it can be readily adjusted to any required size.
Cuts from $\frac{3}{8}$ to $1\frac{1}{2}$ inches, each.......................... $4.50
Machine shanks for same, each.... $ .50 Extra cutters, set... .50

SWINGLE, A., Boston, MA

Inventor and maker of a hub mortising machine patented July 11, 1848, and introduced in 1849. In use, the hub was mounted on a revolving fixture that was located radially by an index at the left end. Boring and mortising tools were fed into the hub as it was stepped across laterally, powered by a hand wheel as shown.

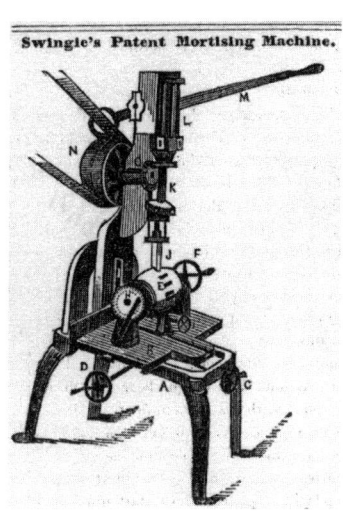

THOMPSON, HIRAM, Worcester, MA

Maker of an improved Blanchard-type spoke lathe, patented March 1, 1870, by Thompson and Charles B. Conant. In operation, a pattern piece was slowly rotated, controlling the path of a rotating cutter head, which then generated the same form on the workpiece. Conant had also patented a more complex spoke lathe on September 29, 1863, but it does not appear to have been made by this firm.

The firm was active as late as 1885, producing a variety of machinery.

MORTISING AND BORING MACHINE.

TRAVIS, N.C., Canastota, NY

Inventor and maker of a hub mortising and boring machine, introduced in 1853. The machine was designed to give a reciprocating motion to the mortising tools, and a rotary motion to the boring tool by the same tool stock. The hub was located radially by an index.

UHLER & BENTON, New York, NY

Maker, in 1883, of the LEWIS axle machine, patented September 21, 1880. The device was designed to "cut back the shoulder, cut the new thread and cut off the end of axle."

UNION FOUNDRY & MACHINE WORKS, Mansfield, OH

A partnership of James A. Niman and his brother John B. Niman. In 1875, the brothers introduced an improved skein setting machine, patented August 18, 1874, by W.K. Stevens, superintendent of the works.

The machine was designed to "turn an axle to a pattern so as to make a perfect fit. At the same time the proper pitch is given to the wheels, all four of which are placed in a plumb spoke. The apparatus also gives any gather required."

In use, the skein to be fitted, or a pattern piece, was located at B and a tracer arm A was rotated inside the pattern. The axle C was clamped in place and a rotating cutter bar, guided by the tracer arm, cut the ends. The firm claimed that skeins for 65 wagons could be fit in ten hours.

By 1897, the machine, slightly improved, was a product of the DEFIANCE MACHINE WORKS.

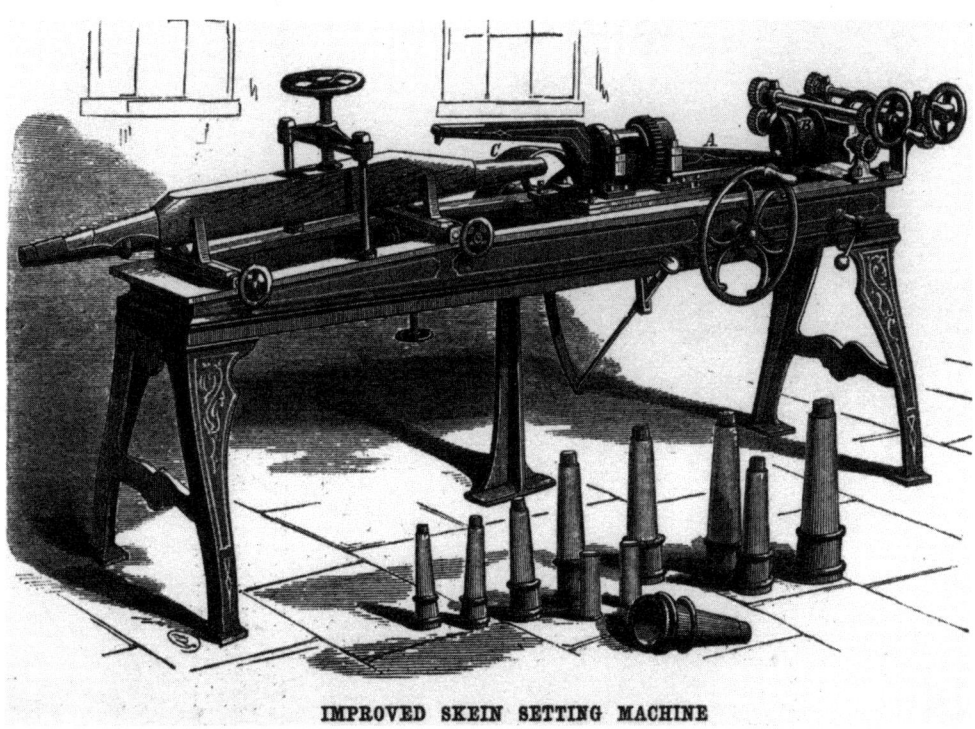

IMPROVED SKEIN SETTING MACHINE

UPDEGRAFF, EDWARD J., York, PA

Inventor and maker of a wood bending machine, patented April 8, 1856. Although claimed fit for bending ship timbers, the machine was used to bend fellies for wagon wheels.

In use, the workpiece was clamped at one end of a semi- circular form, and the form rotated 180 degrees by a crank where the other end was clamped. The workpieces were probably heated, steamed, or both, before bending.

Updegraff claimed that one man and a boy could bend ten sets of fellies per hour. Each set was afterwards divided into eight pieces so production was 80 sections of fellies per hour, or 800 per ten-hour day. The machine sold for $150.

(Illustration on next page)

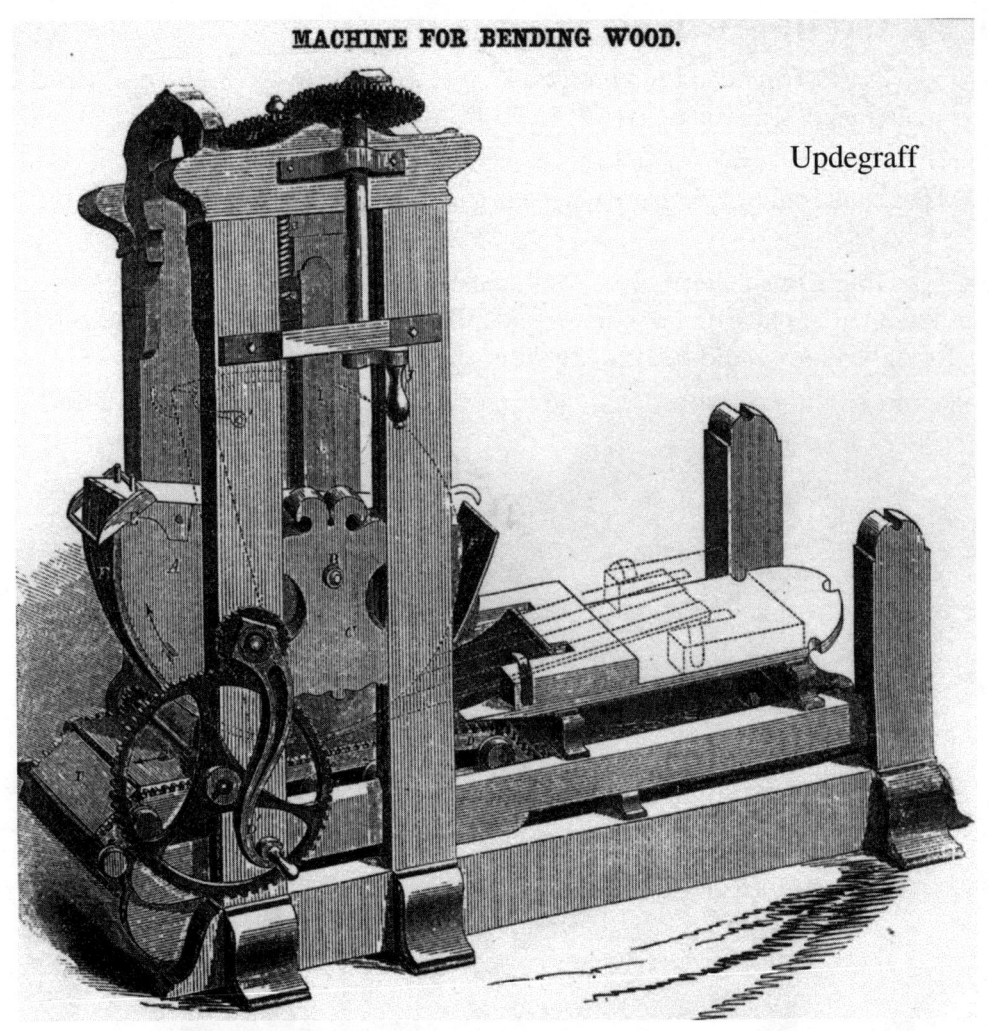

MACHINE FOR BENDING WOOD.

Updegraff

WALKER, RICHARD, Batavia, NY

Inventor and maker of a spoke gauge, patented December 26, 1865. As shown at right, the gauge was mounted with two conical nuts centering it in the bore of the hub. A scriber was set to mark the desired length of the spoke and moved in or out to set the desired dish.

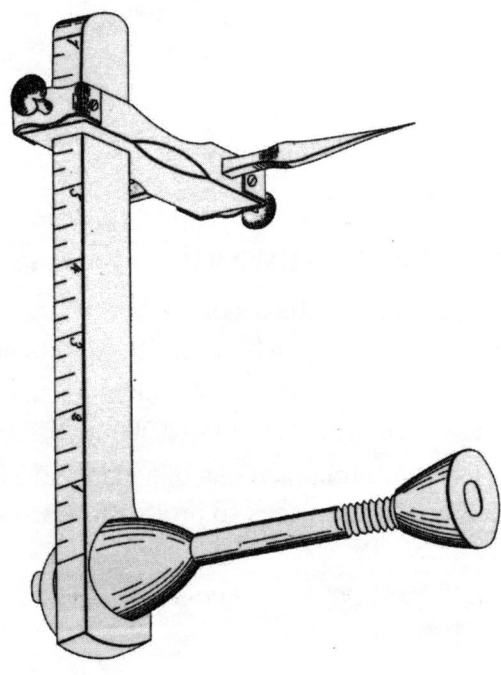

WALKER TIRE HEATER CO., W.H.,
Somerset, OH

Maker, in 1916, of gas tire heaters as shown in the ad at right.

WAPAKONETA MACHINE CO.,
Wapakoneta, OH

Formed in 1890 to make machine knives and mortising chisels for wood working machinery.

By 1910, the firm offered a variety of wheelmaking machinery, including automatic spoke lathes (Fig.1), tenon and mitre machines "for cutting the tenon and mitre on buggy and wagon spokes" (Fig.2), disc spoke facers (Fig.3), rim stretchers, "which straightens rims, bending them to a true circle" (Fig.4), rim rounders, "to round the felloe after it has been bent and drilled" (Fig.5), wheel boring and screwdriving machines (Fig.6), and wheel buffing machines (Fig.7).

Several of the machines look a good deal like those made by J.A. FAY & EGAN, especially the spoke lathe which is clearly covered by a March 2, 1909, patent assigned to J.A. Fay & Egan, the tenon and mitre machine, and the disc spoke facer. The firm appears to have made some or all of its machines under license.

A line of spoke gauges (Fig.8) was also offered in 1910. Such gauges must have been made by several firms, but this is the only documented offering thus far found. *(Illustrations continued on following pages)*

AUTOMATIC IMPROVED SPOKE LATHE.   Pat. Sept. 27, 1909

Fig.1

Fig.2

HEAVY SPOKE TENON AND MITRE MACHINE

Fig.3

DISC SPOKE FACER

Fig.4

RIM STRETCHER

Fig.5

RIM ROUNDER

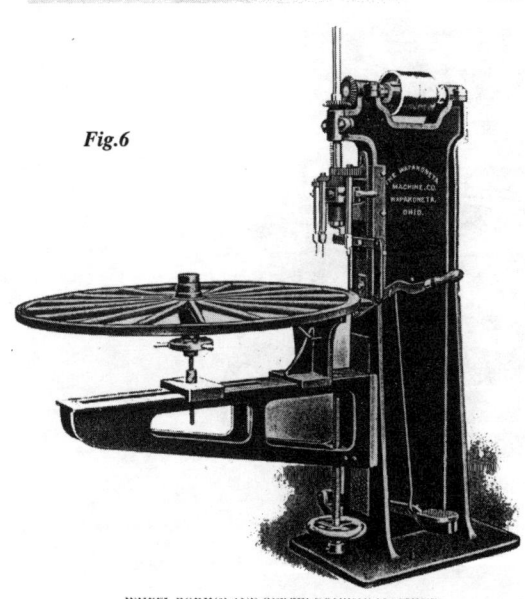

Fig.6

WHEEL BORING AND SCREW-DRIVING MACHINE

Fig.7

WHEEL BUFFING MACHINE

Spoke Gauges

Wapakoneta

Fig. 8

WE MAKE A COMPLETE SET OF GAUGES, which for wheel and Spoke Manufacturers, are indispensable. All Gauges are made of the best steel and tested with the micrometer.

No. 47 is a Spoke Tenon Gauge for measuring the thickness of tenons. Price $6.00.

No. 48 is a light Spoke Mitre Gauge for measuring the mitre bevel on spokes up to ⅞ spoke. Price $4.00. Price of Heavy Mitre Gauge $5.00. Unless otherwise ordered made for 16 spokes.

No. 50 is a Spoke Facer Gauge for measuring the width of spoke tenons. Price of Gauge for light Spokes is $8.00. Price of Gauge for Heavy Spokes is $10.00.

No. 52 is a spoke Pattern Gauge used for proportioning patterns for Spoke Lathe. The ratio used is 3 to 4, which works satisfactory on the Wapakoneta, Egan and Gleason Lathes. Price $8.00.

WAY, THOMAS R., Springfield, OH

Inventor and maker of an improved tire measuring wheel, patented January 21, 1873. Way's improvement was a second pointer, pivoted to the main pointer, which was manually set to deduct an expansion allowance to the measurement.

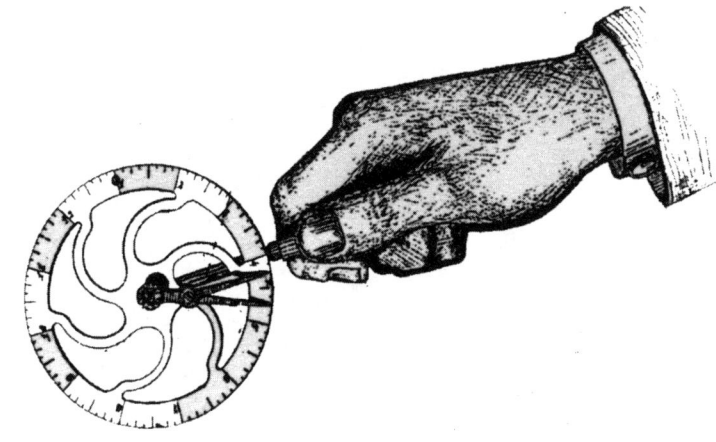

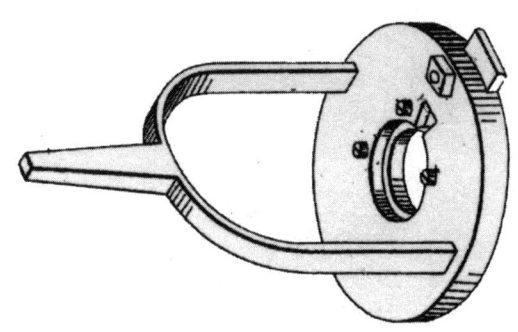

WEATHERINGTON, MELYN, Springfield, OH

Inventor and maker of an "improved method of adjusting round-tenon cutters to certain fixed sizes," patented July 14, 1857. The tenon size was fixed by installing a disc corresponding to the desired diameter and adjusting the moveable cutter as required.

WEBER, FRANCIS J., Carey, OH

Inventor and maker of a self-centering mandrel "designed for use in setting spokes into the hubs of wheels for the purpose of having all the spokes inserted at the proper angle or dish."

Patented September 24, 1867, the device was fitted with two cone-shaped pieces, one inserted in each end of the hub bore as shown below. With the gauge's axle thus centered, a rotating arm, fitted with a rod set to the edge of the spokes, was used to align each spoke to the same angle.

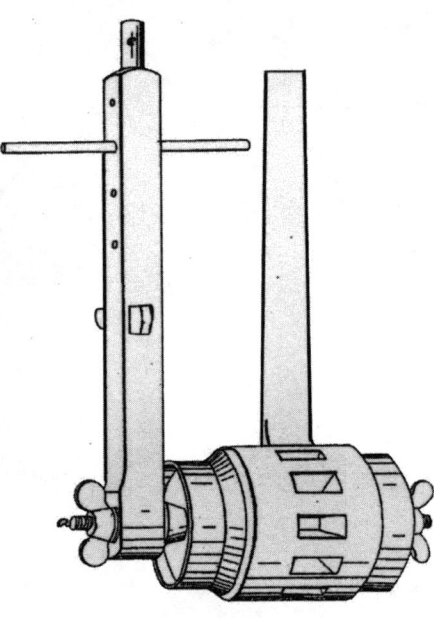

WELLS BROTHERS CO., Greenfield, MA

Founded in 1876 by Frank O. Wells (1855-1935) and his brother Frederick E. Wells (1844-1936) to make a variety of threading devices and blacksmiths' and wagon makers' tools and machinery (Fig.1). On April 1, 1912, the firm merged with the WILEY & RUSSELL MFG. CO. to form the Greenfield Tap & Die Co.

Early production included the SAMSON tire shrinker (Fig.2), patented January 2, 1883, which could shrink a 4"x 3/8" tire; the LITTLE GIANT tire gauge (Fig.3) offered in plain and graduated styles; LITTLE GIANT axle setter and axle straightener (Fig.4); and the LITTLE GIANT tire bolt holder (Fig.5). In 1888, the firm introduced the LITTLE GIANT wheel-holding attachment (Fig.6) for its line of hand operated drills. The attachment was designed to slide up and down to accommodate wheels of various diameters.

In 1894, the firm offered the LYONS tire measurer (Fig.7) which was fitted with a marking pencil for laying out the location of holes for the tire bolts. An improved version (Fig.8) was offered by 1917. Both types were also made without the pencil feature. *(Illustrations continued on following pages)*

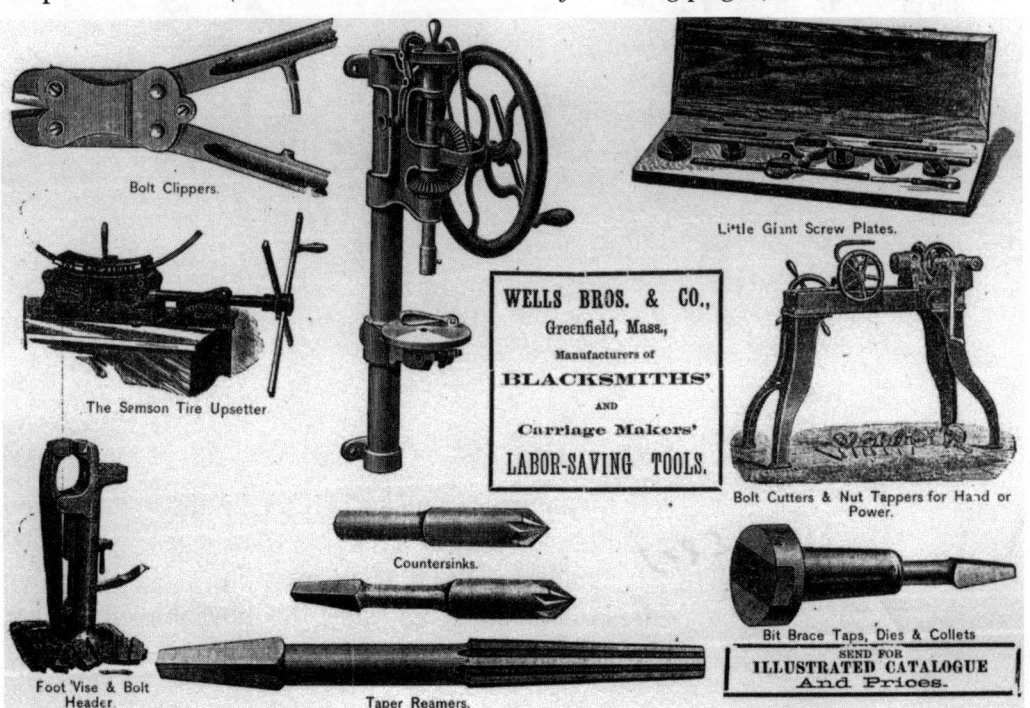

Bolt Clippers.

The Samson Tire Upsetter.

Foot Vise & Bolt Header.

Taper Reamers.

Countersinks.

Little Giant Screw Plates.

WELLS BROS. & CO.,
Greenfield, Mass.,
Manufacturers of
BLACKSMITHS'
AND
Carriage Makers'
LABOR-SAVING TOOLS.

Bolt Cutters & Nut Tappers for Hand or Power.

Bit Brace Taps, Dies & Collets

SEND FOR
ILLUSTRATED CATALOGUE
And Prices.

Fig.1

TIRE SHRINKERS

THE SAMSON

Will shrink tire 4x⅜ or ⅛ inch. Weight 220 lbs. The power is supplied by a screw. The shaft on which the screw is, is cut long enough to let the handle revolve without hitting the tire. Thus giving plenty of speed. The tire is held so that it cannot double up. All that is necessary is to heat the tire, place it in the machine and turn handle until it is upset enough. All slipping and sticking is avoided..$25.00

Fig.2

Fig.3

LITTLE GIANT

Plain...................each $1.25
Graduated............   "   1.50

LITTLE GIANT

"LITTLE GIANT" AXLE SETTER AND AXLE STRAIGHTENER.

A labor and time saving machine that does its work completely, and in a workmanship manner. Axles bent in any shape can be set, without removing the axle, to their original shape; making a perfect job. With the use of this machine it is not necessary to set axles on a new job until it is ready for the paint shop. All four axles can be straightened in less time than is usually required to remove one axle from a job preparatory to setting it. Simple, strong, and practical.

No. 2. For Axles up to and including 1¾ inch.....$6.00

Fig.4

185

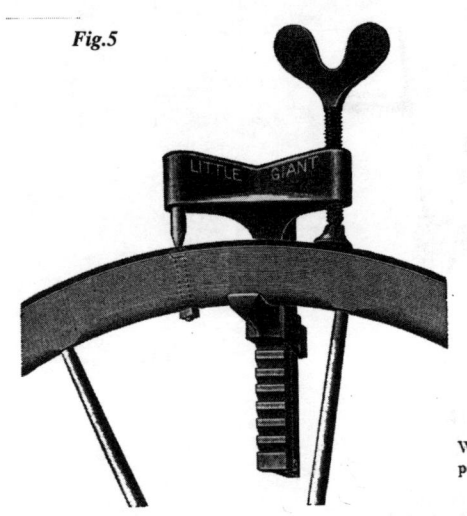

Fig.5

"LITTLE GIANT" TIRE BOLT HOLDERS.

For clamping bolts while nuts are being turned off or on.
With this holder, bolt can be held and holder can be left in
position until work is completed and it will not come off.

Each........................75c.

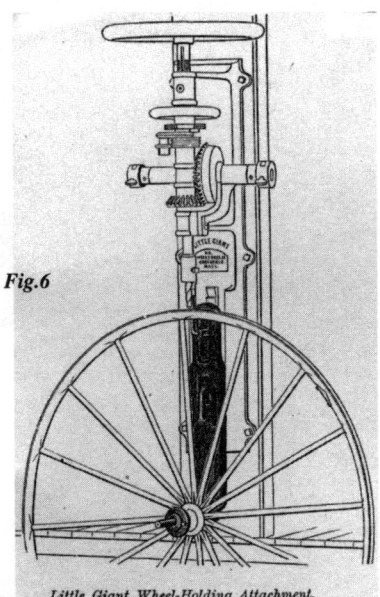

Fig.6

Little Giant Wheel-Holding Attachment.

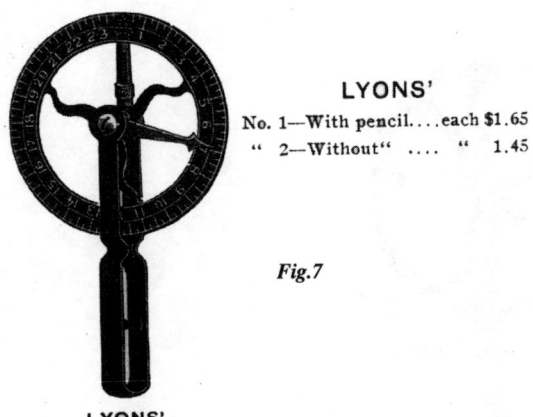

LYONS'

No. 1—With pencil....each $1.65
" 2—Without" .... " 1.45

Fig.7

LYONS'

LYONS' IMPROVED TIRE GAUGE

Fig.8

For Measuring Wagon Wheels and Tire.

WEST PATENT MFG. CO., Elyria, OH

Maker, in 1892, of West's Universal Tire Setter. The device was simply a metal tray for holding oil and a heater for bringing it to a boil. It was believed that tires and other wheel parts could be tightened by soaking in hot oil to expand the wooden parts.

It is quite likely that the West company called it a tire setter to capitalize on the reputation of the WEST TIRE SETTER CO., probably the best known maker of actual tire setting machines.

Fig. 1.—West's Universal Tire Setter.

Fig. 2.—West's Universal Tire Setter in Use.

WEST TIRE SETTER CO., Rochester, NY

Founded in 1869 by Jonathan B. West who had invented the first tire setter. Patented March 29, 1870, it was offered in both hand- and power-operated versions (Fig.1). West spent his time traveling the U.S. selling and setting up the machines which were then made by the MOWRY AXLE & MACHINE CO. with whom he had contracted. In 1873, Mowry failed and West moved to Rochester, NY, where he started the West Tire Setter Co. in 1874.

Rochester products included a steam powered tire setter and hub bander (Fig.2) patented January 6, 1891, offered in 1892; a hand tire setter (Fig.3) offered in 1894; and a hydraulic tire setter (Fig.4) introduced in 1916.

By 1913, West also offered the ROCHESTER helve hammer (Fig.5) in six sizes.

WEST'S AMERICAN TIRE SETTER.

Fig.1

PATENTED MARCH 29, 1870. PATENT No. 101,330.

Sets tire without removing from the wheel—without removing the bolts—without heat—without injury to the paint or varnish—without injury to the wheel—machine always ready—not liable to get out of order—sets either steel or iron tires—in most cases rim-bound wheels can be set without cutting the felloe.

HAND MACHINE.

POWER MACHINE, WITH COUNTER-SHAFT.

SAVES 80 PER CENT. OF TIME ON OLD WORK, AND 40 ON NEW.

The tires can be set more accurately—the dish made exactly uniform—the tread of the felloe can be thoroughly painted, thus excluding moisture and adding materially to the durability of the wheel, &c., &c. Send for circular to

THE MOWRY AXLE AND MACHINE CO.,
SOLE MANUFACTURERS, - - - GREENEVILLE, CONN.

Fig.2

WEST'S HAND TIRE SETTER

WEST'S TIRE SETTER

Will set all light tires up to 1¼ x⅜ inch on wheels from 3 feet to 4 feet 4 inches cold, without removing the tires from the wheels. Easily operated by any man of ordinary mechanical ability from the descriptions and instructions that accompany each machine.

Price ....each, $100.00

Fig.3

WHITE, J.D., Hartford, CT

Inventor and maker, in 1849, of an axle turning lathe as shown below. Patented May 21, 1850, the machine was designed to operate with the axle mounted between two tail blocks and rotated by a center chuck. As the axle rotated, cutters mounted on lathe posts operated on each end simultaneously and traversed at an angle set by adjustable guides mounted on the apron. Thus any desired taper could be machined.

By 1850, White was producing engine lathes and double end railway axle lathes. The firm reorganized as Brown & White in 1853.

IMPROVED COMPOUND SLIDE LATHE FOR TURNING AXLES.---Figure 1.

WHITE, L.& I.J., Buffalo, NY, later
WHITE CO., L.& I.J., Buffalo, NY

A partnership of Leonard White (1810-1893) and his brother Ichabod J. White (?-1880), formed in Monroe, MI in 1836 to make edge tools. In 1844 the brothers moved to Buffalo, NY, where they continued production of edge tools in great variety. Ichabod died in 1880; Leonard continued as proprietor until incorporating in 1892 as the L. & I.J. White Co. where he served as president until his death in 1893.

Joseph W. Best (1848-1902) joined the firm in 1875 and was serving as treasurer and general manager when he died in April, 1902. Officers in 1908 were J.W. White, superintendent; M. White, widow of I.J. White, vice president; and John G.H. Marvin, president. The company went out of business in 1940.

The firm produced a number of edge tools designed for carriage and wagon makers, including the draw knives, carriage body knives, and carriage router knives offered in an 1890 catalog as shown below.

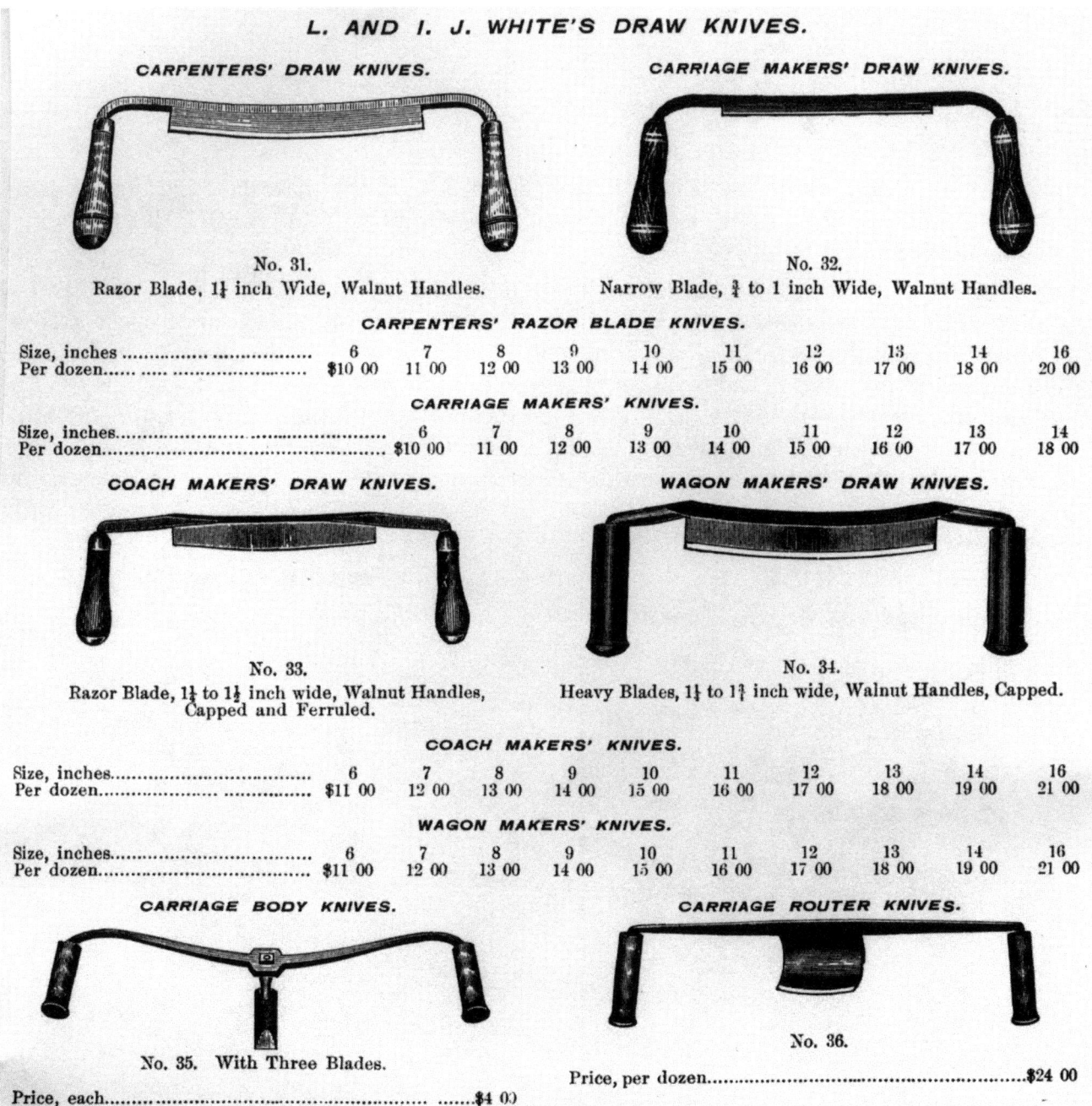

L. AND I. J. WHITE'S DRAW KNIVES.

CARPENTERS' DRAW KNIVES.

No. 31.
Razor Blade, 1¼ inch Wide, Walnut Handles.

CARRIAGE MAKERS' DRAW KNIVES.

No. 32.
Narrow Blade, ¾ to 1 inch Wide, Walnut Handles.

CARPENTERS' RAZOR BLADE KNIVES.

Size, inches	6	7	8	9	10	11	12	13	14	16
Per dozen	$10 00	11 00	12 00	13 00	14 00	15 00	16 00	17 00	18 00	20 00

CARRIAGE MAKERS' KNIVES.

Size, inches	6	7	8	9	10	11	12	13	14
Per dozen	$10 00	11 00	12 00	13 00	14 00	15 00	16 00	17 00	18 00

COACH MAKERS' DRAW KNIVES.

No. 33.
Razor Blade, 1¼ to 1½ inch wide, Walnut Handles, Capped and Ferruled.

WAGON MAKERS' DRAW KNIVES.

No. 34.
Heavy Blades, 1¼ to 1¾ inch wide, Walnut Handles, Capped.

COACH MAKERS' KNIVES.

Size, inches	6	7	8	9	10	11	12	13	14	16
Per dozen	$11 00	12 00	13 00	14 00	15 00	16 00	17 00	18 00	19 00	21 00

WAGON MAKERS' KNIVES.

Size, inches	6	7	8	9	10	11	12	13	14	16
Per dozen	$11 00	12 00	13 00	14 00	15 00	16 00	17 00	18 00	19 00	21 00

CARRIAGE BODY KNIVES.

No. 35. With Three Blades.

Price, each.....................................$4 00

CARRIAGE ROUTER KNIVES.

No. 36.

Price, per dozen.....................................$24 00

WHITING, TRUMAN, Niles, MI

Inventor and maker of "Measuring Wheels for Wagon Tires" patented May 13, 1873. The tool was equipped with a built-in pencil for marking the tire at the point where it was to be cut.

By 1894, measuring wheels incorporating the built-in pencil feature were offered by the WELLS BROTHERS CO.

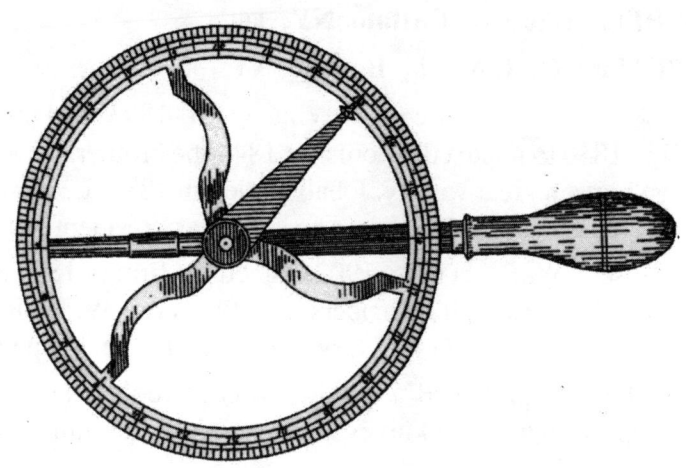

WILEY, RUSSELL & CO., Greenfield, MA, later
WILEY & RUSSELL MFG. CO., Greenfield, MA

A partnership of Solon L. Wiley and Charles P. Russell, formed in 1871 to make threading tools. The firm incorporated in 1874 as the Wiley & Russell Mfg. Co. and merged with the WELLS BROTHERS CO. April 1, 1912, to form the Greenfield Tap & Die Co.

Early products centered around tools and machinery for producing threads, such as taps and dies. By the 1880s, however, the firm had added a number of tools for blacksmiths and wagon and carriage makers. These included the GREEN RIVER tire-bending machine offered in three sizes, No. 1 for tires up to 3"x 1/2" (Fig.1), No. 2 for tires up to 5/8" thick (Fig.2) and No. 3 for tires up to 6"x 1/2" or 4"x 3/4" (Fig.3); GREEN RIVER tire shrinkers in horizontal (Fig.4) and vertical (Fig.5) styles; GREEN RIVER tire-bolt holders (Fig.6); GREEN RIVER patent rim wrenches (Fig.7); GREEN RIVER tire measuring wheels in graduated (Fig.8) and plain (Fig.9) styles; and GREEN RIVER tire markers (Fig.10) for locating holes to be drilled in replacement tires.

GREEN RIVER TIRE-BENDING MACHINE.

FOR LIGHT AND MEDIUM WORK.

Fig.1

GREEN RIVER TIRE-BENDING MACHINE, NO. 2.

FOR LIGHT AND MEDIUM WORK.

Fig.2

GREEN RIVER TIRE-BENDING MACHINE, NO. 3.

FOR LIGHT AND HEAVY TIRES.

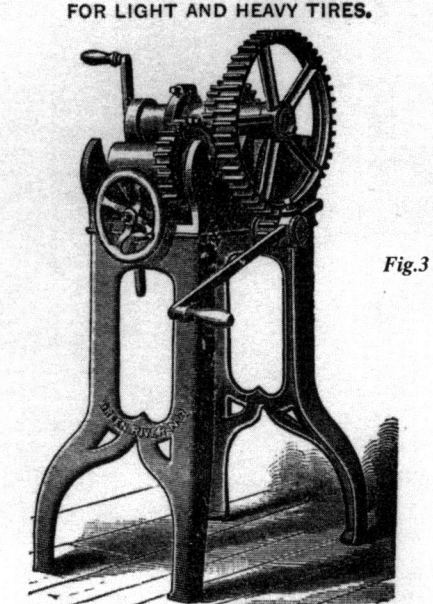

Fig.3

GREEN RIVER TIRE SHRINKERS

HORIZONTAL, NOS. 1 AND 1 1-2.

Fig.4

GREEN RIVER TIRE-BOLT HOLDER

FOR CLAMPING BOLTS WHILE THE NUTS ARE BEING TURNED ON OR OFF.

Fig. 608.

Fig.6

Price, each................................$0 75
Price, per dozen.... .... 8 50

NEW GREEN RIVER UPRIGHT TIRE SHRINKERS, IMPROVED.

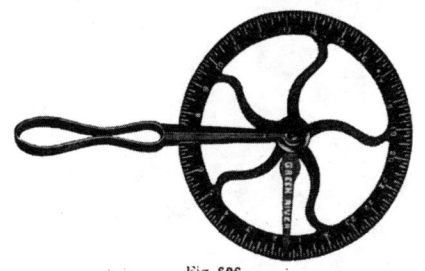

Fig.5

GREEN RIVER PATENT RIM WRENCH.

FOR NUTS ON TIRE BOLTS INSIDE THE FELLOE.

For 1-4 inch size the socket which holds the other wrenches is used.

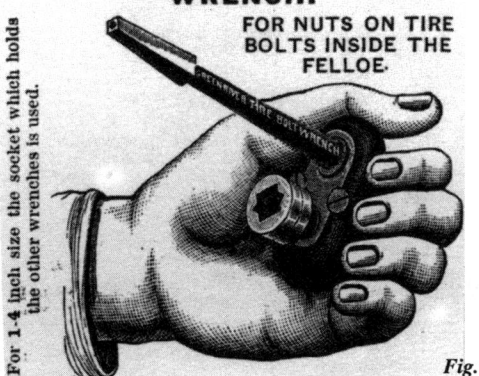

Fig.7

GREEN RIVER TIRE-MEASURING WHEEL, GRADUATED.

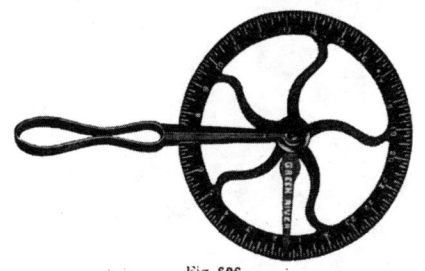

Fig. 606.

The Graduated Tire Wheel, a drop forging, is made so that the figures and lines are raised above the surface of the wheel and cannot be filled or defaced with rust or dirt.   It is a perfect-running wheel, turned carefully in a lathe, exactly 24 inches in circumference, and accurately graduated.

The index hand saves trouble of marking with chalk, and the whole, made of metal, is light, accurately fitted, handy and strong.

   Price $1 50

Fig.8

GREEN RIVER TIRE-MEASURING WHEEL, PLAIN.

Fig.9

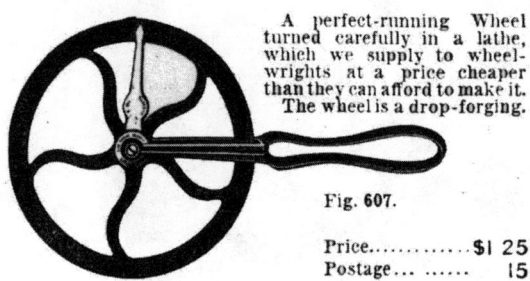

A perfect-running Wheel turned carefully in a lathe, which we supply to wheelwrights at a price cheaper than they can afford to make it. The wheel is a drop-forging.

Fig. 607.

Price............$1 25
Postage... 15

GREEN RIVER TIRE MARKER.

Fig.10

Fig. 604
Indicating where holes should be drilled in new tires on old wheels to save spoiling wood in felloe, so that bolts will go in the old holes without cutting for them.

The pointer below is put in the old hole and the prick-punch above struck with the hammer.
Price...$1 25

WILLIAMS, WHITE & CO., Moline, IL

Founded in 1854 as Williams, Heald & Co. to make steam engines and a variety of machinery for flour mills and sawmills. Henry Ainsworth (1833-1914) bought an interest in 1870 and incorporated the firm as Williams, White & Co. in 1871.

Production of carriage and wagon machinery began in the early 1870s, including skein setters, skein presses, tire rolling machines, and tire welding machinery. By 1900, the firm was specializing in heavy metalcutting machinery and probably made little or no carriage and wagon machinery from that point.

In 1874, the firm introduced a machine for turning carriage axles, patented May 28, 1872, by J.G. Aram (Fig. 1). The machine was designed to turn the axle ends for setting the thimble skeins. A pattern, usually the skein to be used, was mounted on one end of the machine and the axle on the other. A tracer arm, riding inside the pattern skein, was rotated along with a cutter arm B. The cutter arm followed the tracer, thus insuring a near perfect fit between the axle end and the skein.

Drop hammers and spring hammers (Fig.2) were offered in 1887. A cold hydraulic tire setting machine (Fig.3) was introduced in 1894. Using a built-in hydraulic pump, the operator could closely control the action of the pistons as they expanded and contracted the tire.

Fig.1

ARAM'S MACHINE FOR TURNING CARRIAGE AXLES.

WILLIAMS, WHITE & Co. MOLINE, ILL., MANUFACTURERS OF Forging, Forming, and Bending Machines. Drop Hammers, Spring Hammers, Punches and Shears.

Fig.2

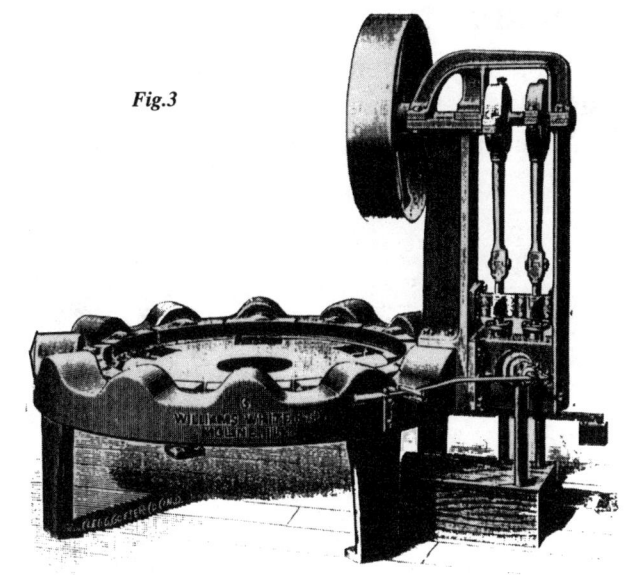

Fig.3

A PERFECTED COLD HYDRAULIC TIRE SETTING MACHINE.

WILLS, WM. W., Janesville, WI

Operator of the Single Center Spring Co., Wills also offered WILL'S automatic micrometer axle gauge, patented June 28, 1881. A clever device, it indicated the exact amount of "gather" of the wheel by deflection of a long pointer that could be read on a scale.

WILLS' AUTOMATIC MICROMETER AXLE GAUGE

By placing the GAUGE upon the TOP side of an axle, as represented in the above cut, it will indicate the exact "GATHER" of the wheel. Keep the Gauge in the same position, and turn the axle up edgewise, and the pointer will indicate the exact "SET" of the wheel..

Testimonial from Studebaker Bros. Mfg. Co.

Dated, South Bend, Indiana, Nov. 9, 1891.

MR. WM. W. WILLS, Janesville, Wis.

DEAR SIR :—We have used the Wills' Automatic Micrometer Axle Gauge for several years, and can say it gives good satisfaction.   H. J. BIERHART, Supt. Spring Vehicle Dept.

Manufactured by **WM. W. WILLS, Janesville, Wisconsin.**

PRICE. $10 00.   WRITE FOR DISCOUNT.

WILSON & DOUGHERTY, Newark, NJ

Maker, in 1866, of Bamberger's axle gauge, patented November 15, 1859, by William C. Bamberger. The gauge was designed for setting axles to the desired "set" and "gather" to wheels of any given dish. It is very unlikely that the gauge was as large and unwieldy as shown in the illustration below.

BAMBERGER'S AXLE GAGE.

WING, CHARLES P., Hinsdale, IL

Inventor and maker of a tire bolt wrench (Fig.1), patented February 9, 1904, and a combined tire and carriage bolt holder and clamp (Fig.2), patented May 3, 1904.

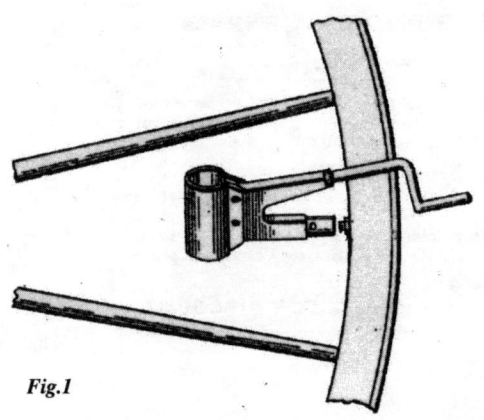

Fig.1

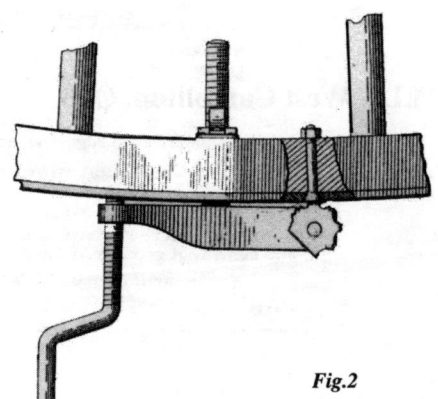

Fig.2

WISELL, E.K., Warren, OH

Inventor and maker of the WISELL lathe for irregular forms, patented March 3, 1863. By 1865 Wisell was advertising himself as a maker of spoke and handle machinery (Fig.1).

The Wisell lathe (Fig.2) was an improvement on the Blanchard design whereby a slowly rotating pattern controlled the movement of a set of rapidly rotating cutters that machined a workpiece also rotating in step with the pattern. The most obvious difference between the Blanchard and Wisell designs was the side-by-side placement of the pattern and workpiece in the Wisell lathe and upper-lower placement in most other machines based on the Blanchard design.

Wisell received patents for improvements on January 14, 1868, and May 28, 1872.

The Wisell lathe was also made by the BASS FOUNDRY & MACHINE WORKS in 1874.

SPOKE AND HANDLE MACHINERY.—THOSE DE-
SIRING to purchase the best machine in the United States for making Spokes, Yankee Ax Handles, Plow Handles, and irregular forms generally, should send for cut and description to E. K. WISELL, Manufacturer and Patentee, at Warren, Ohio.   20 8s

Fig.1

Fig.2

WISELL'S LATHE FOR IRREGULAR FORMS.

WOLFE, M.L., West Carrollton, OH

Maker, in 1916, of the Wolfe tire cooler as shown in the ad below.

THE WOLFE TIRE COOLER
Easiest Operated, non-destructible and safest Tire Cooler made. Wheels can be fastened in or out of dish while the hot tire is being put on wheel.
M. L. WOLFE
West Carrollton, O.

WOOD & SONS, A.A., Atlanta, GA

Maker of a variety of hollow augers for carriage and wagon makers. Wood had received two patents for hollow augers on August 10, 1875, while living in Syracuse, NY, and apparently working for G.N. STEARNS & CO., later E.C. STEARNS & CO. The Stearns companies made hollow augers that incorporated Wood's patent.

By 1901, Wood had started his own firm in Atlanta, GA, where he introduced Wood's UNIVERSAL hollow auger (Fig.1), patented November 27, 1900; and Wood's foreauger (Fig.2), patented December 31, 1901, for use in preparing the end of the spoke for the hollow auger. The hollow auger could cut a tenon up to 4" long and from 1/4" to 1 1/4" diameter.

The IDEAL hollow auger (Fig.3), patented December 31, 1901, and designed to cut larger tenons from 1 1/8" to 1 1/2" diameter, was introduced in 1902. Production of the UNIVERSAL and IDEAL models continued until 1920 or later.

Spoke pointers were offered as the C1 (Fig.4) pointing from 1/4" to 2" and the C2 (Fig.5) pointing from 1/4" to 2 3/4" spokes. The C2 model was fitted with an adjustable shank that formed a gauge for the tenon size.

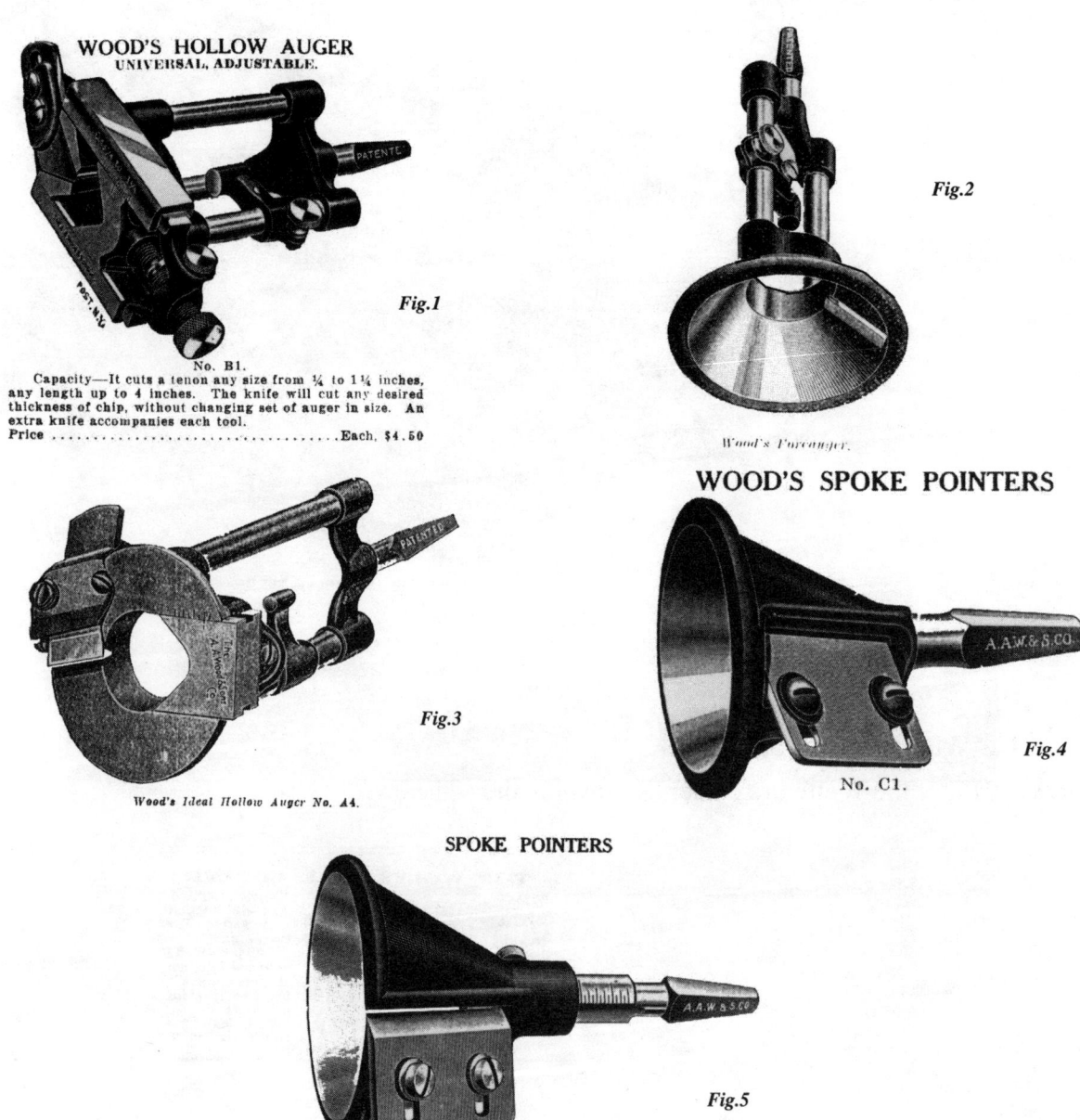

WOOD'S HOLLOW AUGER
UNIVERSAL, ADJUSTABLE.

Fig.1

No. B1.
Capacity—It cuts a tenon any size from ¼ to 1¼ inches,
any length up to 4 inches. The knife will cut any desired
thickness of chip, without changing set of auger in size. An
extra knife accompanies each tool.
Price ....Each, $4.50

Fig.2

Wood's Foreauger.

Fig.3

Wood's Ideal Hollow Auger No. A4.

WOOD'S SPOKE POINTERS

Fig.4

No. C1.

SPOKE POINTERS

Fig.5

No. C2.

WOOLSEY & SON, J.V., Sandusky, OH, later
WOOLSEY WHEEL CO., Sandusky, OH

Founded by Johnston V. Woolsey (1822-1893) in 1851 as a machine shop. In 1855, the firm became Pierce and Woolsey and began making spokes and axe handles.

About 1870 the firm became J.V. Woolsey & Son, specializing in the production of wheels and wheel machinery. Wheel machinery production included spoke machines, patented August 24, 1869; spoke sizing machine, patented December 24, 1872, (Fig.1); and spoke sawing machines also patented December 24, 1872, (Fig.2), all by J.V. Woolsey.

By 1886, the firm had become the Woolsey Wheel Co. which, in 1900, occupied the factory shown in Fig.3. The plant, with all its contents, was destroyed by fire in 1905 and appears not to have been rebuilt.

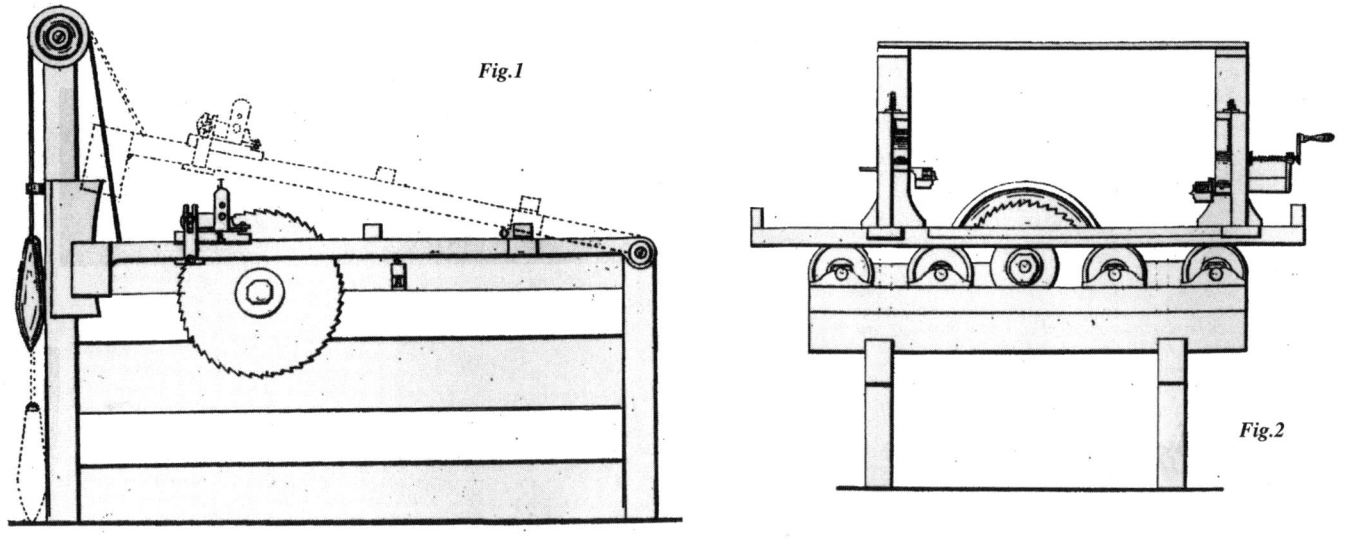

Fig.1

Fig.2

Fig.3

WORDEN, ALVA, Ypsilanti, MI

Inventor and maker of an adjustable tire bolt wrench, shown below, patented November 26, 1889.

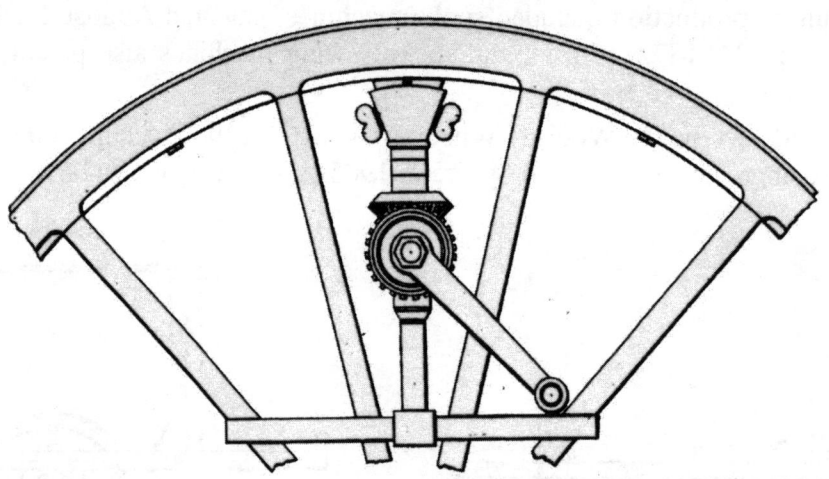

YOUNT, A., Kokomo, IN

Inventor and maker of a tire upsetter, patented October 15, 1872. The upsetter was listed in trade catalogs at least as late as 1882.

YOUNT'S TIRE UPSETTER.

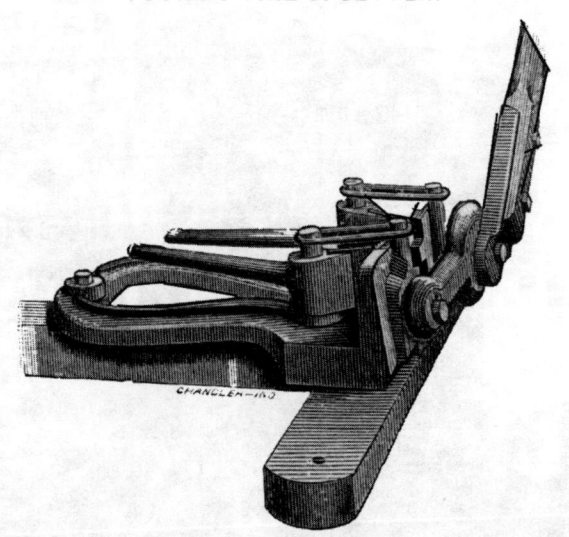

Will Upset Tire from ¼ to 4 inches wide and ⅞ inch thick at one heat.
Will also Upset Bar Iron or Carriage Axles from 1¼ inch down.
Price, each... .... **$16 50**

Multi-Language Technical Dictionary of Wheelwrights Machines

In 1910 R. Oldenbourg of Munich, Germany, published a nine volume technical dictionary illustrating a large variety of machines and machine features, and identifying each in English, German, French, Russian, Italian, and Spanish. Volume IX concerned machine tools for metal working and wood working.

Chapter XIX of Volume IX, reproduced below, covers Wheelwrights' Machines and may be of interest to readers of this book.

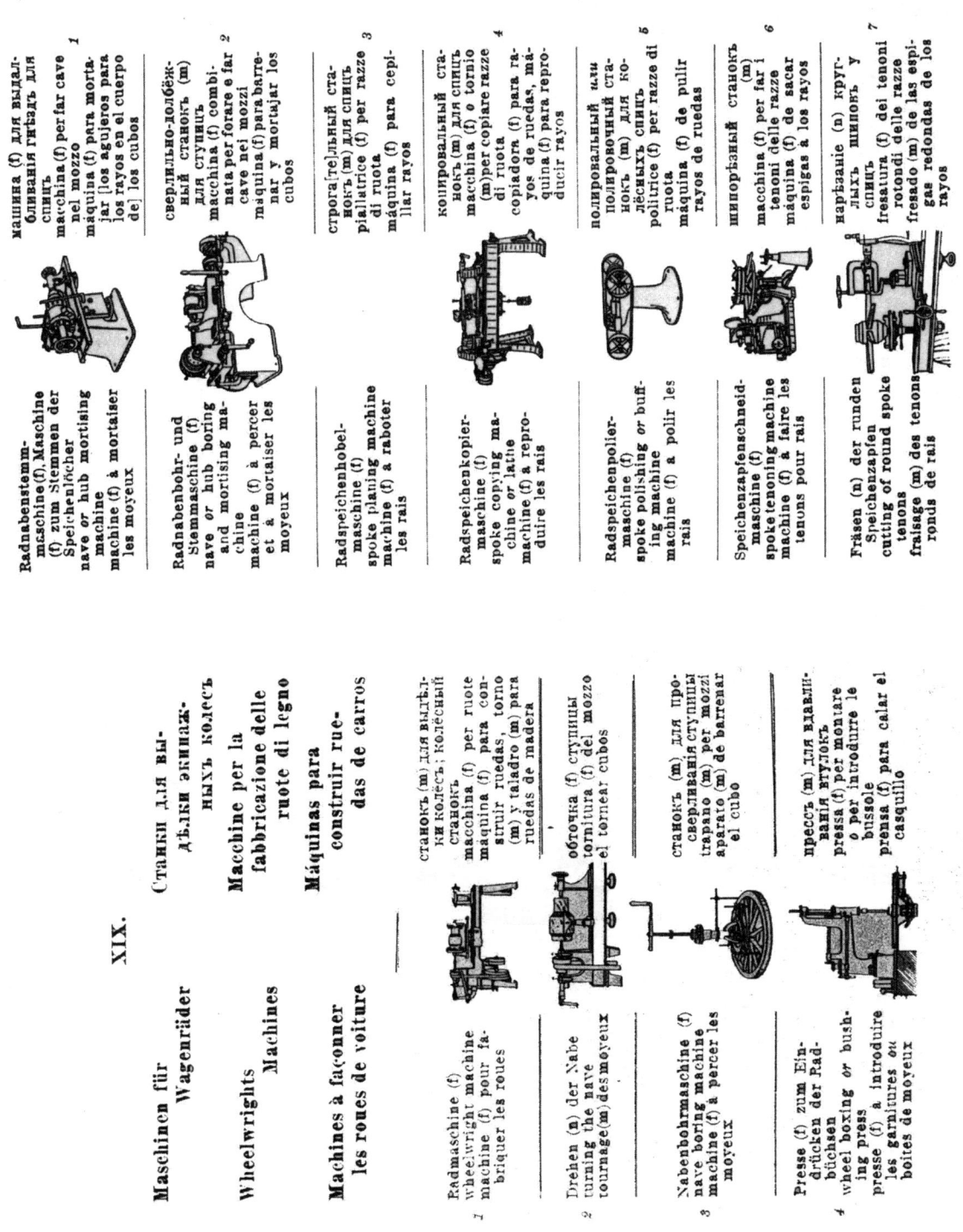

1
die Felgen auf die Speichen drücken (v) oder schieben (v)
to press the felloes on to the spokes
appliquer (v) les jantes sur les rais
mettere (v) o montare (v) il cerchione sulle razze
aplicar (v) las llantas sobre los rayos
надѣть косяки на спицы

2
Rundfräsen (n) der Radbahn
circular milling of wheel tread
fraisage (m) de la surface de la jante
fresatura (f) circolare del cerchione
fresado (m) de la superficie de las llantas
фрезе[р]ованіе (n) колѣснаго обода по кругу

3
Presse (f) zum Aufpressen der Nabenreifen
tyre press
presse (f) pour l'application de la frette sur le moyeu
pressa (f) per montare i cerchioni di ferro
prensa (f) para calar los anillos sobre los cubos
прессъ (m) для насаживанія колецъ на ступицы

1
Fräsen (n) der flachen Speichenzapfen
cutting of rectangular spoke tenons
fraisage (m) des tenons rectangulaires pour rais
fresatura (f) dei tenoni piatti delle razze
fresado (m) de las espigas planas de los rayos
нарѣзаніе (n) плоскихъ шиповъ у спицъ

2
die Radspeichen in die Nabe drücken (v)
to drive the spokes into the hub
forcer (v) les rais dans le moyeu
montare (v) o introdurre (v) le razze nel mozzo
calar (v) los rayos al cubo
вгонять спицы въ ступицу

3
hydraulische Speicheneintreibmaschine (f)
hydraulic spoke driving machine
presse (f) hydraulique pour l'introduction des rais [dans les moyeux]
macchina (f) idraulica per montare le razze
máquina (f) de calar rayos hidráulica
гидравлическая машина для вгонки спицъ

4
Holzfelge (f)
wood felloe
jante (f) en bois
cerchione (m) di legno
llanta (f) de madera
колёсный косякъ (m)

5
Felgenholz (n)
felloe wood
bois (m) pour jante
legno (m) per cerchioni
madero (m) de llanta
лѣсъ (m) для колёсныхъ косяковъ

6
Radfelgenbiegemaschine (f)
felloe bending machine
machine (f) à courber les jantes
macchina (f) per curvare i cerchioni di ruota
máquina (f) de curvar llantas de ruedas
машина (f) для сгибанія колёсныхъ косяковъ

7
Felgenbohrsupport (m)
felloe boring carriage
support (m) pour perceuse de jantes
supporto (m) per forare i cerchioni
soporte (m) de máquina de barrenar llantas
суппортъ (m) для сверленія косяковъ